ROUTLEDGE LIBRARY EDITIONS:
SOVIET POLITICS

Volume 10

THE RISE AND FALL OF
THE SOVIET POLITBURO

THE RISE AND FALL OF THE SOVIET POLITBURO

JOHN LÖWENHARDT,
JAMES R. OZINGA AND ERIK VAN REE

Routledge
Taylor & Francis Group

LONDON AND NEW YORK

First published in 1992 in Great Britain by UCL Press
First published in 1992 in the United States of America by St. Martin's Press, Inc.

This edition first published in 2024
by Routledge
4 Park Square, Milton Park, Abingdon, Oxon OX14 4RN

and by Routledge
605 Third Avenue, New York, NY 10158

Routledge is an imprint of the Taylor & Francis Group, an informa business

British Library Cataloguing in Publication Data
A catalogue record for this book is available from the British Library

ISBN: 978-1-032-67165-9 (Set)
ISBN: 978-1-032-67773-6 (Volume 10) (hbk)
ISBN: 978-1-032-67775-0 (Volume 10) (pbk)
ISBN: 978-1-032-67774-3 (Volume 10) (ebk)

DOI: 10.4324/9781032677743

Publisher's Note
The publisher has gone to great lengths to ensure the quality of this reprint but
points out that some imperfections in the original copies may be apparent.

Disclaimer
The publisher has made every effort to trace copyright holders and would
welcome correspondence from those they have been unable to trace.

THE RISE AND FALL OF THE SOVIET POLITBURO

John Löwenhardt
Leiden University, The Netherlands

James R. Ozinga
Oakland University, Michigan, U.S.A.

and

Erik van Ree
University of Amsterdam, The Netherlands

St. Martin's Press
New York

Scholarly and Reference Division
St. Martin's Press, Inc.
175 Fifth Avenue
New York, NY 10010

First published in the United States of America in 1992

Printed in the United States of America

ISBN 0-312-04784-3

Library of Congress Cataloging-in-Publication Data
Löwenhardt, John.
    The rise and fall of the Soviet Politburo / John Löwenhardt, James R.
Ozinga, and Erik van Ree.
        p.   cm.
    Includes bibliographical references and index.
    ISBN 0-312-04784-3
    1. TSK KPSS. Politbiuro—History. 2. TSK KPSS. Politbiuro—
Registers. I. Ozinga, James R. II. Ree, Erik van. III. Title.
JN6598.K7L627 1992
324.247'075—dc20   91-29623
                                                            CIP

CONTENTS

LIST OF ILLUSTRATIONS

LIST OF TABLES AND FIGURES

Tables

Figure

TERMINOLOGY, DATES AND ABBREVATIONS

From 1952 to 1966 the Politburo was called the Presidium of the CPSU Central Committee, and from 1953 to 1966 the General Secretary was called First Secretary. Between February 1934 and September 1953 the position of General Secretary was not officially used. In the text of this book "Politburo" will be used for the years 1917 to 1952 and 1966 to the present and "Presidium" for the years between 1952 and 1966. In cases when reference is to the body irrespective of a particular period in time, "Politburo" will of course be used. In order to avoid excessive verbiage, the authors have decided not to observe terminological differences with absolute consistency.

Transcription

The transcription of Russian personal names used in this book is an adaptation of the Library of Congress transcription, ignoring diacritic signs. The "soft sign" has not been transcribed.

Dates

To people outside Russia, the (25) October Revolution occurred on *7 November*. This was so because the Russians used the Julian calendar ("Old Style," O.S.) that "lagged behind" the Gregorian calendar (introduced by Pope Gregor XIII in 1582) that was in use in Central and Western Europe. The difference between "O.S." and "New Style" was 12 days in the 19th century and 13 days in the early 20th century. The Gregorian calendar was formally introduced in Russia on 14 (1, O.S.) February 1918. In this book all dates are those of the Gregorian calendar and are noted in the European style (day/month/year).

Abbrevations

		Russian Abbrevation
CC	Central Committee of the CPSU	*TsK*
CCC	Central Control Commission of the CPSU	*TsKK*
CEC	Central Executive Committee	*(V)TsIK*
CO	Central Organ	*TsO*
CPSU	Communist Party of the Soviet Union	*KPSS*
	General Secretary of the CPSU	*Gensek*
	City Party Committee	*Gorkom*
	State Planning Committee	*Gosplan*
	Main Political Directorate	*GPU*
GULag	Main Directorate of Corrective Labor Camps	*GULAG*
JAC	Jewish Anti-Fascist Committee	
KGB	Committee of State Security	*KGB*
MTS	Machine-Tractor Station(s)	*MTS*
	Ministry of Internal Affairs	*MVD*
NEP	New Economic Policy	*NEP*
NKVD	People's Commissariat of Internal Affairs	*NKVD*
	Provincial Party Committee	*Obkom*
PCC	Party Control Committee	*KPK*
Politburo	Political Bureau of the CC, CPSU	*Politbiuro/PB*
RCP(b)	Russian Communist Party (bolsheviks)	*RKP(b)*
RSDWP	Russian Social-Democratic Workers Party	*RSDRP*
RSFSR	Russian Soviet Federal Socialist Republic	*RSFSR*
USSR	Union of Soviet Socialist Republics	*SSSR*
	All-Union Communist Party (bolsheviks)	*VKP(b)*
	Supreme Economic Council	*VSNKh*

PREFACE

The idea of writing a new book on the Politburo was suggested to me as long ago as 1986 by Jim Ozinga of Oakland University. As co-authors we set off and soon found ourselves narrowly trailing the bends and curves of Gorbachev's *glasnost* and *perestroika*. By the late 1980s the institutional changes and the amount of new sources had become all but unmanageable. We were saved from despair by our Amsterdam colleague Erik van Ree, who agreed to write the historical part, using his prolific knowledge of Soviet political history.

What this book does is pull together old and new data so as to provide the history, the sociological and institutional context of the Politburo decision-making process. Our method of clarifying that context is to present in Part I first the history (Chapters 1-6 by Erik van Ree) and the mode of operation (Chapter 7 by me) of the Politburo. In Part II Jim Ozinga (Chapter 8) presents a statistical analysis and profile of the Politburo membership. Having identified the chapters with individual authors, I should haste to add that in the end the book is the result of a truly collective effort of our transatlantic *troika*. So are the two last chapters: a complete list of the composition of the Politburo and a complete alphabetical list of Politburo members and candidate members, presenting for each of the 130 members all sociological data that have been the raw material for the tables and analysis in the earlier chapters.

On the basis of the abundance of new sources and material, it might have been possible to alter the scope of this book and rewrite the history of the Communist Party of the Soviet Union completely. For several reasons, we decided not to take this laborious road, and rather to confine ourselves to the basics and to the red line running through the history of the Politburo. To opt for another road would have meant that this book would have taken even more years of hard work and would have become several times its present size. Besides, the authors are convinced that several of their colleagues are using the new sources to research and write on specific personalities and periods of Soviet political history. Nevertheless, it must be said that had Gorbachev not initiated *glasnost* and the rehabilitation of history, this book would have been much less exciting to research and less fun to write.

I am grateful to Jim and Erik for their enthusiasm and impeccable work ethic, which, in spite of the fact that Gorbachev almost drove us crazy, resulted in a book that in my opinion successfully disproves the thesis that collective works are worse than books written by one solitary author. Collectively, we wish to thank the many people in the Netherlands and the United States who gave of their time and expertise to assist in this project. We are particularly grateful to Marc Jansen of Amsterdam University who critically read most of the manuscript in exchange for an excessive amount of licorice and to Ger van den Berg and William Simons of Leiden University for their free but nevertheless valuable advice.

John Löwenhardt
Leiden, 21 June 1991

INTRODUCTION

"**L**eaving Andropov's office, I glanced at my watch and saw that I needed to hurry to be in time for the Politburo meeting in the Kremlin. The Secretary-General, of course, goes there by car, but I had no transport and had to rely on my very own feet. And it was out of the question that I would be late for the PB meeting, for as a rule they start with personnel questions." In these words Egor Ligachev described his thoughts after he had just been informed by Gorbachev and Andropov in the Central Committee's office building on Old Square in Moscow that his candidacy would be proposed by Secretary-General Andropov to the Politburo for the post of chief of the party Secretariat's Organization Department.[1] "I had no time to peep into Gorbachev's office and tell him about my discussion with Andropov. I was pressed for time, and anyway, Mikhail Sergeevich had surely left for the Kremlin: the Politburo members used to assemble in the Walnut Room before the Secretary-General arrived."

"I hurried downstairs, left the building onto Old Square, and quickly walked down Kuibyshev Street in the direction of the Kremlin. The Politburo members assemble for their meetings in the Kremlin on the second floor of an old building with high ceilings and high windows, which give a view of the Kremlin wall. On the other side is Red Square with the Lenin Mausoleum. Of course, the lay-out of this section of the government building has undergone considerable changes; it has been modernized and all possible sorts of communications equipment have been installed. As a matter of fact, not only is the meeting room of the Politburo located here, but the Kremlin office of the Secretary-General as well. Here there is the so-called Walnut Room with the big round table at which the members of the highest political leadership exchange opinions before the meetings begin. Sometimes the most important and complicated issues on the day's agenda are the subject of an unofficial and preliminary discussion at this round table, with no record or list of decisions being kept. So it can happen that the meeting begins not at eleven sharp, but fifteen or twenty minutes later. Of course, the Candidate Politburo members and the Central Committee Secretaries take part in the meetings as well, but they assemble in the oblong room at the long table where each has his fixed place, according to unwritten rules. Those who have been invited [to the meeting] take their seats behind small tables that are placed alongside the wall."

A candid description such as the one given by Egor Ligachev was, up to 1991, quite exceptional. From 1919 to 1990, the Politburo had been at the commanding heights of Soviet politics. Lodged at the apex of the Communist Party of the Soviet Union (CPSU) this *party cabinet* had for long periods of time been more important than the government, that is, the Council of Ministers or, as it was called up to 1946, the Council of People's Commissars. Politburo decisions both determined the country's direction and settled differences between powerful segments of society, such as the party apparatus, the military, or the KGB. Ultimately, it was the Politburo that decided *who got what, when and how* in the Soviet Union. It was also the Politburo that decided on the most important personnel changes in all sectors of Soviet society, including the Communist Party. These decisions, usually taken at the weekly meetings of the Politburo, had significance far beyond Soviet borders because the Soviet Union was one of the most powerful nations on earth, at least in terms of military capabilities.

But for most of its history the Politburo has operated behind a wall of secrecy so intense that not even when or how often it met was known. Well into the Gorbachev period, its members displayed an extreme sensitivity to the airing of differences that might possibly have the faintest of smells of them trying to split the party.[2] What the *PB* discussed was, up until the late 1980s, not described in the media. Disputes went unrecorded, and Politburo decisions had to be reconstructed from subsequent behavior of lesser party and state bodies rather than from information in the public news. This aversion to publicity characterized all Soviet politics for decades.

Nonetheless, more was known about the Politburo and how it operated in those secret days than was sometimes believed. By the late 1970s enough reliable information had come to light for one of the present authors to write *The Soviet Politburo.*[3] Since the English edition of that book was published a few months before Leonid Brezhnev's death in 1982, political life in the Soviet Union has changed almost beyond recognition. The policy of *glasnost* and what may be called the rehabilitation of history and historiography; the introduction of competitiveness in both intraparty and in Soviet elections, and even between party and state; the withering away of fear as a barrier to political activism; the gradual shifting of the political center of gravity from party to Soviet institutions; and the tremendous upsurge in political activism among the non-Russian nationalities: these developments have made Soviet politics both more interesting and less predictable. For the student of the

Soviet polity, one of the most pressing consequences has been the avalanche of printed (and, for a few lucky ones, audo-visual) material to be read and digested.

In the course of the last eight years, and particularly since 1986 when *glasnost* gained momentum, much new material for the study of the Politburo and the other top organs of the CPSU has become available to the Western specialist. The new situation culminated in 1990 when the Central Committee meetings were thrown open, an extensive report on one Politburo session was published, and in July the press was invited to a session of the Secretariat. Some of the new material is of great value, so that we now know much more about the history and mode of operation of the Politburo than we knew a few years ago. For a start, in December 1982, shortly after Iurii Andropov took over, *Pravda* for the first time printed a report on the weekly Politburo session. This policy has been pursued up to 1990, although the regularity and frequency of reports on Politburo sessions have changed.

Another valuable addition to the source material available to us has been the revival of the journal *Izvestiia TsK KPSS* (*Tidings of the CPSU Central Committee*) in January 1989. This journal quickly became a mine of information: documents and resolutions of the Politburo and Secretariat, reports of Politburo commissions such as the special commission on the repressions of the Stalin period, a serialized chronology of activities of the Central Committee since 1917, and often well-researched and documented reports on burning questions written by historians on the basis of previously inaccesible party archives. *Izvestiia TsK KPSS* has come to be one of the most sought-after journals for the academic student of Kremlin politics. In its second issue it published the verbatim record of the October 1987 Central Committee Plenum (with the aim of further discrediting Boris Eltsin who at the time, February 1989, was much more popular with the population of Moscow than with the leaders and besieged apparatchiki), and in the next issue Khrushchev's "secret speech" of February 1956.[4]

The combination of *glasnost* and the rehabilitation of most of the "remaining" victims of Stalinism has resulted in an increased interest in the Khrushchev period and a growing need of former Politburo members (and others) to justify their behavior ex post facto. A regular flood of memoirs has been the result. Memoirs in the form of books, serialized articles, newspaper or TV interviews and even round-table discussions have added new fact and opinion to our understanding of the Brezhnev, Khrushchev and Stalin periods. Some of them are of great value; others are almost worthless or of value only for the sake of curiosity. Thus, the voluminous memoirs of the longtime Foreign Minister Andrei Gromyko turned out to be a ludicrous disappointment when they were published in 1988.[5] Many former leaders have felt a need to speak out on the rise and fall of Nikita Khrushchev and on the "leadership"-style of Leonid Brezhnev. The serialized publication of Nikita Khrushchev's memoirs started in July 1989 and was, of course, of more interest to the Soviet public than to the Western student of Soviet politics.[6] By that date many persons had, in one way or another, spoken out on the Khrushchev and Brezhnev periods: the former Politburo members Kirill Mazurov, Anastas Mikoian, Petro Shelest, Dmitrii Shepilov and Gennadii Voronov; former Gosplan Chairman Vladimir Novikov; former KGB Chairman Vladimir Semichastnyi; and such diverse personalities as Khrushchev's son Sergei Nikitich; his son-in-law Aleksei Adzhubei; the composer Tikhon Khrennikov; the poet Andrei Voznesenskii; and political scientist and advisor Fedor Burlatskii. No less than 46 articles on Khrushchev, originally published in periodicals in 1988, were collected and published in 1989 in a book of recollections and analyses of Khrushchev and his times.[7] For the first time, documents have been published on crucial periods in Soviet history, such as a letter in which a local secret police official in June 1953 warned Khrushchev of an impending coup attempt of Lavrentii Beriia, or a résumé of the discussions at the first Presidium session after the burial ceremonies of Stalin.[8] Of more passing value are tidbits of new information such as can be read in the letter that former Politburo member and Gorbachev rival Grigorii Romanov sent to the editor of *Pravda* in September 1989, in which he disclaimed the rumor that when in 1974 his daughter married he organized a big party in the Tauride Palace and used Catherine the Great's porcelain from the Hermitage.

The recent event of crucial importance to the subject matter of this book has of course been the fall of the Politburo. It had lost its priviliged position as the main national decision-making body in 1990, one year before the abortive coup attempt triggered the August Revolution. When in that year the Communist Party's Central Committee accepted, on Gorbachev's authority, that there was no other way out of the increasing chaos but to give up its constitutional power monopoly and accept a presidency, the character of the Politburo changed. After the 28th Party Congress the expanded Politburo was no longer directly involved in national policymaking. It had also lost its position at the top of the nomenklatura: no longer were appointments and dismissals of important officials in state and society decided in the Politburo. When on 20 December 1990 Edvard Shevardnadze resigned his post as foreign minister out of disgust over the lack of support he had received from President Gorbachev, the members of the Politburo were as surprised as other mortals all over the world. Finally, the August Revolution of 1991 swept away the communist party, its Central Committee and the Politburo.

At first sight it is surprising that in 1990 so powerful an institution as the Politburo gave up its power so easily; apparently without a fight it succumbed to the President. We have made this event a starting point for our rethinking of the history of this institution. It seems that, in the light of this history, the Politburo's capitulation to Gorbachev is not so surprising after all. From its inception, the history of the Politburo has been characterized by a peculiar duality. On the one hand it established its own dictatorship over the Soviet Union; on the other hand it always tended to subject itself to its own leader. The final demise of the Politburo is the climax of a process that had its roots in the Leninist concept of the party and of the regime inside that party.

NOTES TO THE INTRODUCTION

1. Ligachev, 1991, No. 4: 6.
2. For an interesting episode involving Gorbachev, Ligachev and the *Andreeva Affair*, see Kaiser, 1991: 221-23.
3. Löwenhardt, 1978, 1982.
4. Unfortunately, *Izvestiia TsK KPSS* sometimes suggested comprehensiveness where there was none; the serialized chronologies of activities of the Central Committee that listed data on Politburo and Orgburo sessions were found to be incomplete. The July 1990 issue, for example, mentions in note 3 on p. 170 an Orgburo session on 22 August 1919, a joint Politburo-Orgburo session the next day, and another Orgburo session on 17 September. On pp. 153 and 160 in the February 1990 issue, however, neither of the two sessions is mentioned.
5. Gromyko, 1988 (almost 900 pp.).
6. The first journal to publish Khrushchev's memoirs was *Ogonek*, 1989 No. 27 ff., to be followed by *Znamia* and *Voprosy Istorii*. The first Western publication of the memoirs, *Khrushchev Remembers*, dates from 1970; see Talbott, 1970, 1974 and 1977.
7. Aksiutin, *Nikita Sergeevich...*, 1989.
8. See Gorchakov, 1989; and Barsukov, 1989.

hovered all over the world. Finally, the August Revolution of 1991, when

NOTES TO THE INTRODUCTION

Part I

1

Inner Circle — The Central Committee's Russian Branch

Origins of the Politburo

One day in March 1898 nine men gathered in a small wooden house at the outskirts of the provincial town of Minsk to establish the Russian Social-Democratic Workers Party (RSDWP). Strict conspiracy was demanded because there was a building of the mounted police across the street.[1] Four years later a radical and influential leader of this party, Vladimir Ilich Ulianov (Lenin), published his long pamphlet *What Is To Be Done?* In it he concluded with obvious relish that the workers by themselves would never attain revolutionary consciousness. He claimed the need for the RSDWP to transform itself into a small, closed, conspiratorial and disciplined party of professional revolutionaries. This party was to be the embodiment of the socialist idea. It could educate the workers to become principled opponents of the tsarist and capitalist system. Only such a party had the necessary backbone to resist the onslaught of the police and provide the workers with the necessary leadership. It was to be the vanguard of the proletariat.

Lenin and his good friend and party comrade Iulii Martov saw eye to eye on this matter, but at the 2nd Party Congress in 1903 they split up. Lenin wanted to limit party membership to only the most active and dedicated people — in accordance with his principle of professional revolutionaries. Martov, who was as much of a radical himself, felt that his friend went too far. At the decisive moment Lenin's faction garnered slightly more votes than his rivals. The Lenin group dubbed itself the *Bolsheviki* ("majorityites") and the opposition the *Mensheviki* ("minorityites"). For years to come the two factions battled for supremacy in the RSDWP.

Lenin's second major work on the party, *One Step Forward, Two Steps Back,* appeared in 1904. While the stress in his earlier pamphlet had been on the party's relations with the proletariat, the new book concentrated on the regime within the party. It was an enthusiastic, deliberately provocative song in praise of the virtues of centralism. Lenin as a rule willingly accepted accusations hurled at him to turn them back against his opponents. Martov accused him of setting up "a state of siege" in the party, but so what? "The whole of our centralism, as of now confirmed by the congress, is nothing but a 'state of siege.'" Lenin was not impressed by the accusation that he saw the party "'as a huge factory' with the CC [Central Committee] as its manager." After all, Lenin considered a factory to be the ideal school of proletarian discipline.[2]

Lenin summarized his model of party organization as "proceeding from the top down, defending the broadening of rights and powers of the centre in relation to the part." He acknowledged the "party congress, as the sovereign [*verkhovnyi*] organ of the party" that appoints the "central institutions" and "makes them supreme [*delaet ikh verkhom*] until the next congress."[3] Throughout his life Lenin adhered to the dictatorial principle. Lenin thought that it was undemocratic to provide the party members with too many rights vis-à-vis the Central Committee because the committee, being chosen by the Congress, represented the collective of the members. The more powers the Central Committee had, the more democratic the party was. Thus his views were in line with the old Roman idea of dictatorship that may be defined as the temporary and legal, but nevertheless total, relinquishement of sovereignty by the community to a leader. Once appointed, and for the period of his rule, his powers are total.

In Lenin's system of thought there was no inherent brake on the accumulation of power in the hands of an unassailable and ever smaller group of leaders. One other leader of the RSDWP who disagreed with Lenin was Lev Davidovich Bronshtein (Trotskii). In his pamphlet *Our Political Tasks,* written in August 1904, he sharply attacked Lenin's attitude as elitist and called it a form of orthodox theocracy. Trotskii wrote that the Bolshevik intellectuals were setting themselves up as trustees of proletarian interests and that this "substitutionism" (*zamestitelstvo*) would lead to a narrowing or a shrinking of the active decision makers as the party organization was substituted for the party as a whole, the Central Committee for the party organization, and finally, a dictator for the Central Committee.[4] The subsequent history of the social-democratic party, the communist party and the Politburo in particular testifies to the wisdom of these prophecies even though the prophet would later take a place in the heart of the problem he described in 1904.

At the 2nd Congress of the RSDWP in 1903 a Central Committee of three members was elected. A more prestigious institution (considered to be providing ideological leadership to the party, in contrast to the more practical directions of the CC) was at that time the so-called Central Organ, the party's newspaper *Iskra*. The emigrés Lenin, Martov and G. V. Plekhanov were elected to serve as its editorial board. Compared to them, the members of the CC were not very well known.

THE INNER CIRCLE

It appears that the prehistory of the Politburo goes back to 1903. Its embryonic shapes can be discovered in the unfortunately rather tedious Party Rules and organizational decisions. Soon after the Congress, in July 1903, one member of the CC, G. M. Krzhizhanovskii, established the so-called Russian bureau of the CC. Several of Lenin's relatives took up work for it.[5] The next year, 1904, E. D. Stasova was attached to it as "secretary of the Bureau of the CC." Another member of the CC established the "Foreign department of the CC" in Geneva.[6] The splitting up of the CC in smaller bureaus became one of its enduring features. Pospelov's *History of the Communist Party of the Soviet Union* noted that the five-man-strong Central Committee elected at the 3rd Party Congress in 1905 was soon divided into two parts, Russian and abroad. "Accordingly, two Bureau's of the CC of the RSDWP were established." The Russian Bureau consisted of three CC members (plus another one, recently co-opted), among whom were A. A. Bogdanov and L. B. Krasin. A Secretariat, headed by a "responsible secretary," was attached to it. However, CC member Lenin was part of the Foreign Bureau.[7]

The 5th Party Congress of 1907 elected a new Central Committee, in which the Bolsheviks had a larger vote than the Mensheviks. Accordingly, the new Russian Bureau consisted of three Bolshevik members of the CC and two Menshevik members. According to Pospelov, the Menshevik members, who included Noi Zhordaniia, were not very active. The Bureau was actually the instrument through which the Bolshevik factional center directed its organizations in Russia.[8] The Bolsheviks, who at that time commanded stronger forces in the CC than their rivals, were under the impression that the Mensheviks wanted to weaken decisively the power of the CC. To counter that threat an important decision was taken at the plenary meeting of the Central Committee in Geneva in August 1908. Five Bolsheviks, three

Mensheviks and four representatives of national organizations of the RSDWP attended the meeting. It was decided to strengthen the Russian Bureau.

For the first time the CC adopted its own rules in 1908, called "The Organization of the Central Committee." They noted that "a limited circle [*suzhennyi sostav*] of the Central Committee leads all on-going work in Russia in the periods between the plenary sessions." This "CC in its narrow composition [*v uzkom sostave*]" had five members and was also called the "quintet." It had the duty to consult the other CC members on important decisions; only in cases of extreme urgency could it decide completely on its own. The quintet led the Duma faction. The "Foreign Bureau of the CC" consisted of three members of the CC and was "subordinated to the inner circle [*uzkomu sostavu*] of the CC." Two Bolsheviks were elected into the "limited circle," which was simply another name for the Russian Bureau. Lenin himself was not elected to the Central Committee but to the board of the Central Organ.[9] Although the most influential leaders of the RSDWP were not members of the Russian Bureau, this institution nevertheless became the highest organ of the party, at least on paper.

The party was by now so divided by factional strife that it hardly functioned properly. The Russian Bureau was soon incapacitated because of arrests.[10] In January-February 1910 the Central Committee convened, against Lenin's will, in Paris in a plenary session. The aim was to reunite the party. The plenum adopted "The Rules of the Central Committee." The first paragraph stated: "The collegium of members of the CC working [*deistvuiushchaia*] in Russia has all the rights of the CC." It consisted of seven members of whom four were from the CC. Paragraph 8 of the rules stated that "in the period between general meetings of the CC the Bureau of the CC, elected by the general meeting, leads all business of the CC." This Bureau was presumably the nucleus of the Russian collegium. There was also a Foreign Bureau of the Central Committee.[11] Lenin was again elected to the board of the Central Organ, as was his close collaborator G. E. Zinovev.

Lenin wanted a strong and authoritative collegium in Russia. But the Bolshevik CC members entering the Russian Bureau (among others I. F. Dubrovinskii, I. P. Goldenberg and V. P. Nogin) were too willingly negotiating with the Mensheviks to suit him. Pospelov suggests that due to the Menshevik-Bolshevik conflict, the collegium in Russia did not become a functioning reality.[12] At the Bolshevik Prague conference of 1912 a new Central Committee was elected. A new Russian Bureau of five CC members was created, among whom were G. K. Ordzhonikidze, I. V. Stalin and (candidate CC member) E. D. Stasova. CC member V. I. Lenin was not a member of the Bureau, but became editor of the paper *Sotsial-demokrat*.[13] It is a curious fact to note that, according to the Rules of the Central Committee, Stalin was now in a more authoritative position in the party than Lenin, who was always content with a de facto controlling role from behind the screen of his "Central Organs."

THE BUREAU AND THE REVOLUTION

When World War I broke out all five members of the Russian Bureau were in exile. As a matter of fact, almost the whole of the Central Committee was deported or in jail. Lenin and Zinovev held the fort abroad, but in the autumn of 1915 the new CC member, A. G. Shliapnikov, managed to revive the Bureau of the CC. He was the only CC member in the new Bureau. Soon the Bureau was depleted again to be revived only in November 1916 in its third form under the troika of Shliapnikov, V. M. Molotov and P. A. Zalutskii. The Bureau of the CC succeeded in keeping in touch with the "part of the CC abroad."[14] In March 1917, when tsarist rule was overthrown, the Bureau still consisted of the same troika. Pospelov described it alternately as "the Russian bureau of the CC" or as "the Bureau of the CC," implying that these were two terms for one and the same institution.[15]

The protocols of the Bureau meetings in March 1917 have been published.[16] During this period the Bureau grew sufficiently to elect a five-member Presidium, among whom were CC members Shliapnikov, Stalin, and Stasova. According to the rules adopted in 1910, this Bureau was the leading institution of the party whenever the Central Committee was not in session. That it considered itself to be just that appears from its decision on 31 March to change a paragraph in the Party Rules.[17] In April and May the Bolshevik RSDWP convened in a conference to elect a new nine-member CC. Lenin had returned from abroad. Robert Slusser quotes several Soviet works that state that the Politburo was set up in May 1917 with Stalin as a member.[18] According to the Rules of 1910, the CC was required to appoint such a Bureau. Lenin himself may be assumed to have been a member.

At the 6th Party Congress of the Bolshevik RSDWP in August 1917, new Rules of the Party were adopted. Paragraph 13 noted: "The CC produces from its midst an inner circle of the Central Committee for on-going work."[19] The size of the CC was raised to 21 voting members and 10 candidate members. At its first meeting after the congress on 18 August, with Lenin and Zinovev in hiding, the Central Committee elected a new inner circle, consisting of 11 people: Stalin, Sokolnikov, Dzerzhinskii, Miliutin, Uritskii,

Ioffe, Sverdlov, Muranov, Bubnov, Stasova, and Smilga (until Shaumian's return).[20] When this group met for the first time the next day, it formed a Secretariat consisting of five members, among whom was the eternal Elena Stasova.[21] According to the protocol records, the inner circle met seven times. After 5 September it disappeared from the records.

The first meeting of the CC with Lenin again in attendance took place at 23 October. Between 5 September and 23 October, 15 CC meetings have been recorded. In most of them the great majority of the attending members were also members of the inner circle.[22] What seems to have happened is that the circle was watered down; not all its members showed up, but in their place a small number of other CC members did. At the momentuous meeting of 23 October the Bolshevik Central Committee decided, with only Grigorii Zinovev and Lev Kamenev in opposition, on an armed uprising that would occur in about two weeks. As the meeting was drawing to a close, Feliks Dzerzhinskii, the Polish revolutionary from Wilna, proposed to "establish a Political bureau from members of the CC for political leadership." It was elected and consisted of Lenin, Zinovev, Kamenev, Trotskii, Stalin, Sokolnikov and Bubnov.[23]

Trotskii later wrote that this political bureau never met "in its October membership."[24] There is no reason to suspect this to be untrue, but the qualifying addition deserves attention. There is indeed no evidence that the Bureau worked during the Bolshevik seizure of power two weeks after its establishment. The CC, however, decided at its meeting of 12 December 1917 to expand the powers of the "bureau of the CC (Stalin, Lenin, Trotskii and Sverdlov)." This "quartet" obtained broad decision-making powers, provided it drew in those other CC members present at the administrative headquarters, the Smolnyi.[25] The renewed party journal *Izvestiia TsK KPSS*, discussing this event, notes that "the exact date of the creation [of the Bureau] is unknown."[26] At some date after the seizure of power the Bureau was apparently revived in a more limited and workable composition and re-mained in existence until March 1919.

One reference to it is a cryptic note in the protocols of the CC meeting of 22 January 1918: "Bureau of the CC. 1) The CC to Moscow. 2) The Bureau in Moscow, as it was during the April days. [on a separate line:] Lenin, Stalin, Sverdlov, Sokolnikov, Trotskii."[27] The Bureau of the CC was thus expanded to include Sokolnikov.[28] Recently the protocols of the meeting of the Bureau of the CC of 4 April 1918 have been published by *Izvestiia TsK KPSS*. The Bureau still had the same five members. The same journal informs us of the decision, taken on 30 March, that the "inner circle" of the CC was henceforth to meet regularly on Fridays at 11 A.M. It adds that the "inner circle" was "sometimes called the 'Bureau.' "[29] This is important because it implies that the Bureau, being identical to the "inner circle" of the official Party Rules, was not a coincidental and informal institution. Other meetings of the Bureau took place on 17 and 19 December 1918 and 11 March 1919.[30]

It had been predicted that Lenin's authoritarianism would result in a process of substitution, leading eventually to the downgrading of the Central Committee itself. And indeed, as we have seen, from 1903 onward small bureaus were set up within the CC. In 1908 a "limited circle" within the CC was included in the Rules of the Committee. The available information suggests that the terms "Bureau," "Russian Bureau," "Political Bureau" and "inner circle" were synonyms. The Bureau (in its various shapes) was, however, clearly not able to perform the leading role it was entitled to, until well after the October coup. The main reason was probably not so much the repeated destruction of the Bureau by the police, but that most of the time influential leaders such as Lenin were not Bureau members because they lived abroad or were in hiding. The Bureau has, therefore, not always been recognized as the precursor of the all-powerful Politburo.[31]

On 18 March 1919 the 8th Congress of the Russian Communist Party (bolsheviks) opened in Moscow. At this congress the Politburo was officially established and here the prehistory of the instituition ends. Its history begins.

NOTES TO CHAPTER 1

1. Pospelov, t. 1, 1964: 260-61.
2. Lenin, 1959: 307, 379.
3. Ibid.: 384-85.
4. Trotskii, 1904: 54.
5. There was a predecessor to the Russian Bureau. In January 1902 a meeting of organizers of *Iskra* convened in Samara. It created the formal structure of an organization built up around *Iskra* as a kind of nucleus within the RSDWP. It elected its own Central Committee of 16 people. CC member Krzhizhanovskii, his wife Z. P. Krzhizhanovskaia and M. I. Ulianova (the last two performing secretarial work) formed the "Bureau of the Russian organization of *Iskra*." See Pospelov, t. 1, 1964: 421. This was probably the earliest embryo of the Politburo.
6. Pospelov, t. 1, 1964: 482.
7. Pospelov, t. 2, 1966: 62.
8. Ibid.: 248.
9. Ibid.: 257-58; *KPSS v rezoliutsiiakh...*, 1953: 188-92.
10. Pospelov, t. 2, 1966: 297.

11. *KPSS v rezoliutsiiakh...*, 1953: 238-39.
12. Pospelov, t. 2, 1966: 298-300, 338, 344.
13. Ibid.: 372-73.
14. Ibid.: 484, 543-44, 653.
15. Pospelov, t. 3, 1967: 17.
16. "Protokoly...", 1962.
17. Ibid.: 134, 152, 157n.
18. Slusser, 1987: 95-101.
19. *KPSS v rezoliutsiiakh...*, 1953: 385.
20. *Protokoly...*, 1958: 6.
21. Ibid.: 13.
22. Ibid.: 32-80. At the enlarged session of the CC on 13 September, the presence of a representation of "the Political bureau" is recorded, in addition to a number of CC members who were for the greater part members of the inner circle. Ibid.: 37.
23. Ibid.: 86.
24. Cited in: Slusser, 1987: 227.
25. *Protokoly...*, 1958: 155.
26. "Deiatelnost...", 1989, No. 1:236.
27. *Protokoly...*, 1958: 166.
28. Slusser (1987: 97-98) assumes that the "Bureau in Moscow" and the "Bureau of the CC" were one and the same thing. This may be a misreading. The CC as such moved to Moscow only in early March. The January decision could alternatively be explained to mean that *part* of the CC had to move to Moscow, forming a Moscow Bureau there of the same composition as the Moscow Bureau in April 1917.
29. "Deiatelnost....", 1989, No. 3: 107-113.
30. "Deiatelnost...", 1989, No. 6: 154, 167-71; "Deiatelnost...", 1989, No. 7: 144.
31. An exception in this respect is: Avtorkhanov (1981); see also Slusser (1987) and Van den Berg (1984: 365ff.)

2

Not a Debating Club

The Politburo Under Lenin

In his speech to the organizational section of the 8th Congress on 20 March 1919, V. V. Osinskii, representing the discontented delegates of the Moscow party organization, stated that local party organs never got to hear about the political line laid down by the CC. As a collective organ, Osinskii said, the Committee apparently had no real existence. Decisions were all too often made by a much smaller group of people, Lenin and Sverdlov, with perhaps another official present. Osinskii demanded a stronger CC with 21 members.[1] Grigorii Zinovev, representing the position of the leadership, thought the criticism exaggerated and considered a 21-member CC to be unnecessarily heavy. At the sixth session of the congress on 22 March he proposed: "Nineteen is the number that gives us the possibility to create a Political bureau with a fitting composition, and an Organizational bureau and a Secretariat, as well as a itinerant [*raz''ezdnuiu*] collegium."[2]

In the end, Zinovev's recommendation was carried. The relevant resolution stated: "The Central Committee organizes, first, a Political bureau; second, an Organizational bureau; third, a Secretariat." The Politburo, consisting of only five CC members, was to decide matters that could not be delayed. It was obliged to report on its work to the plenary sessions of the CC at least every two weeks. Other members of the CC could attend Politburo meetings with a consultative voice.[3] Curiously enough, the existing Bureau of the CC did not figure as such in the discussions during the congress. The Politburo was elected at the first plenary session of the CC on 25 March. It consisted of L. B. Kamenev, N. N. Krestinskii, Lenin, Stalin and Trotskii. N. I. Bukharin, M. I. Kalinin and Zinovev were appointed as candidate members.[4]

1. *Protokol of the first Politburo session on 16 April 1919, written in pencil on a piece of brown wrapping paper from a parcel-post package* (Izvestia TsK KPSS, 1989, No. 3).

On 16 April 1919 Lenin opened the first session of the newly constituted Politburo. The broad range of issues on which decisions were taken in this meeting shows the Politburo as the nerve center of Bolshevik rule.[5] It is doubtful whether the enlarged CC had the stronger hold on the Bureau that Osinskii had demanded. During the Civil War centralized leadership became even more essential. Military demands frequently pulled CC members away from Moscow; the Politburo directed and coordinated their movements and actions. During the war the Politburo was a stable nucleus of the CC. Its composition remained unchanged until March 1921. Despite tensions on a personal level, none of the eight leaders of the RCP(b) was engaged in "oppositional" activity before the party crisis of the winter of 1920-21. In the face of the common enemy the ranks were closed.

THE LENIN REGIME

Unity, however, evaporated as the Civil War drew to an end. This was apparent at the 10th Party Congress, which opened on 8 March 1921. The congress met under difficult circumstances. The Kronstadt sailors had rebelled against the party's dictatorship, calling for political and economic freedom and for new soviets elected by secret ballot. While the congress was in session the revolt was being brutally suppressed by Trotskii and M. N. Tukhachevskii, who led military forces and some congress delegates against the sailors. On 9 March a vote was taken on the general policies to be followed by the CC. The Committee was supported by 514 delegates; two opposition platforms demanding more democracy in the party and the country (Osinskii's "Democratic Centralists" and Shliapnikov's "Workers' Opposition") gathered only 92 votes.[6] In this matter the CC stood firm, but the so-called trade union discussion was more serious because it involved a split within the Politburo itself.

The country was in shambles after the Civil War. People's Commissar for Military Affairs, Lev Trotskii, favored the complete merger of the trade unions with the state and the general militarization of labor as a forced solution to the problems. In his authoritarian approach he was supported by two other members of the Politburo: Bukharin and Krestinskii. The Workers' Opposition, on the other hand, favored a quick transfer of the economic administration of the country to the trade unions. Lenin, supported by the remaining four members of the Politburo, produced his own "Platform of Ten." He took a middle course, rejecting absorption of the trade unions by the state while stressing party leadership over state and unions. Lenin won easily, gaining 336 votes on 14 March, while Trotskii had to be content with 50 and the third platform was supported by only 18 delegates.[7] Lenin was, nevertheless, fed up with having to deal with oppositions.

The new Politburo elected on 16 March 1921 was different in several respects. Secretary of the CC V. M. Molotov was added as a candidate member, Zinovev was promoted to full membership and Krestinskii was excluded from the Politburo altogether. Among the full members, Trotskii became isolated, surrounded by Lenin and the three comrades who had followed him in the debate. The more important result of the Congress was the adoption, on Lenin's strong insistence, of the resolution "On unity in the party." It not only forbade "fractionism"—that is the occurrence of organized groups within the party—but stipulated that discussions were henceforth to be waged in a special discussion paper. Participants should take care to make "business-like proposals" because uncontrolled criticism aided the enemies surrounding the party.[8] Any possible misunderstanding of the intentions of the resolution was ruled out by the adoption of another resolution declaring propaganda for the ideas of the Workers' Opposition a ground for expulsion from the party.[9]

The new regime Lenin established in 1921 was not only aimed against organized opposition but also at a drastic restriction of free discussion as such. In his speech on 16 March he acknowledged the necessity of further "theoretical discussion" on moot points, but not of "political struggle. We are not a debating club."[10] In August 1921 he even attempted to have the unfortunate Shliapnikov, leader of the Workers' Opposition and still a CC member, excluded from the party. He failed to gather the necessary support in the Committee. Nevertheless, it remains a valid observation that the new regime accelerated the shift of power from the Central Committee to the Politburo. The centralist side of the "democratic centralist" coin was reinforced. This was, however, also visible within the Politburo: the regime of stifling discussions did not stop at the gates of this most prestigious organ.

Enforced unity on one political line naturally promotes the one embodiment of this line—the leader. Some of the more sinister operations of Lenin and Stalin against Trotskii have been brought to light in the memoirs of Anastas Mikoian, then a local party leader in Nizhnii Novgorod. In January 1922 he was invited to Moscow to meet People's Commissar and member of the Orgburo—Stalin. Stalin expressed his and Lenin's concern that too many followers of Trotskii should be elected as delegates to the forthcoming 11th Party Congress. He invited Mikoian to visit Siberia under the cover of a family visit and secretly inform the Siberian party leader Lashevich of these fears, urging him to prevent such a development. At the end of Stalin's conversation with Mikoian the door quietly opened and in came Lenin, dressed in his usual coat and cap. Stalin informed him that Mikoian was prepared to see Lashevich.[11]

At this next congress, in March-April 1922, Lenin showed no signs of mellowing. By then he was even more convinced that the party needed hard, businesslike work now, no struggles and discussions. The congress confirmed a resolution announcing that it would henceforth be considered a "crime against the party" to inject exaggerated "quarrels and arguments" into party life.[12] In his speech on 28 March Lenin bluntly told critical delegates to shut up or face the consequences.[13] In the same speech he defended Stalin against the accusation of having amassed too many positions; Stalin, he said, was "a man of authority."[14] At the plenum of the new CC on 3 April 1922 Stalin was elected head of the Secretariat, obtaining the title General Secretary. The proposal probably came from Kamenev and Stalin himself, supported by Lenin.[15]

After the congress, Deputy Chairman of the Council of People's Commissars A. I. Rykov and trade union leader M. P. Tomskii were added to the Politburo as full members. Tomskii had been one of the co-signers of the Platform of Ten. Lenin packed the Politburo with loyal followers, making it hard for Trotskii to challenge him again. Lenin and Trotskii had been very close during the early years after the revolution, but nobody had forgotten that Trotskii had joined the Bolsheviks only in 1917— after years of combating Lenin. Mutual tensions between Lenin and Trotskii flared up again with the trade union debate. In a twisted way Trotskii recognized Lenin's closeness to Stalin, Zinovev and Kamenev in his autobiography when he described the three as Lenin's "epigones" on whom Lenin relied to have his orders mechanically executed, "especially during my differences with Lenin."[16] Gradually a new regime crystallized within the Politburo making fundamental opposition to the leader an unusual phenomenon.

LENIN LOSES CONTROL

This regime was to become the rule in the Politburo until the present day, but a historical coincidence temporarily intervened: on 25 May 1922 Lenin was partly paralyzed by a stroke, for a while losing the ability to speak. With their leader disabled, the "epigones," to use Trotskii's term, felt more free to follow their own course, which was not always to Lenin's liking. He started to have doubts about Stalin in the early fall of 1922 when he read his plan for the inclusion of the independent Soviet republics as mere autonomous units in the Russian republic. He formulated a sharp reaction, pointing at the danger of "Great Russian chauvinism." Stalin in turn accused Lenin of "national liberalism." On 6 October the CC, however, accepted a new version of the plan, adopting Lenin's proposal of a Union of Soviet Socialist Republics (USSR) of formally independent republics.[17] This matter was now temporarily closed. But after returning to work that month, Lenin was provoked again by a CC decision, supported by Stalin, to reduce the state monopoly of trade.

Lenin now convinced Trotskii, the leading proponent of economic centralism, to take up the case. Together they made the CC annul the decision on 18 December.[18] Although Trotskii's story that Lenin proposed a joint "bloc" with him in early December was probably an exaggeration, Lenin's rapprochement with him was unmistakable.[19] Then misfortune struck the tormented leader again. During the night of 22-23 December 1922 he had another stroke and was again half paralyzed. From his bed he continued to dictate notes and articles, summarizing his thinking on the situation in the Soviet state and the party.[20] These seemingly antibureaucratic writings can actually be read (with the clear exception of the assault on Stalin's "Great Russian chauvinism") as an argument for more party unity and stricter centralization of the Soviet state. For Lenin combating bureaucracy meant creating discipline, increasing centralized party control, shaking a lax apparatus from above, in order to build a competent machine, able to carry out orders without fail.

The heart of Lenin's ideas consisted of his proposal to create a new, top-heavy cluster of institutions consisting of the Central Committee and the so-called Central Control Commission, assisted by a reorganized apparatus of the People's Commissariat of Workers' and Peasants' Inspection. These organs should absorb several hundred new people, mainly workers and trained specialists. This powerful party-controlled hybrid would have to clean up and take control of the state apparatus that was still largely a leftover from the past. As a good example of the forthcoming reorganization Lenin mentioned the way the Red Army had been built.[21] No one could miss this implicit pointer at Trotskii's former achievements. The efficient organizer of the Red Army, the man who wanted to "shake up" the trade unions in 1920, recaptured Lenin's attention. His revitalized interest in the centralist approach was also evident in his support for Trotskii's old plan to provide the State Planning Commission with legislative powers.

The enlarged Central Committee was also expected to gain sufficient authority to prevent serious conflicts between the highest party leaders. Lenin was aware that his own grip on the Politburo was removed, and so he became even more obsessed with party unity. He feared a split in the Politburo between Stalin and Trotskii, "the two eminent leaders of the present CC." In order to prevent such a split, Stalin, who was "too rude," would have to be transferred to another post because he had obtained too much power as General Secretary.[22] In his "Letter to the Congress" written between 23 December and 4 January, Lenin expressed a change of strategy within the Politburo: instead of rallying Stalin, Kamenev and Zinovev against Trotskii, he now opted for a balancing act between Stalin and Trotskii, dividing his favors. Out of weakness the dictator had become a statesman. But not for long.

For months now, People's Commissar of Nationalities Joseph Stalin was pressuring an unwilling Georgian Central Committee to accept the fact that the Transcaucasian federation (instead of Georgia as a separate unit) would enter the new Soviet Union. When Stalin's ally and leader of the Caucasian party organization, Sergo Ordzhonikidze, in late November 1922 actually struck a Georgian comrade in the face, Lenin was outraged. After months of angry brooding he finally reached a decision. On 5 and 6 March 1923 he wrote two letters, expressing "with all my heart" support for the Georgian leaders against Stalin and asking Trotskii to undertake their defense.[23] At the same time Lenin sent his famous last letter to Stalin threatening to break off all relations if he did not apologize for his rude behavior against his wife, Nadezhda Krupskaia. The next day Krupskaia told Kamenev that Lenin was planning "to crush Stalin politically."[24]

Compared to early 1922, Lenin had now made more than a full turnabout, apparently striving for an alliance with Trotskii against Stalin. Leaving the moral aspect of it aside, it is hard to consider this as anything else than a wild and futile maneuver of a dying leader who had lost his grip on the Politburo. On 10 March a new stroke paralyzed Lenin again. Politically he was now a dead man. The Politburo was left without its leader in a situation where the regime of enforced unity was not yet internalized. The stage was set for a destructive struggle for power.

NOTES TO CHAPTER 2

1. *Vosmoi s''ezd...*, 1959: 164-66.
2. Ibid.: 285.
3. Ibid.: 424-25.
4. Pospelov, t. 3, 1968: 282n.
5. See: "Protokol zasedaniia...", 1989.

6. *Desiatyi s''ezd...*, 1963: 137.
7. Ibid.: 399.
8. Ibid.: 571-74.
9. Ibid.: 574-76.
10. Ibid.: 521.
11. Mikoian, 1972: 188-189.
12. *KPSS v rezoliutsiiakh...*, 1953: 633.
13. *Odinnatsatyi s''ezd...*, 1961: 149.
14. Ibid.: 143.
15. Volkogonov, Kn. 1, Ch. 1, 1989: 132-34.
16. Trotzki, 1930: 461.
17. See for the relevant documents: "Iz istorii...", 1989.
18. Two relevant letters from Lenin to Stalin on this matter can be read in: Lenin, 1964: 220-23, 338-39.
19. Trotzki, 1930: 462-63.
20. See Lenin, 1964: 341-406.
21. Ibid.: 383.
22. Ibid.: 343-46.
23. Trotsky, 1974: 55.
24. Cited in Lewin, 1969: 103.

3

The Entourage of the Leader

The Politburo Under Stalin

Against expectations, the 12th Party Congress in April 1923 was a relatively dull event. The leading "troika" of Zinovev, Kamenev and Stalin, formed immediately after Lenin's first stroke, was in charge. Zinovev delivered the political and Stalin the organizational report of the CC. Trotskii did not dare to put up a fight. The new Politburo of 11 men elected on 26 April differed only in one respect from the previous one: Ia. E. Rudzutak was added as candidate member. Unimportant in itself, this was a sign of changes: Rudzutak was one of the three members of the Secretariat. The other two, Stalin and Molotov, were also on the Politburo. Stalin's secretarial job was now his main one, and the influence of this institution grew in the Politburo. According to Stalin's secretary, Bazhanov, his boss even operated a listening device from his office at the building on *Staraia Ploshchad* (Old Square) to tap his colleagues' telephone calls.[1]

Even Zinovev became alarmed by the secretarial power. In August or September 1923, while in the Caucasian holiday resort of Kislovodsk, he invited his Politburo colleague Bukharin and some other party leaders to discuss the problem how to bring the Secretariat under control of the Politburo. They met in a cave.[2] And they set a tradition: Soviet leaders continued to use their holidays outside Moscow for conspiracies. The result of the meeting was only that Zinovev, Bukharin and Trotskii were elected to the Orgburo, which on paper was superior to the Secretariat, on 25 September 1925.[3] The expected battle broke out on 8 October, with Trotskii taking the initiative. In his memoirs he suggests, though, that he had been provoked because an informal Politburo of seven members had been formed, communicating with its local followers in cipher, that excluded him.[4]

In a letter Trotskii castigated the leadership for their economic policy and for the party regime. At the time the country was hit by an economic crisis; very high prices for industrial goods were an important aspect of that crisis. Peasants were discouraged from selling because they could not buy. Trotskii evidently felt that the liberal New Economic Policy, dating from 1921, went too far. He proposed to make industry work more efficiently through centralization under the State Planning Committee (*Gosplan*) and ruthless concentration. Then he proceeded to attack the "bureaucratization of the party apparatus," pointing at the "secretarial apparatus, created from the top down." The system of nomination of cadres (instead of election) had reached unheard-of proportions. It was much worse than during the Civil War. Furthermore, "the secretarial hierarchy is the apparatus that creates party opinion and party decisions." Free discussion died.[5] Trotskii hoped to break up the ruling cliques and release rank-and-file energies for a more radical economic policy.

One week later, 46 prominent party leaders repeated Trotskii's accusations in even sharper terms in a letter of their own. They claimed that the "regime of factional dictatorship in the party had outlived itself," though they stopped short of demanding an annulment of the resolutions of the 10th Party Congress. The letter noted that the Secretariat controlled the election of delegations to party congresses, thereby perpetuating its rule.[6] Perhaps this was the first description of what has been dubbed Stalin's "circular flow of power."[7] In terms of power politics, the letter was of marginal significance. Only two of the 57 members and candidates of the CC signed it, and many of the dissidents had formerly been in the defeated Democratic Centralist faction. On 19 October the whole Politburo, except the ailing Lenin and (probably for coincidental reasons) Rudzutak, condemned Trotskii's letter in a letter of its own.[8] Trotskii and the 46 dissidents were defeated at the 13th Party Conference in January 1924, receiving only three votes out of 128.[9]

The so-called Left Opposition never had a chance. Its position was based on a fundamental misreading of Bolshevik tradition. The system of "recommendations" for cadres to eligible functions (amounting virtually to nominations) had been established by Lenin, and so was the practice that elected secretaries be "confirmed" by the higher party institutions.[10] In Lenin's last writings one can discover nothing to indicate that he hoped to increase freedom of discussion. It might be said that Trotskii in 1923 reverted to his old anti-Leninist position of 1904, while Stalin guarded Lenin's dictatorial approach. Trotskii had maneuvered himself into a hopeless position. He could draw no relevant support for his declaration of war against the leading apparatus from the apparatus itself; and with his call for freedom of discussion he could not rally the rank and file either because the ordinary members largely shared the Leninist dictatorial premises.

The Left Opposition made another fatal miscalculation. After the disastrous years of the Civil War, a feeling of fatigue prevailed among the party masses and in the country at large. Trotskii's calls to rebel against the apparatus and set the country on a more adventurous economic course found, therefore, no willing reponse. The majority of the Politburo calculated better. It hoped for a breathing span of social and political peace in which the secretarial hierarchy could quietly consolidate its own power, while the economy slowly gathered strength. This was more suited to the spirit of the times.

On 21 January 1924 Lenin died. In a speech at the second All-Union Congress of Soviets on 26 January, Stalin honored his deceased leader. Pledging to fulfill his "commandments" with honor, he noted that the party stood firm "like a rock," despite the many attacks by "scorpions." He pledged to "preserve the unity of our party as the apple of our eye."[11] Stalin added a new, almost religious tone to the Bolshevik tradition. In 1921 he had summarized his view on the party in some personal notes, to be published only in 1947. He described the party as "a kind of order of sword-bearers within the Soviet state" with the "inner weldedness [spaika] and closedness" of "an organism."[12] The order of sword-bearers to which he referred, also called the *Fratres militiae Christi*, had been established in the 13th century. Their image was a red sword supporting a cross on their white cloak, and they had been active in Prussia and the Baltic area for centuries. As all crusading monks, they accepted the vow of absolute obedience.

The comparison of the party to this organization was curious for a communist leader, even counting the fact that Stalin had been a student at a Russian Orthodox seminary. Perhaps too much should not be made of it, but it points at two essential elements of Stalin's thinking on the party. He saw it as a war-making machine and as an almost holy institution, entitled to complete submission by all members.

During 1924 the debate with Trotskii continued. With his brochures *The New Course* and *Lessons of October*, Trotskii dug his own grave by implicitly attacking the Bolshevik tradition. In them he stated that Old Bolsheviks such as Stalin and Kamenev in 1917 had not been up to their revolutionary task. Only Lenin, having gone over to Trotskii's own approach of "permanent revolution," had dragged them into the October coup.

THE TROIKA BREAKS UP

The troika held throughout 1924, but then fear of Stalin's growing power gained the upper hand in Zinovev and Kamenev's minds. The Leningrad party organization, headed by its de facto leader Zinovev, rebelled. In April 1925 Kamenev and Zinovev attacked Bukharin and Stalin at the Politburo for their thesis that socialism could be built "in one country."[13] This was the real starting point of the new debate that was characterized by a surprisingly large dose of dogmatic exchanges. According to Bazhanov, the troika met in April for the last time.[14] The "New Opposition" (as Stalin called it) favored a more radical economic policy. Of the 13 members and candidates of the Politburo, it was supported only by People's Commissar of Finance, G. Ia. Sokolnikov. Trotskii watched silently as his old opponents attacked each other.

At the decisive 14th Party Congress in December 1925, Kamenev complained that the Secretariat had become more powerful than the Politburo itself and added that he now realized that "Stalin cannot carry out the role of unifier of the bolshevik staff." He was shouted down with such remarks as "Now he showed his cards!" and "Nonsense."[15] The Leningrad opposition was overwhelmingly defeated. During this period Stalin made a good impression on the average party leader. Mikoian, already a member of the CC, wrote in his memoirs that Stalin "behaved very comradely when he met ordinary members of the CC and other eminent party workers; he listened attentively, showing no 'leaderism,' capriciousness and arrogance."[16] Stalin's personality was not recognized for what it was. He was excessively power-hungry but preferred not to present himself aggressively. The old underground conspirator posed modestly, secretly pulling the strings from behind the scenes, biding his time.

In the spring of 1926 Kamenev proposed a "bloc" to Trotskii: "It is enough for you and Zinovev to appear on the same platform, and the party will find its true Central Committee."[17] A "United Opposition" was formed, with the so-called Declaration of 13, written in July, as its platform. Of the 14 members of the Politburo, elected on 1 January 1926, only Trotskii, Kamenev and Zinovev signed the declaration. According to a secret document of the CC, handed out in 1927 and in the possession of Avtorkhanov, the opposition was organized along conspiratorial lines. Code names were used: Trotskii was "Tolstoi" and Kamenev "Korolenko"; the Politburo was called "Poland."[18] Trotskii described how in the autumn of 1926 opposition speakers at meetings were met by well-organized shouting, whistling and roaring sirens.[19] Under the rules against factions the CC was authorized to act, and it did not hesitate. On 23 July Zinovev was excluded from the Politburo. Trotskii and Kamenev followed exactly three months later.

The opposition was removed from the Politburo, which from now on worked concertedly toward an overwhelming, final defeat of the remaining opposition forces at the 15th Party Congress in December 1927. During the second half of 1926 the Central Committee appointed a large group of new members to the Politburo, making this the most unstable year in the history of the institution until 1990.[20] After the last reshuffle on 3 November voting members were *Pravda* editor Bukharin, secretaries Molotov and Stalin, people's commissars K. E. Voroshilov and Rudzutak, head of state Kalinin and Prime Minister Rykov, and the leader of the trade unions Tomskii. The candidate members were G. I. Petrovskii, N. A. Uglanov, A. A. Andreev, L. M. Kaganovich, S. M. Kirov, Mikoian and V. Ia. Chubar. This was the winning coalition of the secretarial hierarchy and the state apparatus, based on their shared interests.

EXTRAORDINARY MEASURES

In early 1928 a grain crisis broke out again in the USSR. The countryside did not supply the cities and army with enough grain. The bread lines became longer and longer. It was decided to undertake "extraordinary measures," forceful requisitions of grain stocks that reminded citizens of the Civil War years. This crisis strained relations within the victorious Politburo. As the year progressed, tensions rose between Stalin, who favored a harsh line toward the peasants, and Bukharin, who hoped to preserve the New Economic Policy. On 1 or 2 June the young theoretician of communism wrote his Georgian comrade a letter, addressing him by his old underground pseudonym: "Koba, I write to you, and I don't speak to you because it is very difficult for me to speak, and I'm afraid you won't hear me out."[21] The two senior Politburo members clashed at the plenary session of the CC in July 1928.

In his long speech on 9 July Stalin stated firmly that the state would have to draw a "tribute" from the peasants. Under these circumstances the class struggle would grow fiercer, but that was inevitable in the process of building communism because the resistance of the old exploiting classes would grow more desperate.[22] It has been noted that as soon as Stalin had defeated the Left Opposition, he took over their radical economic program to destroy Bukharin. This is somewhat misleading. First, the continuing procurement crisis rather than tactical considerations was the main reason for Stalin's change of heart. He then met with fierce objections from Bukharin, which caused him to destroy the man politically. Second, Trotskii and Zinovev had fought for more industrial *élan* in order to provide the countryside with more consumer goods. Stalin, however, propagated a "union [*smychka*] based on metals" rather than one on "textiles."[23] With its extraordinary emphasis on heavy industry, Stalin's program stood out against both the old leftists and Bukharin.

Bukharin seems to have been psychologically at a breaking point. Two days after Stalin's speech he contacted the defeated Kamenev and poured out his heart. Bukharin used a "tone of absolute hatred" toward Stalin, calling him an "intriguer without principles." "With this line we will roll into the abyss," ending up with "war communism and death." In the Politburo Bukharin was supported by Rykov, Tomskii, and candidate member Uglanov, First Secretary of the Moscow party committee. Andreev, Voroshilov and Kalinin hesitated, but Stalin had "some kind of hold" on the last two. Molotov and Kaganovich seem to have been Stalin's principal collaborators. Bukharin reported that the security police (*GPU*) listened in on his telephone, so he would have to "conspire." He was convinced that Stalin had to be dismissed.[24] At the July plenum the CC was not yet prepared to support Stalin wholeheartedly, and a compromise was formulated.

This did not please Stalin, and he took action. He was the master of organizational pressure, and he was entitled to use this weapon as chief of the Secretariat. In order to block Tomskii he sent Kaganovich to the Presidium of the Council of Trade Unions.[25] Uglanov was subjected to a virulent campaign and dismissed from his Moscow post in November 1928.[26] Things came to a breaking point when in early 1929 another grain crisis broke out, leading to a rationing of bread.

When "extraordinary measures" were again taken, Bukharin wrote a declaration to the Politburo and the Presidium of the Central Control Commission (*CCC*) on 30 January. The statement was not published, but it probably condemned Stalin's policy as "military-feudal exploitation of the peasantry."[27] Bukharin angrily wrote that free discussion was no longer possible because every criticism was declared "anti-Leninism." As a consequence, party members could only freely debate "'among themselves,' with two or three people." Members ritually approved the line, keeping their doubts to themselves.[28] On 9 February Bukharin, Rykov and Tomskii wrote another critical declaration-making them "factionalists" according to the strict rules against joint operations outside official channels.

On that same day the Politburo met in a joint session with the Presidium of the CCC, headed by Stalin's old friend Sergo Ordzhonikidze, to discuss

Bukharin's meeting with Kamenev and his declaration. It was clever tactics to have the two institutions meet jointly: the nine voting members of the Politburo were divided: Stalin, Molotov and Voroshilov confronted Bukharin, Rykov and Tomskii. According to Avtorkhanov, Kalinin, Rudzutak and chairman of the Supreme Council of the National Economy (*VSNKh*) Valerian Kuibyshev hesitated. The struggle against what Stalin dubbed the "Right Opposition" was therefore not so easy as the battle against the leftists had been. The CCC Presidium, however, sent four Stalin supporters to the meeting, who provided the General Secretary with victory.[29] Bukharin's actions were condemned.[30] In April 1929 a joint plenum of the CC and the CCC confirmed the condemnation of the three opposition leaders. Bukharin lost his seat on the Politburo in November 1929; Tomskii and Rykov lost theirs the next year.

Why did Stalin vanquish them? He and Molotov, with Ordzhonikidze's support from the CCC, controlled the party machine, the secretarial hierarchy. But Prime Minister Rykov was left out in the cold even by his own colleagues: the other representatives of the state bureaucracy—Voroshilov, Kalinin, Kuibyshev and Rudzutak—all swung to Stalin's side, although they reportedly hesitated. Stalin was a master of timing. The moderate New Economic Policy (*NEP*) of the early 1920s had been accepted as a necessary evil as long as the country needed time to restore its strength and the cities profited from it. But as soon as the moderate line seemed no longer to provide economic benefits, the old communist aggressiveness against the "petty-bourgeois class enemy" naturally reasserted itself. The mood changed back to the Leninism of the Civil War. The party cadres felt ready for another real battle.[31] And that is what they got.

STALINISM

Having removed his opponents, Stalin opened his offensive against the peasants in the winter of 1929-30, destroying their independence and often their lives with the dual campaign of "dekulakization" and "collectivization." If one wants to pinpoint a beginning of the Stalinist era, 21 December 1929 is the day. On the day thought to be Stalin's fiftieth birthday, *Pravda* honored the leader with a series of hagiographic articles by prominent personalities, among whom were five members of the Politburo: Kaganovich, Kuibyshev, Voroshilov, Kalinin, and Mikoian.[32] On the front page Stalin was called a "stone-hard Bolshevik" and an "iron soldier of the revolution." He was described as the "chief and leader [*rukovoditel i vozhd*] of the party," standing at the head of the Central Committee. Attacking him, it was said, was synonymous to attacking the party.

A modest Lenin cult had existed prior to 1924, but the formal declaration of a living person as the untouchable leader and embodiment of the party was a new stage in the development of bolshevism.[33] In the winter of 1930 the process of "substitutionism" went a step farther toward submitting the Politburo to one leader as the ultimate decision maker. It may be analyzed as the outcome of the thoroughly militarized Bolshevik ideology: classes were armies, class struggle was a war and the party the general staff, demanding military obedience. It is therefore only natural that an army is subject to one commander-in-chief. The cult of personality was part of an emerging new regime in the Politburo, more severe than that which Lenin had established in 1921. Apart from the cult of the leader, it demanded that members retract their discordant views, reminiscent of the old traditions of the church, which required that heretics recognize their errors.

At the 15th Party Congress in 1927 Stalin had demanded that the opposition "disarm fully and completely, ideologically and organizationally." It had to "take back its anti-Leninist views openly and honestly, in front of the whole world."[34] Kamenev reacted that this was not in accordance with Bolshevik tradition. He was right: Lenin tried to shut up his opponents, not to make them speak against themselves. Curiously enough, however, almost all who opposed him gave in to Stalin's extreme demands. At the 16th Party Congress in the summer of 1930, Tomskii, then still a Politburo member though not to be reelected, proclaimed: "The party was right from beginning to end, and we were wrong from beginning to end." He was "not ashamed to bow his head for the party."[35] In his closing words on 2 July the General Secretary accused him, however, of having (at an earlier occasion) missed "the opportunity to expiate his sins" by not having been sufficiently self-critical.

Expressing an absolute, mystical interpretation of party unity, Stalin demanded that the fallen leaders "come closer to the nucleus of the party leadership and fully merge with it [*slitsia s nim do kontsa*]." They had to "break finally with their past, to re-arm themselves and merge into one [*slitsia voedino*] with the CC of our party."[36] Stalin demanded complete, even inner surrender. Most opposition leaders were prepared to carry out a ritual of repentance. They "capitulated" between 1928 and 1930 without the threat of the firing squad. The best explanation of this is that the thought of expulsion from their revered party was so horrible to them that they were prepared to degrade themselves. In 1928 one of the leftist opposition members, G. L. Piatakov, explained the betrayal of his own opinions to a friend in Paris: "In order to become one with this great party he would fuse himself with it, abandon his own personality, so that there was no particle left inside him which was not at one with the party."[37] A sort of party Nirvana taken very seriously.

Stalin's simplified Leninism with its religious undertones may have appealed to the less educated who were much better represented in the Politburo elected in 1927 than they had been in 1919. Under Lenin, one third of them came from workers' or peasant families; eight years later three quarters of the Politburo members did so. Under Lenin, Kalinin was the only former worker in the Politburo; eight years later over half of the members were.[38] In spite of his victory Stalin could, however, not unconditionally depend on the loyalties of the Politburo. The breakneck industrialization and the killings and deportations in the countryside caused so much suffering that at least one candidate of the supreme organ could not stomach it. Premier of the Russian federation Sergei Syrtsov was appalled by the serious situation of the country and invited V. V. Lominadze, first secretary of the Transcaucasian Regional Committee, to his Moscow home to have a frank discussion.[39] When Stalin heard of this critical exchange, he kicked Syrtsov out of the Politburo on 1 December 1930.

The joint plenum of the CC and CCC of 21 December 1930 made some additional changes in the Politburo. Voting members were secretaries of the CC Stalin and Kaganovich, republican or regional secretaries Kirov and Stanislav Kosior, head of state Kalinin, and the newly elected premier Molotov with his team of Gosplan chairman Kuibyshev, chairman of VSNKh Ordzhonikidze and People's Commissars Voroshilov and Rudzutak. Mikoian, Petrovskii and Chubar were the candidates. This completely Stalinist team remained at the helm of the country with few changes until thinned by the Great Terror in the mid-1930s. By 1932 the "class war" had become so cruel that it caused severe unrest in the CC and lower levels of the party, giving rise to several small opposition groups. On 21 August 1932 former party Secretary of a Moscow district, M. N. Riutin, established the small "Union of Marxist-Leninists," and proceeded to circulate its platform and "Appeal" among former oppositionists and other malcontents.[40]

The appeal "To all members of the VKP(b) [the communist party]" bluntly stated: "Stalin and his clique will not and cannot voluntarily leave their places, therefore they will have to be removed by force [*siloi*]."[41] The small heroic group was soon arrested. On 11 October verdicts of exile and prison were pronounced.[42] Some time later two other brave party dissidents, N. B. Eismont and V. N. Tolmachev, were given prison terms.[43] Rumor has it that on both occasions Stalin demanded capital punishment, but was successfully opposed in the Politburo by a majority headed by the First Secretary of the Leningrad provincial party committee, Kirov, along with Ordzhonikidze, Kuibyshev, Kosior and Kalinin. Molotov, Andreev and Voroshilov supposedly wavered, with only Kaganovich supporting Stalin.[44]

Meanwhile, the Politburo continued on its course, leading the country through a famine of its own making in the winter of 1932-33, causing millions to die in the Ukraine, Kazakhstan, and the Northern Caucasus, and vindicating Bukharin's dire warnings. In a recent interview, Kaganovich, almost one hundred years old, explained how he and his comrades justified the carnage: if an enemy captures our city, we have to take it back, although our own people live in it, "innocent people, who may perish as a result of our attack. But despite that the army will cry out 'To the attack!' because that is how it must always be, in all types of war."[45] In January 1933 a joint plenum of the CC and the CCC convened to discuss the progress of the great communist transformation of the country. The famine, then at its zenith, was passed over in silence. Instead, Kaganovich castigated local authorities for insufficient zeal in collecting grain and punishing peasants who "stole" some grain to feed their families.[46]

According to Stalin, any disruption of his economic plans—be it the grain campaign or the industrialization effort—was caused by deliberate "sabotage" and had to be dealt with by the police. He refused to acknowledge that his own plan to transform agricultural Russia in one decade was the reason for the ensuing chaos. At the plenum "Political Departments" of the so-called Machine Tractor Stations (*MTS*) were established, controlled by the security police and realizing a virtual state of emergency in the countryside.[47] When the worst of the famine was over, the 17th Party Congress convened in January-February 1934 and Stalin was hailed as the victorious genius. Nevertheless, some realism slowly returned. In his speech on 4 February, People's Commissar of Heavy Industry Ordzhonikidze proposed a somewhat more modest rate of industrial growth for the Second Five Year Plan than Molotov had proposed the day before. The Politburo agrees with my proposal, Ordzhonikidze hastened to add.[48]

During the Khrushchev era testimonies were collected to the effect that during the 17th Congress a group of regional secretaries and secretaries of non-Russian Central Committees met with several Politburo members to discuss Stalin's transfer to a position in the government, and his replacement as General Secretary by Kirov. The group met secretly at apartments in Moscow. Among the names mentioned are those of Ordzhonikidze, Mikoian, Kosior and Petrovskii. Kirov refused.[49] Witnesses also declared that almost

300 out of the 1,225 voting delegates crossed out Stalin's name during the elections for the new Central Committee. Kaganovich falsified the results by ordering almost all these ballots destroyed. It has recently been established that indeed 166 ballots are lacking from the archive where the ballots are kept.[50] It is perhaps also noteworthy that Stalin was not elected as General Secretary at the first plenum of the new CC after the Congress but simply as Secretary.[51] Kirov was elected to the Secretariat of the CC.

In November 1934 the Political Departments of the MTS were abolished and so was bread rationing.[52] According to Medvedev, Kirov's pleas in the Politburo were responsible for the abolition of the departments and the revival of the regular Soviet and party organs in the countryside. He also opposed further repression of former opposition members.[53] At the time Kirov and Ordzhonikidze were indeed considered friends and protectors of Bukharin, according to the writer Ilia Erenburg.[54] Such facts have been taken by Robert Conquest to prove that a bloc of moderate Stalinists under Kirov and Ordzhonikidze was in the process of formation.[55] On 1 December 1934 Kirov was shot dead by a young terrorist, Leonid Nikolaev, in the corridor of his office in the Smolnyi Building in Leningrad. Nikolaev probably acted for personal motives, but the Leningrad People's Commissariat of Internal Affairs (*NKVD*) had almost certainly created opportunities for him to execute his plans.

It has been established that Nikolaev had been arrested before and released by the NKVD, that he implicated the NKVD during his first interrogation and that Kirov's bodyguard was killed by the NKVD shortly after the murder.[56] Former Secretary of the CC Aleksandr Iakovlev has revealed that Nikolaev obtained his bullets from an NKVD sports club and that Nikolaev wrote letters to Kirov in July, to Stalin in August, and to the Politburo in October 1934.[57] These facts implicate Stalin and the NKVD, though they leave room for several interpretations. It may have been a murder plan. It may also have been a miscarried provocation: it was standard NKVD practice to let a culprit have his way for some time in order to widen the circle of suspects.

On 21 January 1935 Kuibyshev died, probably of natural causes.[58] The next month Mikoian and Chubar were promoted to full Politburo membership. Two new candidates were added: Andrei Zhdanov (the new Leningrad First Secretary and Secretary of the CC) and First Secretary of the Siberian and West-Siberian District Committee of the party, Robert Eikhe.

THE GREAT TRIALS

The forced confessions at the first two of the great trials against former opposition leaders in August 1936 and January 1937 revealed what was on Stalin's mind. He thought that everything that had been going wrong since he had taken over was the result of a vast conspiracy. Behind all negative phenomena, from hunger to discontent among local youth to economic chaos and failure, loomed a plot to destabilize the country by terror and sabotage. This was a military operation, meant to shake up the USSR so that it would be unable to withstand an invasion by Great Britain and France, Germany or Japan. Stalin thought that the imperialist powers planned to occupy part of Soviet territory, while the former opposition leaders, heading the sabotage and terror groups, returned to power in the rest of the country. He was determined to launch a devastating attack by the NKVD on anyone he perceived to be part of the plot.

Stalin's natural victims were poorly functioning economic organizations and party committees with lax membership policies that were indulgent toward former opposition members and toward criticism. However, he was not supported by all members of the Politburo. It was recently described in *Kommunist* how Ordzhonikidze in 1936 and early 1937 tried to protect the leading personnel of his People's Commissariat of Heavy Industry and how he ridiculed the search for "saboteurs."[59] Stalin expected Ordzhonikidze to condemn the "saboteurs" in his People's Commissariat at the plenary session of the CC that was to open on 23 February 1937. Ordzhonikidze's draft speech has been preserved with Stalin's notes scribbled on it. The boss returned it to be rewritten, "having accompanied it with rude remarks."[60] On 18 February Ordzhonikidze was dead. According to Khrushchev, he shot himself: "Sergo couldn't stand it anymore."[61]

At the plenum Stalin, Molotov, Zhdanov and People's Commissar of Internal Affairs Nikolai Ezhov went out of their way to accuse the saboteurs and terrorist conspirators. Nevertheless, Pavel Postyshev, candidate member of the Politburo and Secretary in the Ukrainian party, dared to say "I don't believe it" when one of his colleagues from the Ukrainian CC was accused.[62] When Ezhov proposed to hand Bukharin and Rykov over to the court and have them shot, Postyshev, supported by Kosior and Petrovskii, proposed to hand them over but not shoot them. Molotov and Voroshilov supported Stalin's "compromise" to have them only arrested by Ezhov's NKVD.[63] All objections were futile, Stalin carried the day. The plenum of February-March 1937 became the real turning point in the development to full-scale terror against the state and party apparatus that was completely ravaged until the storm finally subsided after the 18th Party Congress in March 1939.

Stalin's loyal supporters in the Politburo traveled around the country instructing the local NKVD whom to arrest. A member of the NKVD described how Kaganovich, on a mission in Ivanovo in 1937, telephoned Stalin daily. He was heard to say: "Will do, Comrade Stalin, I'll press on the NKVD Department heads not to be too liberal and to maximally increase identification of enemies of the people."[64] Zhdanov spoke to the plenum of the Bashkir provincial party committee in October of the same year: the CC had become suspicious because it had not received any messages about the fight against the enemy. "Without [the help of] the provincial committee the NKVD unmasks the enemies of the people dug in in very important positions-bourgeois nationalists, Trotskyites, fascist saboteurs, spies, and murderers." Zhdanov came to help.[65] The first Politburo member still in office to be arrested, in May 1937, was Deputy Prime Minister Rudzutak.[66] In October 1937 Ezhov became a candidate of the Politburo, the first time for a police chief since 1926.

In 1938 four more members of the Politburo were jailed: Kosior, Chubar, Postyshev, and Eikhe.[67] Grigorii Petrovskii was relatively fortunate, when he was just not reelected at the congress in March 1939. The other five were killed. Chubar telephoned Stalin in tears to assure the boss of his honesty the day before his arrest.[68] Kosior confessed being an enemy of the people after his sixteen-year-old daughter had been raped before his eyes.[69] It was typical of Stalin's increasingly autocratic behavior toward the Politburo that no official decision to remove Rudzutak, Eikhe and Kosior was ever taken.[70] The real reasons for the removal of the six Politburo members during the Great Purge are unknown. At the CC plenum in January 1938 Postyshev was accused of too much zeal in persecuting people.[71] That charge, however, would be inappropriate for Chubar. Conquest quotes a Soviet biography of Chubar that claims this Ukrainian leader was indignant about the scope of the repression.[72]

The known facts suggest a pattern. Only one of the six was a Russian (Postyshev). The others were Ukrainian, Latvian and Polish. Four of them (Kosior, Chubar, Postyshev and Petrovskii) had been leaders of the Ukrainian party and state. It may be tentatively surmised that the six were victimized for protecting "enemies of the people" in the Ukraine and other areas against Stalin's onslaught from Moscow, as Ordzhonikidze had tried to do for his People's Commissariat. Most of the Politburo was, however, on Stalin's side. His first power base was the central party apparatus: during the years of the Great Terror all five secretaries of the CC (Andreev, Ezhov,

Zhdanov, Kaganovich, and Stalin) were on the Politburo.[73] Ezhov was also the chairman of the Commission of Party Control, the successor to the CCC.[74] The second and most important of Stalin's instruments was the NKVD, headed again by "iron commissar" Nikolai Ezhov.

Ezhov once told one of his deputies: "We must now educate the chekists [security police personnel] in such a way that [the NKVD] will become a closed sect, tightly welded together and unconditionally fulfilling my instructions." His words were reminiscent of Stalin's with reference to party unity.[75] After his victory, Stalin became concerned about Ezhov's tightly organized power. At a meeting of the so-called Council of Elders of the triumphant 18th Party Congress, Stalin accused Ezhov of plotting to kill him. The boss advised the Elders to "think about" keeping Ezhov on the new CC, though he himself had "doubts."[76] Ezhov was soon arrested. Stalin later told a Soviet general: "Ezhov was a scoundrel. In 1938 he killed many innocent people. We have executed him for this."[77] He may well have meant this, thinking that the terror reached unacceptable proportions for the stability of the USSR. Lavrentii Beriia was nominated as the new People's Commissar of Internal Affairs. Having confirmed his power over the NKVD, Stalin's position was secure.

The new Politburo elected after the 18th Party Congress was small. It consisted of nine voting members: Andreev, Voroshilov, Zhdanov, Kaganovich, Kalinin, Mikoian, Molotov, Stalin, and Nikita Khrushchev. The two candidate members were Beriia and N. M. Shvernik. Comparing the Politburo elected after the 18th Party Congress in March 1939 with the one from 1934, it appears that the share of Russian nationals had sharply gone up, and so had the representation of institutions of a central level, as opposed to republican or provincial institutions.[78] Institutions outside Moscow were represented only by Khrushchev, First Secretary of the Ukrainian party, and Zhdanov, Secretary of the CC and of the Leningrad City and Provincial Committees.

This points to a paradox regarding the Politburo as a nucleus of power. On the one hand, centralized power was firmer than it had ever been: the majority of the Politburo had literally killed the majority of the CC. The CC was no longer a working organ; it met only five times in 1939 and 1940.[79] The victory of the Politburo was, on the other hand, more Stalin's victory than its own. Perhaps the General Secretary triumphed in the twenties because he expressed the mood of the party elite better than his opponents. But the triumph of 1937-38 was scored against this elite, by killing it off. Although the extent of genuine adoration for the genius-hero and the hysterical sweep of the "purge" atmosphere should not be underestimated, Stalin's main source of strength was the NKVD. He could kill any Politburo member if he so wished. If there was ever a Pyrrhic victory, this was one.

In February 1941 a plenary session of the CC decided to strengthen the Politburo by nominating three new candidate members: Gosplan Chairman Nikolai Voznesenskii, Secretary of the CC Georgii Malenkov, and First Secretary of the Moscow City and Provincial Committees Aleksandr Shcherbakov. However, the outbreak of the war on 22 June accelerated the demise of the Politburo. On 30 June the Politburo decided to establish the so-called State Committee of Defense as the supreme organ of power in the country. Stalin chaired this committee that soon comprised nine members, all of them from the Politburo except N. A. Bulganin.[80] In addition to the Committee and the Politburo, the *"Stavka"* (General Headquarters) was the third leading institution. According to Marshal Zhukov, in practice the boundaries between such institutions were indeterminable: "The *Stavka* was Stalin and the State Committee of Defense was basically also Stalin. He commanded everything."[81] When something needed to be decided, Stalin called together a group of leading political officials and military. When a decision was reached he decided whether this was to be formalized as an extended meeting of the Politburo, the Committee or the *Stavka*.[82] The Politburo ceased to exist as an independent institution. Instead, it became one of the names for the leader's entourage.

THE FINAL YEARS

In December 1945 the Politburo decided to resume regular meetings.[83] At the first plenum of the CC after the war in March 1946, it was even strengthened. Beriia and Malenkov were promoted to full membership; Deputy Minister of the Armed Forces Bulganin and Deputy Prime Minister A. N. Kosygin were nominated as new candidates. Nevertheless, the Polit-buro did not become a permanently working institution again. From 1946 to 1952 it convened less than eight times a year on the average.[84] According to Khrushchev, Stalin used the Politburo "as little more than a rubber stamp."[85] He established "quintets," "sextets" and other informal groupings within the Politburo according to his liking.[86] This does not mean that Stalin was completely autonomous. No formal institution limited him, but he had to reckon with the powerful men around him. Politics took the shape of dark intrigues between informal clans, striving to gain Stalin's support against each other.

coffin. (Photo Dmitrii Valtermants, Ogonek, 1990, Nr. 30)

According to Mikoian, the *vozhd* (leader), while on a Caucasian holiday in 1948, expressed the wish to be eventually succeeded as premier by Voznesenskii, and as leader of the Secretariat by Secretary A. A. Kuznetsov.[87] Voznesenskii and Kuznetsov had begun their careers in Leningrad under Andrei Zhdanov. On 31 August 1948 their powerful patron died from, Khrushchev thought, excessive drinking.[88] This enabled the two most powerful men after Stalin (Malenkov and Beriia) to attack their young rivals, creating the so-called Leningrad affair, the arrest and trial of a group of Leningrad and former Leningrad officials. It ended in October 1950 with the execution of Politburo member Voznesenskii, Secretary Kuznetsov and a number of other former Leningrad officials. Some of them seem to have proposed the establishment of a Russian Communist Party and the transfer of the capital of the Russian federation to Leningrad. This was interpreted by Stalin as "Russian nationalism," a threat to Moscow's central powers. Voznesenskii in particular was accused of criminal mismanagement of Gosplan.[89]

Beriia and Malenkov, themselves of the middle generation, simultaneously launched an indirect attack against some of the old guard. In 1944 and again in 1947 the Jewish Anti-Fascist Committee (JAC), established during the war, proposed to Stalin the creation of a Jewish republic in the Crimea. According to a witness, the committee was supported in its proposal by Molotov, whose Jewish wife was active in the JAC, and Kaganovich, who was Jewish.[90] In 1948 Malenkov and Beriia, again working through the Ministry of State Security, convinced Stalin that the proposal was part of a Zionist-American separatist conspiracy.[91] Arrests and executions followed. Molotov's wife was exiled.[92] In 1949 Molotov lost his position as Minister of Foreign Affairs. Other Politburo members with Jewish wives, such as Voroshilov, Andreev and Bulganin, may also have been in trouble. Stalin forbade Andreev to attend Politburo meetings, accusing him of being a "British agent."[93]

In the final years of his life Stalin came to be more obsessed than ever with the integrity and strength of the Soviet state. All "affairs" from 1948 onward were directed against a specter of national separatism-Russian, Jewish, or otherwise. At one point Stalin seems to have been afraid that he lost control to Beriia, suspecting him of treasonous plans. In June 1951 the latter's confidant, Minister of State Security V. S. Abakumov, was suddenly excluded from the party.[94] Five months later a case was opened against a group of Georgian party leaders, Mingrelians like Beriia. They were accused of forming a nationalist conspiracy in league with Turkey. The case was not discussed in the Politburo, but concocted personally by Stalin out of, Khrushchev thought, fear of Beriia's growing power.[95] The inner circle, where the ghost stories were developed, became ever smaller. In the end the quintet consisted of three secretaries of the CC: the boss himself, Malenkov and Khrushchev; and two deputy prime ministers: Beriia and Bulganin, responsible for the police and the army. They met at one of Stalin's dachas for "interminable, agonizing dinners" where policy was decided.[96]

The grand finale came after the 19th Party Congress in October 1952. At the first plenary session of the newly elected CC on 16 October, an old and gray Stalin climbed the rostrum and poured out his venom for one and a half hours. The writer Konstantin Simonov was there to witness how he passionately urged his listeners to be hard and fearless. Then he violently attacked Molotov and Mikoian, who sat listening to him with "white masks" for faces, for "capitulationism" to the capitalist camp.[97] He proposed to expand the

3. Mikoian, Khrushchev, Stalin, and Malenkov strolling in the Kremlin. (Ogonek, 1989, Nr. 36)

Politburo to a new Presidium of 36 members and candidates, with a small Bureau as its leading nucleus.

The Bureau consisted of secretaries Stalin and Khrushchev and seven deputy prime ministers: Malenkov (simultaneously Secretary of the CC), Beriia, Bulganin, Voroshilov, Kaganovich, M. Z. Saburov and P. G. Pervukhin.[98] Stalin probably intended the large Presidium as a reservoir of young people to replace those he was about to kill. On 13 January 1953 *Pravda* announced that Politburo members Shcherbakov and Zhdanov, who died in 1945 and 1948, had been murdered by their doctors, most of them Jews, who also intended to wipe out a number of marshals, generals and admirals. This was said to be part of an American-Zionist conspiracy to undermine the USSR. In the same edition *Pravda* reminded its readers of Stalin's old thesis that the class struggle intensifies during the building of communism, castigating the lack of vigilance in the state organs and accusing "the State Security organs" for not uncovering in good time the "wrecking terrorist organization." State Security had been under Beriia's control in 1945 and 1948.

The old leader had not yet lost his touch. He was about to unleash his Ministry of State Security against Soviet Jews and the "rotten" parts of the state and the party, sweeping out in the process many of his comrades. This time, however, fate was merciful. On 1 March Stalin suffered a stroke at his Kuntsevo dacha. The alarmed guards called Malenkov. After a delay of many hours, he and Beriia arrived at three in the morning on 2 March. One of Stalin's former bodyguards remembers Beriia crying out when he saw the boss: "Why are you creating a panic? Can't you see that comrade Stalin is fast asleep?" He forbade doctors to be summoned. They came only at 10 A.M.[99] Stalin died on 5 March.

NOTES TO CHAPTER 3

1. Baschanow, 1977: 37, 50-51; Kirilina et al., 1990: 22.
2. *XIV s''ezd...*, 1926: 455-56, 398-99, 950.
3. Kirilina et al., 1990: 23.
4. Trotzki, 1930: 484.
5. Trotskii, 1990: 169-70.
6. "'Zaiavlenie...", 1990: 190.
7. See Hough/Fainsod, 1979: 144.
8. "Otvet chlenov...", 1990.
9. See Carr, 1969: 339-48.
10. See for the relevant resolutions, adopted in September 1920 and December 1921: *KPSS v rezoliutsiiakh...*, 1953: 509, 595-96.
11. Stalin, t. 6, 1947: 47.
12. Stalin, t. 5, 1947: 71.
13. Pospelov, t. 4, 1970: 361.
14. Baschanow, 1977: 162.

15. *XIV s'' ezd...*, 1926: 274-75.
16. Mikoian, 1987: 6.
17. Trotzki, 1930: 505.
18. Avtorkhanov, 1983: 268-69.
19. Trotzki, 1930: 33.
20. See Table 8.27.
21. Cited in Bordiugov/Kozlov, "Nikolai...", 1988: 98.
22. Stalin, t. 11, 1949: 159, 171.
23. Ibid.: 162.
24. "Bolsheviki...", 1929.
25. *KPSS v rezoliutsiiakh...*, Ch. II, 1953: 443.
26. See Chizhova, 1990.
27. *KPSS v rezoliutsiiakh...*, Ch. II, 1953: 438.
28. Cited in Bordiugov/Kozlov, "Nikolai...", 1988: 100.
29. Avtorkhanov, 1983: 411, 436.
30. See the resolution in *KPSS v rezoliutsiiakh...*, Ch. II, 1953: 436-47.
31. See also: Bordiugov/Kozlov, "Povorot...", 1988: 21-22.
32. In reality Stalin was probably born on 18 December 1878. See "Sostav...", 1990: 124n.
33. See Tumarkin, 1983.
34. *Piatnadtsatyi s'' ezd...*, 1961: 90.
35. *XVI s'' ezd...*, 1930: 142, 148.
36. Ibid.: 292-93.
37. Schapiro, 1971: 385.
38. See Table 8.21.
39. Medvedev, 1989: 295-96.
40. See "O dele...", 1989: 107.
41. Riutin, 1988: 25.
42. "O dele...", 1989: 107.
43. "O tak...", 1990: 73.
44. For a survey of such rumors: Conquest, 1990: 24-25, 27; see also Volkogonov, Kn. I, Ch. 2, 1989: 86; Medvedev, 1989: 297.
45. "Lazar...", 1990.
46. See Bordiugov/Kozlov, "Vremia...", 1988.
47. Ibid. For the relevant resolution: *KPSS v rezoliutsiiakh...*, Ch. II, 1953: 733.
48. *VII s'' ezd...*, 1975: 435.
49. See Medvedev, 1989: 331; Tselms, 1990: 13; Mikhailov, 1991: 81 ff.; Shatunovskaia, 1990.
50. See Mikhailov/Naumov, 1989; Mikhailov, 1991.
51. "Sostav...", 1990: 75n.
52. For relevant resolution: *KPSS v rezoliutsiiakh...*, Ch. II, 1953: 799-808.

53. Medvedev, 1989: 330.
54. Erenburg, 1988.
55. Conquest, 1990: Chapter 1.
56. Shatunovskaia, 1990: 6; Tselms, 1990: 13. For another opinion: "Vokrug ubiistva...", 1990.
57. Iakovlev, 1991.
58. See Gerasimov, 1988: 147n.
59. Khlevniuk, 1989: 100-103.
60. "Chelovek i simvol", 1988.
61. Talbott, vol. 1, 1977: 106.
62. Khrushchev, 1989: 140.
63. "O partiinosti...", 1989: 79-81.
64. Shreider, 1988.
65. Ilishev, 1988: 126.
66. "Sostav...", 1990: 120.
67. See their biographies in ibid.
68. Talbott, vol. 1, 1977: 128.
69. Medvedev, 1989: 490.
70. "Sostav...", 1990: 75.
71. Volkogonov, Kn. I, Ch. 2, 1989: 248-50.
72. Conquest, 1990: 420.
73. Kirilina et al., 1990: 31-32.
74. "Sostav...", 1990: 93.
75. Viktorov, 1988.
76. Medvedev, 1989: 459.
77. Iakovlev, 1966: 179.
78. See tables 8.7 and 8.26.
79. Pospelov, t. 5, 1970: 666-69.
80. Ibid.: 164. Beriia's membership is omitted here.
81. Pavlenko, 1988: 97.
82. Volkogonov, Kn. II, Ch. 1, 1989: 271.
83. Aksenov, 1990: 99.
84. Ibid.: 100. For the individual years, see table 7.6.
85. Talbott, vol. 1, 1977: 297.
86. Khrushchev, 1989: 163.
87. Kutuzov, 1989: 65-66.
88. Talbott, vol. 1, 1977: 305.
89. "O tak nazyvaemom 'Leningradskom...", 1989; Talbott, vol. 1, 1977: 276; Kutuzov, 1989: 56; Bardin, 1988: 10; Dzhirkvelov, 1989: 256-57.
90. "O tak nazyvaemom 'dele...", 1989: 37; Rapoport, 1990: 122.
91. "O tak nazyvaemom 'dele...", 1989: 37; Talbott, vol. 1, 1977: 280.

92. Talbott, vol. 1, 1977: 281; Allilueva, 1967: 182.
93. Khrushchev, 1989: 163.
94. Ibid.: 50n; Talbott, vol. 1, 1977: 334.
95. Talbott, vol. 1, 1977: 334-35; Khrushchev, 1989: 153-54.
96. Talbott, vol. 1, 1977: 322.
97. Simonov, 1988: 96-99.
98. Talbott, vol. 1, 1977: 301.
99. Rybin, 1988: 92-93; Alliluyeva, 1990.

4. *Stalin's funeral in the mausoleum (on the frieze his name has been added to that of Lenin), Red Square, 9 March 1953 (Ogonek, 1989, Nr. 37).*

4

The Era of Conspiracies

The Presidium Under Khrushchev

At the joint session of the Central Committee, the Council of Ministers and the Presidium of the Supreme Soviet on 6 March 1953, a new Presidium of the CC was elected, consisting of Beriia, Bulganin, Voroshilov, Kaganovich, Malenkov, Mikoian, Molotov, Pervukhin, Saburov and Khrushchev. Candidates were M. D. Bagirov, L. G. Melnikov, P. K. Ponomarenko and Shvernik.[1] The meeting took place at the Kuntsevo dacha with Stalin's body still there. His daughter was crying.[2] The event constituted a revolt of the old Politburo against their dead leader. The large Presidium was abolished and apparently agreed to step aside without a fight. Real power was in the hands of a small group of oligarchs, representing the security police, the party apparatus and the state bureaucracy. Their conspiratorial power struggle raged until June 1957. Georgii Malenkov, a puffy man with an odd baby face, served as Stalin's successor, being nominated Prime Minister while keeping his seat at the Secretariat. Khrushchev was the only other Secretary of the CC on the Presidium.

According to Khrushchev, Stalin had never considered Malenkov as more than a "good clerk," with "no capacity at all for independent thought or initiative." Malenkov was close to Beriia, and always played up to him, "though he knew Beriia pushed him around and mocked him."[3] There is reason to assume that Malenkov did indeed not have the ambition to become a second Stalin. On 10 March *Pravda* carried a fake photograph of Stalin, Mao Zedong and Malenkov. It was assumed to have been published on orders of Malenkov to support symbolically his claims for leadership. A recent article, however, describing a Presidium meeting in the evening of the same day based on notes taken by a participant casts a different light on the event.

5. *The Politburo in the early 1950s. Back row (left to right): Khrushchev, Mikoian, Malenkov, Kaganovich, Beriia, Bulganin; between Mikoian and Malenkov: Suslov; vague in front, with handlebar moustache: Marshal Budennyi (Ogonek, 1990, Nr. 6).*

Malenkov angrily described the photograph as "a provocation." He did not want to be separated from his colleagues and noted: "We consider it our duty to end the policy of a cult of personality."[4] On 14 March he resigned as Secretary of the CC.

Minister of Internal Affairs Beriia was "radiant" after Stalin's death. "He was regenerated and rejuvenated. To put it crudely, he had a housewarming over Stalin's corpse before it was even put in its coffin."[5] The security police, now part of Beriia's Ministry of Internal Affairs (*MVD*), had been Stalin's main power base, enabling him to finish off his colleagues in the Politburo if he so wished. This power lay now in the hands of Beriia, a sinister man who was politically responsible for the GULag, personally directed beatings of prisoners, and raped hundreds of women.[6] After Stalin's funeral Beriia kept the special MVD divisions that he had sent to Moscow to maintain order at the funeral in the capital.[7] On 4 April *Pravda* announced that a commission appointed by the MVD had discovered that the case against the murderer-doctors had been a frame-up. Thus Beriia succesfully destroyed the case that had been intended to destroy him.

In the Presidium he also proposed to fire Russian first secretaries in the non-Russian republics and bring in more local personnel in the governing bodies of Ukraine, Belorussia and the Baltic states. This was accepted. As a result, Melnikov lost his post as Ukrainian First Secretary.[8] In this way Beriia turned Stalin's antiseparatist "cases" around, trying to gain support among the non-Russians. There are indications, founded on archival materials, that this was part of a plan for a coup d'état and that Khrushchev was informed of these intentions on 21 June.[9] In his memoirs Khrushchev described his own conspiracy against the police chief, secretly winning over one Presidium member after another by warning them: "Beria is sharpening his knives."[10] Khrushchev obtained support from the whole Presidium (except Mikoian) for Beriia's arrest. On 26 June an extended Presidium of the Council of Ministers convened.

The conspirators enlisted the support of the army, which had hated the MVD since 1937, when the General Staff had been murdered by the NKVD, the precursor of the MVD. Army units were in control of the Kremlin and MVD buildings.[11] A group of high-ranking officers, including Georgii Zhukov and commander of Moscow Military District General K. S. Moskalenko, hid in a waiting room. When the meeting opened, Khrushchev, according to his own accounts, accused Beriia of being an "agent of imperialism" and a former British spy. Beriia was startled, grabbed Khrushchev's hand and cried, "What's going on, Nikita?" When all had spoken Malenkov pushed a button and in came the officers. "Hands up," Zhukov commanded Beriia. The minister was taken out. His briefcase was found to contain a sheet of paper with the words "alarm, alarm, alarm" in red pencil.[12] Beriia was executed in December 1953: the power of the MVD over the party and the state was broken.

DUAL POWER

In March 1954 the Interior Ministry's security branch was reduced in status to a Committee for State Security (KGB). Its chairman remained outside the Presidium until 1967. This was the precondition for a reassertion by the Presidium of old collective rights as they had existed before the Great Terror. The minutes of the plenary session of the CC of July 1953, discussing the Beriia case, have now been published. Apparently soon after Stalin's death a consensus was reached on the necessity of a retreat from Stalinism. On 2 July Khrushchev boldly stated at the Plenum that *all* so-called conspiracies detected within the past ten years had been faked, and even many of those from 1937 onward.[13] In his final words on 7 July, Malenkov said that the CC and Politburo had not functioned properly for years due to the "cult of personality of com. Stalin."[14] The plenum replaced Beriia's comrade Bagirov as candidate of the Presidium by the new Ukrainian First Secretary, A. I. Kirichenko, a client of Khrushchev's who had made his career under him.[15]

In September 1953 Khrushchev was elected to the new position of First Secretary of the CC. From then on Malenkov chaired the Presidium meetings, but Khrushchev signed the decisions.[16] It was an unstable system of dual power. Now that the Beriia threat had been dealt with, the question arose what new policies to follow. The Presidium was confronted with Stalin's heritage in the form of international isolation and desperate food, housing, and general living situations. At the July plenum Beriia had been accused, among other evil deeds, of plans to restore comradely relations with the traitor Tito and to abandon the socialist German Democratic Republic in favor of a neutralized united Germany.[17] Paradoxically Beriia was the first to have pleaded for more moderate policies after Stalin's death. Opinions varied on solutions to the problems.

In his speech to the Supreme Soviet on 8 August, Malenkov spoke out in favor of a more rapid development of light industries.[18] Khrushchev stressed continued primacy for heavy industry, although complemented by new agricultural initiatives. According to A. Adzhubei, Khrushchev first presented his idea of opening up the Virgin Lands in Kazakhstan and Siberia in a note to the Presidium in January 1954 in which he declared grain to be Problem Number One.[19] Having successfully dealt with Beriia, Khrushchev became self-confident. In August-September 1954 the First Secretary, while on vacation at the Crimea, secretly met with Minister of the Armed Forces Bulganin and with Kirichenko, and with several other leaders not on the Presidium. He secured their support for Malenkov's demotion.[20] Bulganin's support may have expressed the army's discontent against Malenkov's patronage for light industry that slighted arms production.

At the plenary session of the CC in January 1955, Malenkov was attacked for his responsibility for the Leningrad affair.[21] Apart from that, Khrushchev ominously compared Malenkov to Rykov.[22] As in the Beriia case, Secretary Khrushchev operated in league with the ministers and was supported by first deputy prime ministers Molotov and Kaganovich.[23] Malenkov resigned as Prime Minister in February. In a statement he expressed the hope to be succeeded by "another comrade who possesses greater experience in state work."[24] That comrade was Nikolai Bulganin. Khrushchev and Bulganin formed a new duumvirate. They succesfully combined a traditional emphasis on heavy industry, new agricultural initiatives, and the continuation of the new policy of opening up to the outside world as initiated earlier by Malenkov. Together they visited Yugoslavia, India, Burma, and Afghanistan.

Minister of Foreign Affairs Molotov, however, could not adapt to the new approach in foreign policy, nor could he overcome his old anger against Tito. At the plenary session of the CC in July 1955 he was heavily criticized for this by Bulganin, Mikoian, and others as a man "who lives only in the past" and a "hopeless hair-splitter."[25] At the plenum Kirichenko was promoted to full membership of the Presidium; so was Mikhail Suslov, Secretary of the CC since 1947, which strengthened the Secretariat in the Presidium. In October 1955 Molotov was forced to publicly criticize himself for having said that only the "foundations of socialism" had been built in the USSR, instead of socialism as such. According to Molotov, Khrushchev organized this humiliation by ordering Secretary P. N. Pospelov to write a letter to the Presidium against Molotov's dogmatic mistake.[26]

The Presidium now had 11 voting members, representing the coalition of the Secretariat and the state apparatus. Bulganin headed the majority with his phalanx of six deputy prime ministers and Chairman of the Supreme Soviet's Presidium Voroshilov. But among them Malenkov and Molotov had already been humiliated. On the other hand, the Secretariat's position had numerically improved and Khrushchev had proved to be the more dynamic intriguer. He was now ready for a masterstroke to catapult himself as a leader of historic proportions, figuring that for former Stalinists the best defense was offense.

Investigations into the repression under Stalin had started. Sometime after the July 1955 plenum Khrushchev called Procurator Rudenko to his office and was informed that all of Stalin's executions had been juridical frame-ups. The First Secretary informed the Presidium of this and proposed to establish a commission under Secretary Pospelov to investigate Stalin's crimes further.[27] Khrushchev remembers that "Voroshilov, Molotov, and Kaganovich weren't very enthusiastic about my suggestion." Mikoian remained neutral.[28]

But Khrushchev had his way because he was supported by Bulganin, Saburov, Pervukhin, Kirichenko and Suslov.[29] The duumvirate apparently had the support of other relatively young members of the Presidium who had less blood on their hands than Stalin's oldest comrades. On the eve of the 20th Party Congress Khrushchev, supported by the Pospelov report, noted at a Presidium meeting that Stalin was guilty of "incredible abuses of power."[30] According to the historian Aksiutin, he proposed to condemn Stalin publicly at the Congress; but Molotov, Kaganovich, Voroshilov and Malenkov protested. This time Khrushchev was not supported by the Presidium.[31] The congress started peacefully. In his report on 14 February 1956 Khrushchev put a new dogmatic basis under the new foreign policy, declaring that "peaceful coexistence of states with a different social system was and remains the general line of our country's foreign policy."[32]

During a recess of the congress, Khrushchev again brought up the difficult question in the Presidium: "Comrades, what are we going to do about Comrade Pospelov's findings?" He again proposed to tell the Congress about Stalin's "reign of repression." Kaganovich and Molotov violently objected. Voroshilov called out: "What's the matter with you? How can you talk like that? [...] Word will get out about what happened under Stalin, and then the finger will be pointed straight at us." Bulganin, Mikoian, Pervukhin, Saburov, "and possibly Malenkov" supported Khrushchev this time.[33] Molotov remembers: "There was a majority. We all voted."[34] Khrushchev could go ahead. When he spoke in the night of 25 February "it was so quiet in the huge hall you could hear a fly buzzing."[35] Molotov was criticized later that he did not object then and there. But he knew it would have been futile: "Nobody would have supported [me]. No, nobody."[36]

How could this historic event happen? Perhaps the answer lies in the contents of the speech itself. Khrushchev concentrated on Stalin's crimes against party leaders, against the delegates of the 17th congress, against Stalinists such as Chubar and Rudzutak, against the Leningrad leaders after the war. The Stalin age had actually been a comparatively stable one in terms of the turnover rate of tenure in the Politburo, but if one was evicted from high office as Chubar and Rudzutak had been, the cellars of the NKVD or MGB were often the next place of residence.[37] By subjecting party and state to the police, Stalin had terrorized his own comrades. They were determined not to let such a thing happen again. The speech was their revenge.

On 27 February the new CC confirmed all full members of the Presidium but dropped candidate Ponomarenko. Shvernik, chairman of the Committee of Party Control, was confirmed as candidate, and five new candidates were nominated, among whom were three secretaries of the CC (L. I. Brezhnev, E. A. Furtseva and D. T. Shepilov), the Uzbekistan First Secretary N. A. Mukhitdinov, and Defense Minister Zhukov. The position of the Secretariat further improved.

Khrushchev and Bulganin released the great majority of the inhabitants of the concentration camps and allowed a cultural thaw, but their policies ran into deep trouble in Central Europe where the communist regimes in Poland and Hungary were shaken by the unexpected de-Stalinization. Khrushchev, however, kept the initiative. In February 1957 he proposed to abolish most of the central industrial ministries and replace them by regional economic councils, the *sovnarkhozy*. The Supreme Soviet approved the reform in May. Thus Khrushchev unilaterally destroyed the alliance with

6. *A Presidium banquet in the mid-1950s. From left to right: Shepilov, Pospelov, Mikoian, Molotov, Bulganin speaking, Khrushchev, Kaganovich, Suslov, and Malenkov (Photo: Dmitrii Valtermants, Ogonek, 1990, Nr. 13).*

Bulganin by directly undermining the institutional basis of the ministers. At the same time he earned the enthusiasm of the provincial party secretaries, a strong contingent in the CC, because under the new system they would be controlling industrial planning indirectly.

KHRUSHCHEV THREATENED AND VICTORIOUS

At the plenary session of the Presidium on 18 June 1957, Khrushchev unexpectedly met a solid front of opponents headed by Molotov and Malenkov.[38] According to former Presidium member Mukhitdinov, they demanded limits to the de-Stalinization, reduction of the role of the party to ideological and cultural matters, more power for the government over the republics and Khrushchev's resignation for indecent language and drinking habits.[39] Out of 11 voting members, Khrushchev was supported only by Mikoian, Suslov, and Kirichenko. All of the candidate members supported him, except for Shepilov, who jumped ship in the middle of the debate.[40] The new candidate member, Frol Kozlov, First Secretary of the Leningrad Provincial Committee, was absent. A vote was taken and Khrushchev was removed from office. According to this same account, the debate was stormy. Kaganovich attacked Brezhnev so rudely that the latter almost fainted.[41] This is Molotov's account when he was asked how Khrushchev reacted: "He shouted and became very excited... But we had already agreed. We were 7 out of 11."[42]

The conspirators never stood a chance. Khrushchev refused to resign, demanding to let the CC have the final word. He was backed by his own secretarial hierarchy, the army and the KGB. Zhukov is quoted as having said: "The army is against this decision, and not one tank will move from its place without my order."[43] He ordered his air force to fly in members of the CC from all over the country. Kozlov, supported by Suslov and Furtseva, rallied the other CC members. A group of 21 members demanded access to the Presidium session. KGB chief Ivan Serov was one of them. He grabbed Voroshilov at the collar of his jacket and demanded an immediate end to the Presidium session. On 21 June 100 angry CC members besieged the Presidium.[44] From 22 to 29 June the CC met. The revolt turned into victory. Molotov and most of his comrades lost their seats on the Presidium, though Bulganin and Voroshilov were graciously allowed to keep theirs until 1958 and 1960.

Many CC members were rewarded with a seat on the new, large Presidium of 24 members and candidates. Among the 15 voting members were 10 secretaries of various levels. Never in Soviet history has there been a Politburo with such a large percentage of officials from the party apparatus.[45] The ministers were pushed to the sidelines of the Presidium. At the same time the victory of the Secretariat in the struggle for power subjected the Presidium again to a new leader demanding submission: all of the oppositionist group except stubborn Molotov admitted their mistake and voted for the resolution that condemned them as an *"anti-party group."* The next day Kaganovich telephoned Khrushchev, begging him not to have him executed.[46]

The new leader had a coherent vision of the future of the USSR. He wanted to reduce state centralization and increase the role of various collectives of citizens, mobilized and controlled by the party. He had already abolished many ministries. In 1958 he decided to have the state-owned Machine Tractor Stations sell their equipment to the collective farms, the *kolkhozy*. The First Secretary also supported the establishment of voluntary citizen police (*druzhiny*) and citizen's courts. In 1958 a theoretical project was started to prepare a change of dogma, corresponding to the new policies. The new Presidium member Otto Kuusinen was appointed to organize the writing of a theoretical exposé explaining why the Soviet state, having completed the liquidation of the exploiting classes, had now outgrown the "dictatorship of the proletariat" and should be transformed into a "state of the whole people."[47] This was supposed to be a first step toward the disappearance of the state under full communism.

The notion that the state need no longer repress a complete class corresponded to the end of the killing and locking up of millions of people, as had been done under Stalin. This change of dogma enraged many members of the Presidium. Furtseva phoned Kuusinen, accusing him of "an outrageous attack on the holy of holies—the dictatorship of the proletariat!"[48] Meanwhile Khrushchev strengthened his position by dismissing many of his supporters and accumulating new positions. In October 1957 he dismissed Zhukov, who was abroad, because of his "Bonapartist aspirations" directed at "a South American-style military takeover," as he claimed absurdly.[49] In 1958 the First Secretary took over the post of Prime Minister as Stalin had done. In May 1960 he ousted five members of the Presidium, among them Furtseva, A. B. Aristov and N. G. Ignatov, from their seats in the Secretariat—often for apparently irrelevant reasons.[50]

Former Gosplan chairman Novikov described how one day in 1960 Aristov dared to suggest to Khrushchev ways of improving his speeches for his forthcoming trip to France. The leader reddened and angrily retorted: "What, what, what?" The unfortunate secretary was demoted to the post of ambassador to Poland.[51] One other victim was Second Secretary of the CC Kirichenko, who had to relinquish his seat in favor of Kozlov who took over as second in command.[52] According to Mukhitdinov, after 1960 Khrushchev formed a small group with whom he discussed in advance Presidium and Secretariat affairs. It consisted of himself, secretaries Kozlov and Suslov, and First Deputy Prime Minister Mikoian.[53]

The 22nd Party Congress in 1961 saw further revelations on Stalin's crimes. A new, utopian party program was adopted, promising the introduction of full communism in 1980. The United States was to be surpassed in per capita production by 1970, and all remaining market elements in the Soviet economy were to be abolished.[54] On 31 October 1961 a new Presidium was appointed. Many secretaries appointed in 1957 lost their seats, making the Presidium again a more select body. It retained, however, the preponderance of the party apparatus. It consisted of 11 voting members: secretaries of the CC Kozlov, Kuusinen, Suslov and Prime Minster Khrushchev; the Ukrainian First Secretary N. V. Podgornyi and members of the Russian Bureau of the CC Brezhnev (who was also chairman of the Supreme Soviet's Presidium) and G. I. Voronov; chairman Shvernik of the Committee of Party Control; deputy prime ministers Kosygin and Mikoian and the Russian Prime Minister D. S. Polianskii. Candidate members were V. V. Grishin, K. T. Mazurov, V. T. Mzhavanadze, Sh. R. Rashidov and V. V. Shcherbitskii. This

Presidium remained largely unchanged until Khrushchev's fall in October 1964; contrary to conventional wisdom, the Khrushchev era was one of relative cadre stability for the Presidium. The average turnover rate in the Presidium in the years 1958 to 1963 was actually below the total average.[55]

In November 1962 Khrushchev decided that the party should lead the economy even more directly than before. The provincial and local party machines were therefore split up into two branches: industrial and agricultural. According to Khrushchev's son Sergei, Brezhnev, Podgornyi and Polianskii pretended to be enthusiastic about this "great idea" when they heard about it.[56] Khrushchev took the traditional position that his word was final, expecting support for his policy. He allowed only limited opposition, as for instance from conservatively oriented Secretary Suslov when he opposed the publication of Solzhenitsyn's *One Day in the Life of Ivan Denisovich* in 1962.[57] Former Belorussian First Secretary Mazurov remembers that he and Khrushchev "struggled all the time." He was a man "with whom one could argue." Mazurov claims that he opposed Khrushchev's ill-fated policies to curtail the peasants' ownership of cows and their small plots. When he criticized the division of the party apparatus, however, Khrushchev threatened to have him replaced.[58]

THE LAST CONSPIRACY

Paradoxically, the plan, intending to further enhance the power of the party, undermined the authority of the provincial secretaries because it broke up their apparatus. This eroded their support for Khrushchev. The army was antagonized by cuts in the defense budget. This was accepted by the Soviet elite as long as the policy paid off. In 1963, however, a drought resulted in grain shortages. Khrushchev received a further blow when Second Secretary Kozlov suffered a stroke in April 1963. His position was taken over by Brezhnev.[59] Khrushchev's position was not so firm as it had seemed. There was room for one more conspiracy—and he fell victim to it. It crystallized during 1964 around four secretaries of the CC: Presidium members Brezhnev, Podgornyi, Suslov and Aleksandr Shelepin, who was not then part of the Politburo. The accounts contradict each other on who took the initiative, but it is clear that it was the Secretariat that brought down its own leader. KGB Chairman V. E. Semichastnyi and Defense Minister R. Ia. Malinovskii supported the conspirators.[60]

They met under various covers, for instance during a football match and in Brezhnev's hunting lodge in Zavidovo. A meeting was organized in

September by Stavropol regional secretary F. D. Kulakov during a hunting trip.[61] The "bomb" went off when Khrushchev was on holiday at his favorite Pitsunda peninsula on the Black Sea, accompanied by his friend Mikoian. On 13 October he was summoned to Moscow where he appeared the same day in a session of the Presidium. In addition to the 17 Presidium members and candidates, Malinovskii, Minister of Foreign Affairs Andrei Gromyko, and three provincial secretaries attended the meeting.[62] Foreign policy did not figure prominently in the accusations. Khrushchev was accused of a mistaken agricultural policy. The establishment of the *sovnarkhozy* and the division of the party apparatus was also criticized. He was accused of rudeness toward his colleagues, of organizing a cult of personality through photographs in the press, and of nepotism—presumably a hint at the comfortable positions of his son, daughter, and the son-in-law, *Izvestiia*-editor Adzhubei.[63]

Khrushchev defended himself fiercely but only Mikoian gave him some support. After he had gone home late in the evening, he phoned Mikoian to tell him he was prepared to step down, but he added that nobody could ever have dreamed of telling Stalin that he should go. He considered it his achievement that the fear had gone.[64] The next morning the Presidium met again to hear Khrushchev's "swan song," as he called it himself. He announced his resignation but bitterly remarked that "none of you [...] ever said anything about my deficiencies, you always confirmed everything and supported me. You lacked principle and courage." He only asked to be allowed to make a request to the plenary session of the CC that was about to meet. When Brezhnev answered, "That won't happen," tears came to Khrushchev's eyes.[65] Brezhnev was recommended as the new First Secretary and Kosygin as Prime Minister. The plenum of 14 October met in deep silence. Khrushchev sat with his head bowed and his eyes downcast.[66]

Suslov repeated the accusations in his speech, describing Khrushchev as an arrogant leader with overly rigid policies in agriculture, and wild reorganizations of industry and the party. His speech was accompanied by shouts: "He was like the Iranian Shah, he did what he wanted!"[67] There was no discussion. First Secretary Brezhnev noted in his short closing speech that while Khrushchev ended the cult of Stalin's personality only after the latter's death, the cult of Khrushchev's personality had been ended while the leader was alive.[68]

Khrushchev had upheld the regime according to which the First Secretary had almost the status of a dictator in the Presidium and could not be openly resisted for too long; but he failed to inspire enough fear. He fell victim to the rebellious spirit against personal dictatorship that he had himself encouraged. For once the Presidium, normally lacking courage, dared to face its leader and brought him down for his policy of radical economic and administrative reorganizations.

NOTES TO CHAPTER 4

1. *KPSS v rezoliutsiiakh...*, Ch. II, 1953: 1149.
2. Talbott, vol. 1, 1977: 346.
3. Ibid.
4. Barsukov, "Mart 1953-go", 1989.
5. Talbott, vol. 1, 1977: 345.
6. Gnedin, 1977: 135ff.; Golovkov, 1988: 30.
7. Medvedev/Medvedev, 1977: 9.
8. Talbott, vol. 1, 1977: 353-54.
9. See Gorchakov, 1989.
10. Talbott, vol. 1, 1977: 354.
11. Medvedev/Medvedev, 1977: 10.
12. Talbott, vol. 1, 1977: 360-62; Aksiutin, *Nikita...*, 1989: 12-14; Moskalenko, 1990; Ivanova, 1990: 42-45.
13. "Plenum TsK...", 1991, Nr. 1: 150.
14. "Plenum TsK...", 1991, Nr. 2: 195.
15. "Sostav...", 1990: 101.
16. Barsukov, "Eshche...", 1989.
17. "Plenum TsK...", 1991, Nr. 1: 157, 162-65.
18. *Pravda*, 9 August 1953.
19. Aksiutin, *Nikita...*, 1989: 298.
20. Barsukov, "Eshche...", 1989.
21. Ibid.
22. *Pravda*, 3 February 1955.
23. Barsukov, "Eshche...", 1989.
24. *Pravda*, 9 February 1955.
25. Barsukov, "Eshche...", 1989.
26. Ivanova, 1990: 47.
27. Schecter/Luchkov, 1990: 41-42.
28. Talbott, vol. 1, 1977: 369.
29. Aksiutin, *Nikita...*, 1989: 33.
30. Schecter/Luchkov, 1990: 42.
31. Aksiutin, *Nikita...*, 1989: 33-34.
32. *XX s''ezd...*, 1956: 34.

33. Talbott, vol. 1, 1977: 372-75; Aksiutin, "N. S. Khrushchev:...", 1989: 107.
34. Ivanova, 1990: 50.
35. Talbott, vol. 1, 1977: 376.
36. Ivanova, 1990: 48.
37. On stability of tenure, see Table 8.27.
38. Kuptsov, 1988: 636.
39. Ivanova, 1990: 92.
40. For Shepilov's own account: "Problemy...", 1989: 55.
41. Kuptsov, 1988: 637.
42. Ivanova, 1990: 53.
43. Burlatskii, 1990: 176.
44. Kuptsov, 1988: 637-38; Ivanova, 1990: 53; *Politicheskii dnevnik...*, 1972: 107-8.
45. See Table 8.25.
46. Kuptsov, 1988: 638-39.
47. Burlatskii, 1990: 37-38.
48. Ibid.: 41.
49. Talbott, vol. 2, 1977: 44.
50. "Sostav...", 1990: 78.
51. Novikov, 1989, Nr. 2: 104-5.
52. Burlatskii, 1990: 266; Sergei Khrushchev in: Aksiutin, *Nikita...*, 1989: 250; Novikov, 1989, Nr. 2: 112.
53. Ivanova, 1990: 94.
54. *XXII s''ezd...*, 1962: 276, 295.
55. See Table 8.27.
56. Chroesjtsjov, 1990: 25.
57. Schecter/Luchkov, 1990: 198, 201.
58. Bondarenko, 1989: 3.
59. Chroesjtsjov, 1990: 33-34, 61.
60. See: Medvedev in Kuptsov, 1988: 641-42; Burlatskii, 1990: 263, 275; Chroesjtsjov, 1990: 61-63; Voronov in Lynev, 1988; Shelest in "O Khrushcheve...", 1989, and in "So I said...", 1989; Semichastnyi in Svetitskii/Sokolov, 1989: 25-26; Rodionov, 1989: 185; Novikov, 1989, Nr. 2: 115.
61. Burlatskii in Aksiutin, *Nikita...*, 1989: 211; Lynev, 1988; Kuptsov, 1988: 641-42.
62. Kuptsov, 1988: 643.
63. Aksiutin, *Nikita...*, 1989: 278-81; Novikov, 1989, Nr. 2: 116.
64. Kuptsov, 1988: 643; Aksiutin, *Nikita...*, 1989: 281-82.
65. "O Khrushcheve...", 1989: 5.
66. Adzhubei, 1989: 8.

67. Kuptsov, 1988: 644-48; Voronov in Ivanova, 1990: 121;
    Adzhubei, 1989: 8.
68. Adzhubei in Aksiutin, *Nikita...*, 1989: 342.

5

Stability of Cadres

The Politburo Under Brezhnev, Andropov and Chernenko

During the Khrushchev period a new generation came to power that had played no part in the revolution. In 1953 the average year of birth of members of the Presidium was 1896. The leaders under Lenin and Stalin were of the generation that lived through the revolution and the ensuing Civil War as adults. In 1961, however, the average Presidium member was born in 1905.[1] Such persons were only 16 when the Civil War ended. This second generation had World War II as its main life experience and carried out the "de-Stalinization." It continued to rule after Khrushchev's fall.

The most powerful men in the USSR were secretaries Brezhnev, Podgornyi and Shelepin (who joined the Presidium in November 1964) and Prime Minister Kosygin. This new team immediately started to undo Khrushchev's administrative reforms. In November 1964 the undivided party apparatus was restored.[2] The new leaders had the avowed aim of "collective leadership." Brezhnev and Podgornyi even shared a past; they had both been Khrushchev's clients, making their career in the Ukraine under him. They were both his *vydvizhentsy*, functionaries promoted under his *pokrovitelstvo*, his protection. But this did not ensure an automatic mutual sympathy any more than it had ensured loyalty toward their patron; the new leading group had coalesced on a negative rather than a positive platform. Quarrels broke out almost immediately.

Shelepin's program was reactionary in all respects. He represented the "tough wing" opposed to Brezhnev.[3] In February 1965 he wrote the draft for a speech by Brezhnev on the occasion of the 20th anniversary of the victory in the war. Burlatskii read the text, disapprovingly called a "dissertation" by

Brezhnev. It called for the restoration of Stalin's "good name"; revision of many decisions of the 20th and 22nd Party Congresses; restoration of the industrial ministries and more labor discipline; revocation of the principle of "peaceful coexistence" as Khrushchev had interpreted it; and restoration of the ties with Mao Zedong's China—where Stalin was still in good standing. "Iron Shurik" stood for order and class principles and played the "Chinese card." His "shadow cabinet" consisted of young people he knew from the Komsomol where he had made his career.[4] He had also been chairman of the KGB. His strongest point was that KGB Chairman Semichastnyi was his client who had succeeded him as head of both organizations.[5]

Suslov and Mzhavanadze, the Georgian First Secretary, supported him in his plea for a reconsideration of Stalin's role, but he was opposed by Mikoian. Brezhnev, however, accepted the proposal of Secretary of the CC Iurii Andropov to give no judgment on Stalin at all.[6] According to Georgii Arbatov, Secretary Suslov (nicknamed the "gray cardinal") did not aspire to the role of top leader. He was content to influence events from behind the scenes.[7] Kosygin supported Shelepin in his China policy. The Vietnam war had broken out and he hoped to restore unity with the Chinese party in a common effort to support their Vietnamese comrades. In a meeting of the Presidium in early January 1965, Kosygin and Shelepin jointly criticized a foreign policy report made by Andropov and Gromyko for being lenient on imperialism. Brezhnev was so irritated about Kosygin's wish that he should visit China that he said: "If you find that so utterly necessary, then go yourself."[8]

Arbatov describes Kosygin as a man "open for new economic ideas. But in political questions he was, unfortunately, a conservative." Rodionov, though, calls Kosygin an outspoken proponent of détente and trade with the West.[9] In September 1965 the Central Committee abolished the *sovnarkhozy*, restoring the industrial ministries. Prime Minister Kosygin presented the report. He also announced that individual enterprises should operate more freely, taking profits as one of their aims. This reform program was never realized, and Brezhnev was responsible for the failure. According to Burlatskii, he was "an active opponent of the reform proposed by Kosygin." In the apparatus Brezhnev was quoted: "Well, what did he think up? Reform, reform...Who needs this and who will understand this? We have to work better, that's the whole problem."[10] Brezhnev's obstruction of the Kosygin reforms was confirmed by several former Presidium members and other highly placed Soviet leaders.[11] According to Shelest, Brezhnev considered Kosygin a "schemer" because he insisted on expanding light consumer industries.[12]

In 1965 investments in agriculture were substantially raised. Simultaneously an ambitious program was adopted to expand all services of the Soviet army, not only missiles and submarines as under Khrushchev with his predilection for a cheap army. In the 1970s this program resulted in Soviet nuclear parity with the United States and a capability for military intervention in the Third World. According to George Breslauer, this was Brezhnev's approach, reflecting his dual emphasis on agriculture and defense industries, while Kosygin tried to cut the shares of these two sectors in favor of light industry.[13] Podgornyi was characterized by Arbatov as "even darker and more conservative than Brezhnev."[14] He had some support in the Presidium: Ukrainian First Secretary Petr Shelest was a client of his, having made his career under him in the Ukraine.[15] Podgornyi lost his seat on the Secretariat in December 1965. Nevertheless, he remained a powerful man as chairman of the Supreme Soviet's Presidium and CC Presidium member.

In March and April 1966 the 23rd Party Congress convened. It restored the old names *Politburo* and *General Secretary*.[16] The new Politburo had 11 voting members: secretaries of the CC Brezhnev, A. P. Kirilenko, Suslov and Shelepin; Ukrainian First Secretary Shelest, and chairman of the Committee for Party Control A. Ia. Pelshe; Prime Minister Kosygin with his deputies Mazurov and Polianskii, and Russian Prime Minister Voronov; and finally Podgornyi. The eight candidates were Grishin, P. N. Demichev, D. A. Kunaev, P. M. Masherov, Mzhavanadze, Rashidov, D. F. Ustinov, and Shcherbitskii. Six of them were secretaries of the CC or republican first secretaries. A basic characteristic of Khrushchev's Presidium was retained: the party apparatus and the republics were much better represented than they had been during the latter years of Stalin's rule, when central state institutions predominated. This continued to be so throughout Brezhnev's rule.[17] After the congress Brezhnev quickly consolidated his position.

In April 1967 Andrei Grechko was appointed the new Minister of Defense. He had commanded the Kiev Military District when Brezhnev worked in the Ukraine as leader of various party organizations.[18] In May 1967, with Shelepin hospitalized, the Politburo convened. Semichastnyi was invited. Brezhnev announced that he, Podgornyi, and Kosygin, supported by Suslov, proposed to fire him as chairman of the KGB. In order to bring the KGB closer to the CC, they proposed Secretary Andropov as his successor. Semichastnyi was crushed: "What do you mean, bringing closer? Was I far away then? I am a member of the CC, I... Dear comrades..." Brezhnev reacted: "It is not necessary to discuss this, comrades, not necessary to discuss." It was over in a few minutes.[19] Andropov was loyal to Brezhnev.[20] He was promoted to Politburo candidate in June 1967. The General Secretary now had a former collaborator for Minister of Defense and he, rather than Shelepin, more directly controlled the KGB.

In September he struck: Shelepin lost his seat on the Secretariat and was appointed trade union chairman. Brezhnev had now removed his two rivals, Podgornyi and Shelepin, from the Secretariat, and until his death he controlled it as his main power base. According to Arbatov, Brezhnev did not nominate one Second Secretary, but used Suslov and Kirilenko as his two permanent deputies in the Secretariat.[21] Kirilenko had been Brezhnev's client from his days in Zaporozhe and Dnepropetrovsk.[22] The USSR was now ruled by a triumvirate of General Secretary Brezhnev, Prime Minister Kosygin and Chairman of the Supreme Soviet's Presidium Podgornyi.

THE PROFITEERS

After Andropov joined the Politburo, no change occurred in it for almost four years. Similar stability had been achieved only during the war years when the Politburo did not really function. During the Brezhnev era the Politburo had the lowest turnover rate in Soviet history.[23] Stability of cadres became an absolute demand in reaction to the deadly threats in Stalin's days and Khrushchev's organizational turmoil. Burlatskii describes the ruling generation in Brezhnev's time as people who had not participated in the revolution but had often made a "fairy-like career making a leap in a few years from ordinary workers to ministers."[24] The Politburo elected in 1971 was indeed the most proletarian of Soviet history: more than three quarters of the members and candidates had started their working careers as manual workers.[25] The Brezhnev Politburo profited more from the revolution than any other in terms of social mobility. At no other point in Soviet history was the distance in social milieu so great between where the leaders began and where they ended.

These leaders formed the generation of profiteers. They wanted their peace to enjoy what had been built. The concept reflecting this was "developed socialism," proposed by Burlatskii in 1966 but given a different interpretation by Brezhnev.[26] It was finally included in the new Constitution of 1977. It was defined as "a society of mature socialist social relations" in which on the basis of a drawing together and equality of all classes and nations "a new historical community of people has been formed: the Soviet people."[27] Khrushchev's program of a speedy building of full communism implied the urgency of reforms. Brezhnev's celebration of the "maturity" of Soviet socialism stressed the relative perfection of the system as it was. It vocalized satisfaction and aversion to change. The Soviet system was frozen in a state of immobility.

The conservative slant of the regime caused concern among the public, and in a speech in March 1968 Brezhnev called for "turning the nuts tightly" against the rising "dissident" movement.[28] Meanwhile, a dissident form of communism made itself felt in Czechoslovakia, but it was also crushed. According to Arbatov, Brezhnev and Suslov hesitated to send in the troops but Shelest, Ustinov, and others pressed for an invasion.[29] The actual decision seems not to have been taken by the whole Politburo but by Brezhnev, Podgornyi, Kosygin, Andropov, Shelest, and some others. Only Voronov may have objected to the invasion.[30]

Soon after the invasion had restored the status quo ante, *détente* triumphed. The USSR opened up to the West, trying to obtain economic aid to modernize its economy, but without any reforms. During this age there was a strong tendency, both in the Politburo and elsewhere in politics and society, toward a suffocating conformism and consensus. There was no room for antagonistic policy programs. Brezhnev even established the rule that members needed permission from the Politburo for trips around the country.[31] Nevertheless, there were collisions, often over style and sometimes over content. Brezhnev, after all, was a rather silly man. He insisted that his comrades stand up and applaud him during his public speeches and demanded that he be awarded several medals.[32] He raced his cars as if he were an 18 year-old boy and was sentimental to the point of weeping to impress his audience, even foreign visitors like Willy Brandt.[33] Some irritation was to be expected. Voronov even mentions "a fierce struggle [that] was waged in the leadership for all these years."[34]

BREZHNEV'S VICTIMS

On 4 April 1971 a new Politburo was elected after the 24th Party Congress. It had 15 voting members of whom eight were secretaries of various levels plus Pelshe. The seven others were Podgornyi, ministers Kosygin, Mazurov, Polianskii, Voronov, and Shcherbitskii, and trade union chairman Shelepin. Except for Shcherbitskii and with the addition of Ukrainian Secretary Shelest, precisely these names are mentioned by various sources as not of one mind with Brezhnev.[35] With Kosygin in particular, Brezhnev is said to have had "fundamental differences of opinion" on economic and foreign policy.[36] And so these seven, roughly representing the government machine, all fell victim to Brezhnev's march to power during the new decade.

According to Gelman, Shelest favored a more strident anti-imperialist policy in relation to Western Germany and the Vietnam war and was also accused of Ukrainian nationalism.[37] Shelest himself confirms that he demanded more republican autonomy and often clashed with Brezhnev on issues ranging from selling cattle cakes abroad to the closing of Ukrainian mines. One day in 1972 during a Politburo meeting, Brezhnev invited him into a separate room and declared that "we have decided" that he should leave the Ukraine and become a Deputy Prime Minister in Moscow. He insisted: "you'll be a friend of my family." But Shelest refused, saying that he did not want to be turned into Brezhnev's "pet dog." The Politburo, however, supported Brezhnev. Although he realized "This is the end," Shelest gave in: "In the party, discipline is the main thing." The affair ended with his retirement from the Politburo on 27 April 1973.[38]

Russian Prime Minister Voronov claims repeatedly to have criticized the building of gigantic factories, power stations, and irrigation projects as too expensive and too damaging to the environment. Instead he favored the introduction of independent teams in the *kolkhozy*. He was part of a commission that cancelled a hydropower station planned to flood 90 villages. Thereafter commission chairman Kirilenko gave all members a separate working-over, resulting in a reversal of the decision. In 1971 Voronov was transferred to the post of chairman of the Committee of People's Control where he again clashed with Brezhnev. In his new capacity he was informed of widespread corruption in Uzbekistan and Azerbaidzhan, but he was ordered personally by the General Secretary to disregard such signals. He was dismissed from the Politburo together with Shelest. Brezhnev sighed: "Voronov has left—now we have unity."[39]

At the same plenary session of the CC in April 1973 three voting members were added to the Politburo: KGB chairman Andropov, and ministers of Defense and Foreign Affairs Grechko and Gromyko. Brezhnev fought for the dominance of the Secretariat, but at the same time he shrewdly bound some crucial branches of the state bureaucracy with ties of gratitude to him. Grechko's Politburo membership was particularly noteworthy for the rising status of the army under Brezhnev: it was almost 20 years earlier that a defense minister had been on this highest body. This was a corollary of Brezhnev's policy of favoring military investment as developed in the 1960s. Grechko, however, could be bothersome: he criticized the SALT-1 Treaty in the Politburo, though he was later made to apologize to Brezhnev.[40]

After the 25th Congress a Politburo was elected on 5 March 1976 with 16 voting members. It included five secretaries of the CC (Brezhnev, Suslov, Kirilenko, Ustinov, and F. D. Kulakov) and four provincial and republican secretaries. Ustinov succeeded Grechko as Minister of Defense when the latter died soon after taking office.

According to Mazurov, the five secretaries of the CC "and others" decided all important matters beforehand. "Brezhnev relied on the Secretariat and not on the Politburo."[41] The General Secretary used to announce that "we" proposed something. The others had no choice but to accept the proposals. Politburo meetings often took no longer than 15 to 20 minutes.[42] Out of the seven dissidents, only Kosygin, Mazurov, and Podgornyi remained on the Politburo. Their fall was a matter of time. In May 1977 Podgornyi lost his seat on the Politburo, and soon Brezhnev himself took over the post of chairman of the Supreme Soviet Presidium. Mazurov had the temerity to inform Brezhnev of his daughter Galina's involvement in "speculation" during a trip to France. He paid for his frankness with his Politburo seat in November 1978.[43]

Meanwhile, relations between Brezhnev and Kirilenko cooled in 1978-79.[44] In November 1978 Secretary Konstantin Chernenko, who had worked under Brezhnev in Moldavia, acquired full Politburo status. According to Arbatov, Chernenko replaced Kirilenko as one of Brezhnev's two deputies in the Secretariat because of Kirilenko's "complete incompetence" and frequent illness.[45] By this time Brezhnev was himself a very sick man. Once in 1976 he had been clinically dead.[46] This did not, though, slow down his drive to acquire full power: in October 1980 at last Kosygin's turn came. He was succeeded as Prime Minister by Nikolai Tikhonov, Brezhnev's associate from his days in Dnepropetrovsk. The Secretariat and its leader were victorious.

THE BREZHNEV CULT

As after the disappearance of Lenin and Stalin, "collective leadership" had once more been reduced to the dominance of one leader. The tradition of one-man rule was apparently engrained in the heads of the Soviet elite. Mazurov explains the relative lack of resistance to Brezhnev as a consequence of three ingrained feelings: an old belief in a "good lord"; out of fear to harm the unity and authority of the party; and out of fear to lose one's priviliges if fired.[47] Shelest more clearly pronounced the dictatorial principle when asked why he, after all, assisted in strengthening Brezhnev's authority: "Once we have elected the General Secretary, we are responsible for his activities." Otherwise "there would be no order."[48] The Politburo that overthrew Khrushchev resigned to a new leader from its own midst. Time and again it was hypnotised by the snake it had itself reared.

Brezhnev strongly identified with the army: he made himself a marshal in 1976 and presented himself as a war hero in his memoirs. When he received the marshal title he proudly pointed to the stars on his shoulder straps, saying: "I've earned this."[49] The military profile of the Brezhnev cult was part of a new militant tendency in Soviet foreign policy that became apparent with the Soviet support for the Cuban intervention in Angola in 1975. The invasion of Afghanistan in December 1979 marked its climax. The decision was probably made by Brezhnev, Ustinov, Andropov and Gromyko. There were rumors that the KGB chairman had doubts. The other members of the Politburo were only informed of the decision. It is not clear whether a formal vote even took place.[50] Arbatov describes the policies of the second half of the decade as a revival of revolutionary "messianism," backed up by the "military-industrial complex over which control was basically lost." Brezhnev gave in to all demands of the military. Andropov and Gromyko seem to have been afraid of quarreling with Ustinov.[51]

Meanwhile, the Soviet posture in the Third World and new arms projects such as the SS-20 missiles caused grave concern in the West and in China. Its ambitious military policies isolated the USSR and placed it in dire financial straits. This was a regime in its death throes. Under the new Cold War conditions, economic stagnation could no longer be mitigated by technological influxes from abroad. More and more often, therefore, problems in resource allocation emerged. Forced to make a choice between his two favorite sectors of heavy industry and agriculture, Brezhnev in the early 1980s opted for an expensive "Food Program" to the detriment of investments in machine-building industries. There are indications that this caused estrangement between the party leader and the army.[52] Corruption became widespread, much more so, according to Telman Gdlian, than it had ever been under Stalin.[53] The policy of cadres stability allowed the Soviet elite to engage without punishment in the lucrative protection of illegal economic enterprises on an ever greater scale.[54]

In February 1981 the 26th Party Congress convened. On 3 March the new CC elected a Politburo. Voting members were secretaries of the CC Brezhnev (who also remained head of state), M. S. Gorbachev, Kirilenko, Suslov, and Chernenko; first secretaries Grishin, Kunaev, G. V. Romanov, and Shcherbitskii; chairman of the Committee of Party Control Pelshe; Prime Minister Tikhonov; and ministers Andropov (KGB), Gromyko, and Ustinov. Candidate members were G. A. Aliev, Demichev, T. Ia. Kiselev, V. V. Kuznetsov, B. N. Ponomarev, Rashidov, M. S. Solomentsev, and E. A.

Shevardnadze. This was Brezhnev's victorious team. Except for Kirilenko, nobody was dropped from it until Gorbachev's take-over. But several dropped themselves: death took a heavy toll. The policy of cadre stability had led to a gerontocracy. The youngest member was 50 years old: Gorbachev. The average age in the Politburo was 68.

THE GLORIOUS SEXTET

According to Brezhnev's former assistent V. A. Pechenev, a "glorious sextet" emerged in the late 1970s. It consisted of secretaries Brezhnev, Suslov, and Chernenko, and ministers Ustinov, Gromyko, and Andropov. The KGB and the ministries of Defense and Foreign Affairs played "the leading role in the definition of our strategic policy."[55] The Prime Minister was not on the sextet. It was a coalition, but only between the Secretariat and the national security branch of the state apparatus. Within a few years this power structure crumbled. The members of the sextet, with an average age of 73, began to fall away like autumn leaves. During their final years the ministers among them, especially Andropov, grew concerned about the spread of corruption. They did not shrink from measures that threatened to undermine the position of the old secretaries around Brezhnev and Chernenko. Nevertheless, as we will presently see, the septuagenarians remained the team they were until the bitter end.

In January 1982 Andropov's KGB initiated a drive against corruption. It started with the case of the singer Boris Buriatse, who was charged with theft of a large collection of diamonds. Brezhnev's brother-in-law Semen Tsvigun, who as Deputy Chairman of the KGB headed the investigation, informed Suslov of the case. It concerned a smuggling network and "speculation" in diamonds. All the direct suspects were close friends of Galina Brezhneva's, daughter of the leader who was herself engaged in the same activities. The case was potentially far-reaching: it involved the Minister of Internal Affairs (an old acquaintance of Brezhnev's from Dnepropetrovsk and Moldavia); Galina's husband, who was also Deputy Minister of Internal Affairs; and Brezhnev's own brother, a Deputy Minister of Foreign Trade. After their discussion Tsvigun committed suicide. Suslov died on 25 January. Several of the less powerful suspects were soon arrested.[56]

Suslov's death created a vacancy in the Secretariat. Arbatov has written that Brezhnev himself proposed to make Andropov a Secretary of the CC. He took up this new job in May. At the same time Andropov was afraid that Brezhnev's motive was to remove him from the KGB. Suslov had been considered the most powerful of the two deputies of the General Secretary (*Gensek*). According to Zhores Medvedev, the heated Politburo meeting that decided to give Andropov the job of second-in-command in the Secretariat lasted six hours. Brezhnev and Tikhonov wanted Chernenko to be the second man, but Ustinov and Gromyko did not consider him fit for the job. The ministers carried the day, supported by secretaries Gorbachev, Romanov, Shcherbitskii and Kunaev.[57] The KGB intensified its campaign: during the summer for the first time a powerful First Secretary, Sergei Medunov of the Krasnodar Territory, was dismissed on charges of corruption. He protected the illegal caviar trade. He was a personal friend of Brezhnev's, who had a dacha in Pitsunda in his territory.[58]

Neverthess, in October 1982 Andropov, according to information he provided to Arbatov, again received Brezhnev's blessings: "You are the second man in the party and the country, proceed from that, use all your powers."[59] On 10 November the *Gensek* died. An enlarged Politburo meeting convened the same day. According to Pechenev, the procedural rules of the game dictated that the second man in the party be appointed the new General Secretary.[60] Medvedev has it that Andropov was elected almost immediately at the proposal of Ustinov, who is rumored to have said about a Chernenko alternative: "It will not be understood by the army."[61] Among the voting members Ustinov and Gromyko were supported by Gorbachev, Shcherbitskii and Kunaev. Chernenko stood no chance, although according to Rodionov, Tikhonov, Kunaev and Romanov supported him.[62] On 12 November the CC elected Andropov the new *Gensek*. Chernenko was nominated, apparently without problems, to the informal position of Second Secretary.[63]

INTERREGNA

During his short reign Andropov continued to fight corruption. In the spring of 1983 an investigation was started against the First Secretary of the Bukhara Provincial Party Committee. Comrade Karimov was accused of bribe taking. Trunks full of gold coins, jewelry and money were discovered. Karimov had gold busts made for Uzbek First Secretary Rashidov and for Brezhnev.[64] Rashidov himself turned out to be the boss of a network that drew its main income from cheating the state by falsifying reports on cotton production. It was covered up by the bribed leaders of the Ministry of Internal Affairs—Brezhnev's friends and relatives. The investigation culminated in Rashidov's death in October 1983, possibly by suicide.[65] The anticorruption campaign now potentially threatened the Politburo itself. Some of the other most corrupt areas of the country were directly ruled by Politburo members or candidates: Kazakhstan (Kunaev), the Ukraine (Shcherbitskii), Moscow (Grishin) and Georgia (Shevardnadze).[66]

Meanwhile, Andropov quickly "started to raise the political weight of Gorbachev"—as Egor Ligachev expresses it. Secretary of Agriculture Gorbachev had been a client of the deceased Kulakov, and had made his whole career in the latter's wake.[67] Until Romanov became a Secretary of the CC in June 1983, he was for a time the only full Politburo member on the Secretariat besides Andropov and Chernenko. Andropov involved him in the cases against corrupt cadres such as Rashidov, and in the nomination of new cadres. The young and dynamic Gorbachev seems to have enjoyed Andropov's full confidence.[68] Nevertheless, when Andropov's illness came in a terminal stage in September 1983, Second Secretary Chernenko took over his work.[69] According to Andropov's assistent, A. I. Volskii, his boss expressed the hope that Secretary Gorbachev should succeed him, but this was impossible as long as Chernenko was Second Secretary.[70] The Gensek died on 9 February 1984. The next day the Politburo convened.[71]

It now appeared that the team spirit of the old Brezhnev group was decisive. Ustinov, his hand on Tikhonov's shoulder, remarked, while entering the room: "Kostia [Chernenko] will be more obliging than this one [Gorbachev]." A few days later the CC elected 73-year-old Chernenko General Secretary "without problems."[72] The three remaining members of the "glorious sextet" were not prepared to give a relative newcomer the highest position. Pechenev and Ligachev agree that at the first Politburo session after his election, Chernenko himself proposed that Gorbachev be nominated to preside over the Secretariat—that is, be Second Secretary. He was supported by Ustinov but resisted by Tikhonov who warned: "Well, Gorbachev will turn the meetings of the Secretariat into a collegium of the Ministry of Agriculture." Gromyko proposed diplomatically to postpone a decision, but Chernenko insisted—and he was obeyed.[73]

Apart from Ustinov's death in December 1984, nothing changed in the Politburo during Chernenko's rule. The struggle against corruption was slowed down. The Politburo was frozen, as the USSR was. When Chernenko was absent due to illness, as he often was, Gorbachev chaired the meetings of the Bureau.[74] According to Aliev, the "inner circle [krug]" of the most powerful men in the Politburo now consisted of

Chernenko, Gorbachev, Tikhonov and Gromyko.[75] Chernenko appeared on Soviet TV screens, visibly unable to walk without support. On 10 March 1985 the Gensek died, the third one within three years. Of Brezhnev's sextet, only Gromyko was left.

NOTES TO CHAPTER 5

1. See Table 8.4.
2. See *Pravda*, 17 November 1964.
3. Rodionov, 1989: 188.
4. Arbatov, September 1990: 207; Burlatskii, 1990: 319.
5. See Kirilina et al., 1990: 255; Svetitskii/Sokolov, 1989: 24.
6. Burlatskii, 1990: 284-85, 291.
7. Arbatov, September 1990: 208.
8. Burlatskii, 1990: 315-16, 318; Arbatov, September 1990: 205-6.
9. Arbatov, September 1990: 208; Rodionov, 1989: 194.
10. Burlatskii, 1990: 295-97.
11. Rodionov, 1989: 194; Lynev, 1988; Bondarenko, 1989.
12. "So I said...", 1989.
13. Breslauer, 1982: Chapter 8.
14. Arbatov, September 1990: 208.
15. See Kirilina et al., 1990: 185, 256.
16. *XXIII s'' ezd...*, 1966: 319-20.
17. See Tables 8.25 and 8.26.
18. See Kirilina et al., 1990: 77, 93.
19. *Politicheskii dnevnik...*, 1972: 243-44; Svetitskii/Sokolov, 1989: 25.
20. Arbatov, October 1990: 204.
21. Ibid.
22. Kirilina et al., 1990: 77, 128.
23. See Table 8.27.
24. Burlatskii, 1990: 303.
25. See Table 8.21.
26. Burlatskii, 1990: 297.
27. *Konstitutsiia i zakony...*, 1983: 6.
28. Arbatov, September 1990: 214.
29. Ibid.: 215.
30. Rodionov, 1989: 195-96.
31. Bondarenko, 1989: 4.
32. Ibid.; "O Khrushcheve...", 1989: 6.

33. Medvedev, 1988: 8-9.
34. Lynev, 1988.
35. Rodionov, 1989: 194-95; "So I said...", 1989; Bondarenko, 1989: 4; Lynev, 1988.
36. Rodionov, 1989: 194.
37. See Gelman, 1984: 123, 157.
38. "O Khrushcheve...", 1989: 6; "So I said...", 1989; Ivanova, 1990: 148-50.
39. Ivanova, 1990: 110-112; Lynev, 1988; Rodionov, 1989: 195.
40. Arbatov, September 1990: 220.
41. Bondarenko, 1989: 4.
42. "So I said...", 1989; "O Khrushcheve...", 1989: 6; Bondarenko, 1989: 4; Rodionov, 1989: 197.
43. Bondarenko, 1989: 4; Rodionov, 1989: 195.
44. Rodionov, 1989: 193.
45. Arbatov, October 1990: 204.
46. Medvedev, 1988: 8-9.
47. Bondarenko, 1989: 4.
48. "So I said...", 1989.
49. Medvedev, 1988: 8.
50. Arbatov, September 1990: 219; Burlatskii, 1990: 363; Borovik, 1990: 4-7; Medvedev, 1984: 105.
51. Arbatov, September 1990: 217-22; and October 1990: 220.
52. See Gelman, 1984: Chapter 5.
53. Gevorkyan, 1989.
54. Khokhryakov, 1988.
55. "Vverkh po lestnitse...", 1991.
56. Medvedev, 1990; Medvedev, 1984: Chapter 9.
57. "Vverkh po lestnitse...", 1991; Arbatov, October 1990: 210-11; Medvedev, 1984: 8-12; Medvedev, 1986: 119.
58. Medvedev, 1984: 15-16, 96, 139-41.
59. Arbatov, October 1990: 210-11.
60. "Vverkh po lestnitse...", 1991.
61. Murarka, 1988: 91.
62. Medvedev, 1984: 21, 112; Rodionov, 1989: 201-02.
63. "Vverkh po lestnitse...", 1991; Arbatov, October 1990: 210; Ligachev, 1991, Nr. 3: 6.
64. Loshak, 1988.
65. See for one report Likhanov, 1989.
66. Gdlian/Ivanov, 1988: 27.
67. Kirilina et al., 1990: 91, 149.
68. Ligachev, 1991, Nr. 4: 5; Nr. 5; Medvedev, 1986: 121-27.
69. "Vverkh po lestnitse...", 1991.

70. "Treugolnik...", 1990; see also Wishnevsky, 1991: 33; "Vverkh po lestnitse...", 1991.
71. Gromyko, 1988, vol. 2: 392.
72. "Treugolnik...", 1990; see also: "Vverkh po lestnitse...", 1991; Ligachev, 1991, Nr. 6.
73. Ligachev, 1991, Nr. 6; "Vverkh po lestnitse...", 1991.
74. Arbatov, October 1990: 221.
75. "Ia vsegda...", 1990: 7.

6

Abdication

The Politburo Under Gorbachev

During the years 1985 to 1990 a third generation of relatively young leaders came to power. These leaders may be distinguished from their predecessors by the fact that they had not experienced World War II as adults. In July 1990 the average Politburo member was born in 1929.[1] Although they came from blue-collar families, almost none of these highly educated people had a personal history of manual labor.[2] Their ties with the working class were thinner than those of the leaders of the era of Khrushchev and Brezhnev. Their leader was Gorbachev.

The Politburo convened immediately upon Chernenko's death, late in the evening of 10 March 1985. Republican first secretaries Shcherbitskii and Kunaev, and Russian Prime Minister Vorotnikov were not in Moscow.[3] This left the decision to the remaining seven voting members of the Politburo: secretaries of the CC Gorbachev and Romanov, Moscow city First Secretary Grishin, Chairman of the Committee of Party Control Solomentsev, and ministers Tikhonov, Aliev and Gromyko. According to Aliev, everybody naturally supported Gorbachev because he was already the second man.[4] Rumor has it, though, that Romanov, supported by Tikhonov, proposed Grishin as the new *Gensek*. Candidate member and KGB Chairman Chebrikov is said to have objected to Grishin because of the corruption in the Moscow trade system. Grishin (who himself denies having coveted the top position) apparently stood no chance because the same rumors have it that he rejected Romanov's proposal.[5]

At the plenary session of the CC the next morning, Gromyko, the last surviving member of the Glorious Sextet, nominated Gorbachev on behalf of the Politburo, warmly noting that he "has a nice smile, but he has iron teeth."[6] According to Aliev, everybody supported Gorbachev.[7] Boris Eltsin confirms that Grishin, who had made a list of his supporters on the Politburo, did not dare to take any initiative at the plenum, so that the election went ahead smoothly. It seems, however, that covert operations were undertaken to avert the danger of Gorbachev not being elected. Ligachev and Eltsin mention as Gorbachev's staunchest supporters Chebrikov, Solomentsev, Gromyko and a large group of first secretaries such as Eltsin himself.[8] According to Aliev, "nobody thought that [Gorbachev] would be a reformer" when he was elected.[9] He rather picked up where Andropov had left off. At the first plenary session of the CC in April 1985, his catchword was "acceleration" of the social and economic development, rather than reform.

The new party leader started in May 1985 with a campaign against the excessive use of alcohol that undermined the population's health and labor productivity. Gorbachev, a man of order and discipline, flirted with the labor campaigns of the Stalin era and called for a continuation of the great traditions of the Stakhanov movement.[10] In his opening speech to the 27th Party Congress on 25 February 1986, he castigated the stagnation of the past decade. He was mainly concerned with raising the rate of economic growth. Acceleration was expected to be accomplished by a substantial investment program in technologically crucial sectors such as machine-building. The need for a "reorganization [*perestroika*] of the economic mechanism" and a "democratization of society" were mentioned-but not in much detail.[11]

The new Politburo elected after the congress had 12 voting members. The party apparatus was represented by CC secretaries Gorbachev, Ligachev (responsible for ideology) and L. N. Zaikov (responsible for the military-in-dustrial complex); republican first secretaries Kunaev and Shcherbitskii; and Chairman of the PCC Solomentsev.[12] The state apparatus, improving its position, was represented by the new chairman of the Supreme Soviet's Presidium, Gromyko, the new Prime Minister, N. I. Ryzhkov, with ministers Aliev, Shevardnadze and Chebrikov (KGB), and Russian Prime Minister Vorotnikov. The KGB was again represented by a full member, reflecting Gorbachev's concern with social discipline. Six of the members had been promoted to leading positions during the short Andropov interregnum: Ligachev, Ryzhkov, Solomentsev, Aliev, Vorotnikov, and Chebrikov. This was a forceful Politburo, carrying Andropov's posthumous mark. The next four years the Andropov *vydvizhentsy*, the people who had been promoted by him and were now clustering around Ryzhkov and Ligachev, would, however, gradually be crowded out by newcomers.

According to Aliev, the Secretariat of the CC, with its powerful nucleus of Gorbachev and Second Secretary Ligachev, dominated.[13] "They usurped the Politburo and decided practically all matters themselves."[14] Aliev opposed the alcohol campaign which harmed the Azerbaidzhan vineyards. His feelings were shared by Ryzhkov and candidate member of the Politburo Eltsin, the new Moscow city First Secretary, who defended his city's breweries. But they were overruled by the powerful duo and Solomentsev, another vigorous puritan. Aliev was accused of being "a supporter of the alcoholics."[15] The new leaders continued to stress discipline and struggle against corruption, arresting officials of the Ministry of Internal Affairs and the Moscow trade system who had been protected by Brezhnev and by Grishin, who had himself been deposed as Moscow secretary in December 1985.[16]

The new Politburo faced grave problems. The explosion at the Chernobyl nuclear power plant in April 1986 was not only a human tragedy but also an economic disaster. Falling oil prices and decreasing income from alcohol sales combined with the ambitious investment program to enhance economic difficulties. This caused strains in the Politburo over questions of the budget. They were usually solved in favor of heavy industry—in accordance with Gorbachev's initial stress on industrial technology. Secretary of Agriculture Viktor Nikonov, Politburo member since June 1987, favored a conservative but financially lavish policy toward the farms. He was supported by Ligachev, but always conflicted with the friends of the heavy and military industries, such as Ryzhkov and Zaikov, who accused Nikonov of being interested in pigsties only. According to Nikonov, there was always "superiority of the defense people and industrialists" in the Politburo.[17]

PERESTROIKA

It became clear that "acceleration" was impossible without reforms. At the plenary session of the CC of January 1987, a political "democratization" was promised. After the plenum, *perestroika* of the economy became the prime slogan. During 1987 new rules were adopted to place industries on a self-financing basis and to create space for cooperatives. Unfortunately, most of the reforms were as ineffective as Kosygin's 1965 plans had been. The Soviet economy remained stagnant. Gorbachev was more successful in his simultaneous expansion of *glasnost*. In December 1986 Andrei Sakharov received permission to return from his exile to Moscow. Censorship was gradually lifted during 1987.

The Politburo of the Gorbachev era was notable for its high percentage of Russians and low representation of republican and local institutions. In that respect it was strangely reminiscent of the Politburo as it had been during the late Stalin era.[18] After the 27th Congress this centralizing trend expressed itself in an ever-increasing share of the Secretariat of the CC in the Politburo, continuing until the fall of 1988. Apparently, the breakthrough of *glasnost* and *perestroika* during 1987 and 1988 was effected by the Moscow Secretariat, the institution that profited the most from it in terms of influence in the Politburo-to the detriment of members from the state apparatus and local or republican secretaries.

In January 1987 the corrupt First Secretary of Kazakhstan, Kunaev, was at last dropped from the Politburo. This Kazakh was replaced by a Russian— Gennadii Kolbin—which caused riots in the republican capital Alma Ata in December 1986. Kolbin was not adopted into the Politburo. On 21 October 1987 Deputy Prime Minister Aliev was dropped after Gorbachev called him to his office and said, without an explanation: "You have to go." Aliev answered: "If the General Secretary does not want me to work, I will go."[19] However, Eltsin was the Secretariat's most celebrated victim. Grishin's popular successor as First Secretary of Moscow had put his predecessor's mafia network under strong pressure. Interestingly he had the same complaints about Ligachev as Grishin himself had had: the Second Secretary mistrusted him and organized too many checkups on his work.[20] In the Politburo he used to quarrel with Ligachev and Solomentsev about the privileges of the party elite. Gorbachev generally took a neutral stand.[21]

At the plenary session of the CC on 21 October 1987, Eltsin took the floor to criticize the slow tempo of the *perestroika*. He blamed the work style of the Secretariat and Ligachev, who showed little appreciation for the local party committees. He said he was alarmed because of the "hymns of praise by several members of the Politburo [...] to the General Secretary" and announced his resignation. As if by instinct, the CC members, including those Politburo members not on the Secretariat, hurled themselves upon him. Eltsin was accused of being overambitious and incompetent. Ryzhkov noted that in Gorbachev's Politburo there was real discussion. And as to Gorbachev: "Yes. We all respect him. And I, I say it openly, am glad to work with him. Glad. And happy for working." According to Vorotnikov, there was no cult in the Politburo, only "the most complete unity," which was a "Leninist heritage."[22] The Politburo closed ranks around its leader, and soon Zaikov replaced Eltsin as First Secretary of Moscow.

Meanwhile, the economy did not pick up. Unrest grew. In February 1988 a violent conflict broke out over the ethnically Armenian enclave Nagornyi Karabakh in Azerbaidzhan. On 13 March the newspaper *Sovetskaia Rossiia* published a letter by an alarmed Stalinist from Leningrad, Nina Andreeva.

It became a cause célèbre, bringing differences within the Secretariat to the surface. Rumor had it that after reading it, Ligachev happily exclaimed, "This is what we need!"[23] Nikonov claims even to have proposed to reprint it in regional papers. He angrily accused another Secretary of the CC, Aleksandr Iakovlev, in the Politburo since June 1987, of having ruined the press with his "social-democratic" blackening of Soviet history. Gorbachev defended Iakovlev, calling Nikonov a rightist.[24] Three weeks later *Pravda* carried a rebuke to Andreeva's piece, probably written by Iakovlev, the man who is said to have favored *perestroika* even before Gorbachev.[25] By now, relations between Ligachev and Iakovlev were explosive.[26]

Gorbachev decided to go ahead with democratization. At the 19th Party Conference in June-July 1988 he introduced a constitutional reform providing for the establishment of a Congress of People's Deputies, elected more democratically, which would appoint a new, working Supreme Soviet. In his opening speech Gorbachev laid out his new political philosophy: the people could not be expected to participate in economic reconstruction if they were not granted "socialist self-administration" in which "the decisive, final word will always be for the people," represented by their soviets. The executive branches of the state, such as the ministries, would have to give up much of their power, but the party would continue to be the "political vanguard," inspiring the sovereign people voluntarily to follow its lead.[27] From a traditional Leninist perspective (that would soon enough prove right), the idea that the people would voluntarily follow the communists was a naive and unwarranted assumption: Lenin had taught that the workers were no natural communists but tended to turn to "trade unionism" and reform capitalism.

Gorbachev's plan aimed at a coalition of the party secretaries with the soviets against the bureaucracy of the ministries. The heart of this idea was his proposal that the first secretaries be elected to preside the soviets. This would make the *Gensek* Chairman of the Supreme Soviet, a step closer to a real presidency; until now the Soviet "president" had been Chairman of the Supreme Soviet's Presidium. New strong soviets provided Gorbachev with a power base of his own, next to the Secretariat.

Since the end of 1987 there were strong rumors that Ligachev disagreed with the new trend that stressed additional civil rights rather than discipline as the way to increase citizen participation. Moscow intellectuals reportedly considered Ligachev a conservative, the "Darth Vader of *Perestroika*."[28] In an interview with the French newspaper *le Monde* in December 1987, however, Ligachev denied that there were any differences with the *Gensek*, though he acknowledged that he was discontented with some journals, such as *Ogonek* and *Moscow News*, that carried *glasnost* too far.[29] It is interesting that neither Eltsin, nor Aliev, or Nikonov reports significant opposition by Ligachev in the Politburo against Gorbachev. It is tempting to assume that Ligachev, despite his misgivings, played along with Gorbachev because the Secretary General defended their joint secretarial interests against the other sectors of the Politburo.

After the plenary session of the CC in September 1988, the Politburo counted among its 12 voting members no less than eight secretaries of the CC: Gorbachev, Ligachev, Zaikov (who was simultaneously Moscow city First Secretary), Chebrikov (who lost his post as director of the KGB), Nikolai Sliunkov, Iakovlev, Nikonov, and Vadim Medvedev, many of them relative newcomers. Only Shcherbitskii was left to represent the republican party apparatus. With only two other ministers (Vorotnikov and Shevardnadze), Prime Minister Ryzhkov's institutional position had become very weak. The chairman of the KGB, Vladimir Kriuchkov, was not even a candidate member of the Politburo. While this was a collective triumph for the Secretariat, Gorbachev profited in particular. He took over Gromyko's (old style) "presidency." Ligachev lost his ideological portfolio in the Secretariat and was demoted to be head of the Secretariat's agricultural commission. Ligachev became gloomy because Solomentsev was ousted.[30]

CRISIS

Ligachev had every reason for concern. The elections for the new Congress of People's Deputies in March 1989 resulted in the defeat of many official candidates, suggesting that democratic elections would spell the end for CPSU rule. Even Gorbachev, the powerful Chairman of the new Supreme Soviet, could not easily control the violent debates in his new parliament. The forces of order now raised their heads. On 9 April troops of the MVD and the army attacked a peaceful demonstration in Tbilisi with shovels and poison gas, killing at least 19 people. Investigations established that the whole Politburo was involved in the decision to send the troops or at least endorsed it. Evidence suggests that Defense Minister (and candidate member of the Politburo) Dmitrii Iazov and Secretary Chebrikov (responsible for the KGB) decided to use the troops.[31]

In 1989 the USSR plunged into a general crisis. In the summer the Soviet miners went on strike, demanding inter alia the abolition of article 6 of the Constitution in which the leading role of the party was fixed. Many republics, most prominently the Baltic, headed for separation from the USSR. In his book *On Perestroika and New Thinking,* published in 1987, Gorbachev had announced that class struggle no longer directed foreign policy. Every country was entitled to choose its own system. In 1989 he lived up to this promise in Central Europe—and lost it as the USSR's security zone. The economy was partially liberated from the suffocating grip of the ministries and the party but was left without a functioning market. Additionally struck by the Armenian earthquake in December 1988, the USSR moved in 1989 from stagnation to a crash.[32] Even the party started to crumble: on 20 December the Lithuanian Communist Party split off from the CPSU. Then the Union itself began to fall apart as Lithuania declared its independence on 11 March 1990. The party had to respond.

In September and December 1989 the CC reshuffled the Politburo. Two secretaries, Chebrikov and Nikonov, were dropped. Shcherbitskii was replaced by the new Ukrainian First Secretary Vladimir Ivashko. Two ministers were added: KGB Chairman Kriuchkov and Gosplan Chairman Iu. D. Masliukov. Thus, Gorbachev's clear preference for the Secretariat of the CC was a thing of the past. He moved toward a new coalition with the state apparatus and the KGB. Ryzhkov, heading what was left of the state-planning bureaucracy, gained in stature when in December 1989 he successfully prevented the adoption of a program of radical economic reform. In the last period before the Politburo's de facto demise in July 1990, the state apparatus came again to be very well represented, reflecting the new concern with order.[33] Yet Gorbachev did not allow his own position to be weakened by the crisis. Instead, he cleverly turned it around to serve his own interests, playing on the feelings of emergency among his colleagues.

On 5-7 February 1990 the CC met in a plenary session. There was an acute awareness of crisis. Ligachev stated, as always, his support for *perestroika,* but desperately declared that here and there "a situation of dual power has been established," suggesting the presence of a (counter)revolutionary situation. He complained bitterly about the "devouring of the German Democratic Republic" and engaged in an unprecedented, nervous quarrel with Shevardnadze about the responsibility for the Tbilisi massacre.[34] The Politburo presented a platform in which it, on the one hand, repeated Gorbachev's philosophy of the soviets as "sovereign organs" and suggested abolition of article 6. Henceforth the CPSU would earn its "vanguard role" through democratic competition with other parties. At the same time it noted that the stable functioning of the country demanded "the creation of the post of head of state in the person of a president, responsible to the Congress of People's Deputies and equipped with the full completeness of executive-commanding power."[35] Gorbachev's presidential system was intended to make the President the sole, undisputed leader of the country, relying on the new-style soviets.

THE END

The Politburo was not undividedly enthusiastic. Shevardnadze, Sliunkov, Medvedev and Iakovlev supported the proposal. Vorotnikov also considered the new system imperative because the "foundations of the state are subjected to a siege."[36] But Prime Minister Ryzhkov, although he passionately pleaded for more "hardness," suggested that he disagreed. He proposed instead to widen the powers of the Chairman of the Supreme Soviet and simultaneously strengthen the Council of Ministers.[37] Ryzhkov in effect pleaded for retaining two powerful leaders: the Prime Minister and the Chairman of the Supreme Soviet. Ligachev, Kriuchkov, and Ivashko did not specifically endorse the presidential system either. The plenum, nevertheless, accepted the platform with only a slight reduction of the powers of the President.[38]

The platform also proposed henceforth to elect the party leader at the Congress. This new rule made the leader almost untouchable for the Politburo. His status would be higher than that of the Politburo, which after all was not elected by the Congress. On 11 March 1990, the fifth anniversary of Gorbachev's taking office, the CC met again in plenary session. In this unprecedented national crisis the instinct to rally around a strong leader got the upper hand. On 14 March Ryzhkov notified the plenum that it was the "unanimous opinion" of the Politburo that Gorbachev should be elected President because "only he can lead the country today." That did not mean that they "only stroked each other's heads," but their differences were only of a tactical nature.[39] On 15 March the Congress of People's Deputies elected President Gorbachev. The next day Zaikov hailed him as "the initiator of *perestroika,* the leader of our party and the state."[40]

The March plenum also adopted draft Party Rules calling for a new Politburo that consisted, apart from the party leader and his deputies, mainly of the republican party leaders.[41] This formula suggested that it would become a federal conglomerate of republican first secretaries instead of the junta of most powerful men of the country that it had always been. From 2 to 13 July 1990 the 28th Party Congress convened to ratify the new system. Ryzhkov and Ligachev, the most powerful counterweights to Gorbachev in the Politburo, did not oppose it. From the tone of their speeches from 1988 onward, it seems evident that they had doubts about Gorbachev's wisdom, about both his democratic and his autocratic leanings. But they could never find the courage to face Gorbachev head-on because they saw no realistic alternative to him. In his speech to the Congress on 3 July, Ligachev meekly repeated what he had said so many times before: "I see no alternative for *perestroika*."[42]

On 10 July Gorbachev was elected without problem as General Secretary. The next day the election of the new Deputy-General Secretary (fulfilling the tasks of the old "Second Secretary") was on the agenda. Gorbachev proposed Ukrainian President Ivashko, with whom he had a "mutual understanding" and no "cracks" in their relations. Unexpectedly Ligachev offered himself for the post, the first time he ever publicly provoked his boss. In his explanatory speech he admitted that he had "tactical differences" with Gorbachev, though no strategic ones.[43] But it was too little and too late. Ivashko got 3,109 votes and Ligachev only 776.[44] Ligachev's career was over. The new CC convened on 13 and 14 July, electing a new Politburo of 24 members with only Gorbachev and Ivashko left of the old one. With 15 republican first secretaries and no other major power holders outside the party apparatus, it had only one thing in common with its predecessor: its name.[45]

The history of the Politburo as we knew it had ended. This history has been characterized by a cycle. Every time a leader was replaced or died, an oligarchic coalition came to power. Soon mutual struggles broke out, ending in the victory of one of the contenders: the new leader. Three weapons have been used:

1. To gather support of one or more of the powerful institutions represented in the Politburo. The leaders *in spe* tended to start their climb to undivided power by gaining support among the secretarial hierarchy. After this first step they stabilized their rule with the support of the police or the military. Khrushchev neglected the second stage-and he fell from power.
2. To present a political program adapted to the mood of the Soviet elite,
3. To place clients in strategic positions.

Two leaders have been able to crown the cycle with the complete submission of the Politburo—Joseph Stalin and Mikhail Gorbachev—though their personal victories over their colleagues resulted in very different forms of rule. It is the tragedy of the Politburo that it subjected the whole USSR to its ruthless dictatorship, but itself bowed time and again to the leader of its own making. The Politburo came to an inglorious end when it could think of nothing better to overcome the historic crisis than to abdicate in favor of the leader whom the members, from an orthodox Leninist perspective, must have perceived as having triggered that crisis.

<hr>

NOTES TO CHAPTER 6

1. See Table 8.4.
2. See Table 8.21.
3. Medvedev, 1986: 4-5.
4. "Ia vsegda...", 1990: 7.
5. Grishin, 1991; Medvedev, 1986: 5, 15, 172-73.
6. Cited in Medvedev, 1986: 17.
7. "Ia vsegda...", 1990: 7.
8. *XIX vsesoiuznaia...*, t. 2, 1988: 85; Eltsin, 1990: 58.
9. "Ia vsegda...", 1990: 7.
10. Medvedev, 1986: 195.
11. *XXVII s''ezd...*, 1986: 24, 42, 46, 54, 77.
12. Medvedev, 1986: 169; Zaikov speech in *Pravda*, 4 July 1990.
13. Eltsin, 1990: 60; "Chelovek", 1990: 102; Ligachev's speech in *Pravda*, 5 July 1990.
14. "Ia vsegda...", 1990: 10-11.
15. Ibid.; Eltsin, 1990: 55, 61.
16. Rodionov, 1989: 204; Likhanov, 1989, Nr. 4: 22; Murarka, 1988: 255-56.
17. Gavriliuk, 1990: 22-26.
18. See Tables 8.7 and 8.26.
19. "Ia vsegda...", 1990: 8.
20. Grishin, 1991.
21. Eltsin, 1990: 8n., 10, 50-51, 55, 60. See also Tretyakov, 1989.
22. "Plenum TsK...", 1989: 239-41, 256, 258.
23. "Chelovek", 1990: 102.
24. Gavriliuk, 1990: 23-24.
25. Tretyakov, 1990: 8.
26. Eltsin, 1990: 63; See also: Tretyakov, 1990: 8.
27. *XIX vsesoiuznaia...*, t. 1, 1988: 46-49, 53, 77, 91.
28. Keller, 1988.
29. Tatu/Vernet, 1987.
30. Eltsin, 1990: 61.
31. On Chebrikov's responsibility see: Kirilina et al., 1990: 246. See for various accounts of the Tbilisi massacre: Sobchak, 1989; Fuller, 1989; A. Romanov, 1989; *Pravda*, 7 and 8 February 1990.

32. Grigorev, 1991.
33. See Table 8.25.
34. *Pravda*, 7 February 1990: 6; 8 February 1990: 3.
35. "Proekt platformy...", 1990: 104, 111.
36. *Pravda*, 7 February 1990: 6; 8 February 1990: 3-5.
37. *Pravda*, 7 February 1990: 4.
38. *Pravda*, 13 February 1990: 2.
39. *Pravda*, 18 March 1990: 2.
40. *Pravda*, 19 March 1990: 3.
41. *Pravda*, 28 March 1990: 2.
42. *Pravda*, 5 July 1990: 2.
43. *Pravda*, 12 July 1990: 2.
44. *Pravda*, 13 July 1990: 1.
45. See *Pravda*, 15 July 1990: 1-2.

7

The Politburo at Work

Mode of Operation

Over a period spanning 20 party congresses between Lenin and Gorbachev, the destiny of the Soviet Union and its peoples was basically decided by the 130 individuals who sat on the Politburo. For seven decades the Politburo was the most powerful organ in the Soviet political system, because its members were the top office-holders in party, government and state institutions that had been imbued with the bolshevik tradition of concentration of power. The Politburo's power showed itself in the fact that through other institutions, it could manipulate its political, economic and social environment. Concealment, fear, manipulation, scheming and stringpulling were its instruments. After dealing with the history of this institution, the reader is now invited to take a closer look at its central place in the Soviet power structure and at the way in which it operated. Inevitably, we will have to start with the formal rules and procedures that governed the relations between the Politburo and other institutions.

In formal terms, the highest organs of the Communist Party were the Party Congress, the Central Committee and the Committee for Party Control. However, the Party Congress met only once every few years for little more than a week. The Central Committee was responsible for laying down party policy in the intervals between congresses, and the Committee for Party Control for maintaining party discipline. The few hundred members of the Central Committee made up the top echelon of the political, economic, cultural, social and military elite of the country. Membership of this Committee conferred prestige and gave access to the only real decision-making institutions-the Politburo and the Secretariat. In addition, during the years between 1919 and 1952, the *Orgburo* (Organization Bureau) dealt mainly

Table 7.1

Membership of the Communist Party, Central Committee, Politburo, Orgburo and Secretariat, 1919-1990

Year	Party Congress	Party* M	Party* C	CentrComm M	CentrComm C	Politburo M	Politburo C	Orgburo M	Orgburo C	Secretariat M	Secretariat C
1919	8th	0.3		19	8	5	3	5	1	2	
1920	9th	0.6		19	12	5	3	5		3	
1921	10th	0.7		25	15	5	3	7	3	3	
1922	11th	0.5	0.1	27	19	7	3	7	3	3	
1923	12th	0.4	0.1	40	17	7	4	7	3	3	
1924	13th	0.7	0.1	53	34	7	6	11	6	5	
1925	14th	0.6	0.4	63	43	9	5	11	5	5	2
1927	15th	0.9	0.3	71	50	9	8	13	7	5	3
1930	16th	1.3	0.7	71	67	10	5	11	4	5	2
1934	17th	1.9	0.9	71	68	10	5	10	2	4	
1939	18th	1.6	0.9	71	68	9	2	9		4	
1952	19th	6.0	0.9	125	110	25	11			10	
1956	20th	6.8	0.4	133	122	11	6			8	
1959	21st	7.6	0.6								
1961	22nd	8.9	0.8	175	155	11	5			9	
1966	23rd	11.7	0.8	195	165	11	8			11	
1971	24th	13.8	0.6	241	155	15	6			10	
1976	25th	15.0	0.6	287	139	16	6			11	
1981	26th	16.7	0.7	319	151	14	8			10	
1986	27th	18.3	0.7	307	170	12	7			11	
1990	28th	18.8	0.4	412		24				18	

* in millions.

M—Members; C—Candidate Members

with organizational questions: the recruitment and allocation of personnel, the coordination of the activities of party, government and social organizations (e.g., trade unions and youth organizations), improvements to the party structure, the distribution of information and reports within the party, and so on. These tasks were taken over by the Secretariat in 1952.

As we have seen in earlier chapters, only on rare occasions, when for instance there appeared to be marked disagreement within the Politburo, did the Central Committee in fact make a decision on its own account. In recent decades the Central Committee had been elected once every five years by the Party Congress. For these "elections" the candidates were nominated by the Secretariat. Those attending the congress had little choice: one single list of candidates was offered to them, and at best they could cross out one or more candidates. Few chose to do so. It was traditional for the congress to support the candidates unanimously. Either immediately afterward or on the following day the Central Committee would elect the Politburo, once again in the familiar undemocratic manner. This was the usual course of events under normal conditions, when the *Gensek* was securely seated in the saddle and there was no acute struggle for power.

Initially paragraph 25 of the party Rules had said no more about the formation of the Politburo than that this was to be carried out by the Central Committee. Until 1961 there was no mention of "election." The successive versions of the rules used the words "the Central Committee 'forms' or 'organizes' the Political Bureau....," thereby indicating the less than formal status that this "inner circle" of the Central Committee originally had. In 1961 the terminology of the party Rules was noticeably democratized. In place of "organizing," it now spoke of "secret elections." It was moreover laid down that at least one quarter of the membership of the Politburo (known at the time as the Presidium) as also of the Central Committee must be replaced at each election, while members of the Politburo could not as a rule be reelected more than twice. This meant that 12 years (three four-year terms) was set as the maximum term of membership.

Khrushchev, who initiated these changes, had actually at that time himself been a member for 22 years. A simple solution to this problem was found by stipulating that party leaders who enjoyed great authority and possessed exceptional ability might, by way of exception, remain members for more than 12 years as long as they scored at least 75 percent of the votes.

These stipulations have since been cut from the party rules. Under Brezhnev they were replaced by the following formula: "In the election of all party organs, from the primary party organization to the Central Committee of the CPSU, the principle of the systematic replacement of personnel

Table 7.2
Positions Held by Full Members of Politburo

Year (31 December)	1941	1951	1961	1971	1981
Number of members	9	11	11	15	14
Offices					
Party					
General Secretary	Stalin	Stalin	Khrushchev	Brezhnev	Brezhnev
Party Secretaries	Zhdanov	Malenkov	Kozlov	Suslov	Suslov
	Andreev	Khrushchev	Suslov	Kirilenko	Kirilenko
	——	——	Kuusinen	Kulakov	Chernenko
	——	——	——	——	Gorbachev
Chrmn Control Commission	Andreev	Andreev	Shvernik	Pelshe	Pelshe
PL Ukraine	Khrushchev	——	Podgornyi	Shelest	Shcherbitskii
PL Moscow	——	Khrushchev	——	Grishin	Grishin
PL Leningrad	Zhdanov	——	——	——	Romanov
PL Kazakhstan	——	——	——	Kunaev	Kunaev
Chrmn RSFSR Bureau	——	——	Khrushchev	——	——
Frst VcChrmn RSFSR Bureau	——	——	Voronov	——	——
VcChrmn RSFSR Bureau	——	——	Brezhnev	——	——
Government					
Premier USSR	Stalin	Stalin	Khrushchev	Kosygin	Tikhonov
VcChrmn,	Molotov	Molotov	Kosygin	——	——
Council of Ministers	Mikoian	Malenkov	Mikoian	Mazurov	——
	Voroshilov	Beriia	——	Polianskii	——
	Kaganovich	Voroshilov	——	——	——
	——	Bulganin	——	——	——
	——	Kaganovich	——	——	——
	——	Andreev	——	——	——
	——	Mikoian	——	——	——
	——	Kosygin	——	——	——
State Security / IntAffairs	——	——	——	——	Andropov
Min Defense	Stalin	——	——	——	Ustinov
Min Foreign Affairs	Molotov	——	——	——	Gromyko
Min Foreign Trade	Mikoian	——	——	——	——
Min Transport	Kaganovich	——	——	——	——
Min Light Industry	——	Kosygin	——	——	——
Chrmn Comm Peoples Control	——	——	——	Voronov	——
Premier RSFSR	——	——	Polianskii	——	——
Premier Ukraine	——	——	——	Shcherbitskii	——
State & other					
Chrmn Presdm SuprSoviet USSR	Kalinin	——	Brezhnev	Podgornyi	Brezhnev
Chrmn Trade Unions	——	——	——	Shelepin	——

Abbrevations:

Chrmn —	Chairman	Presdm —	Presidium
(Frst) VcChrmn —	(First) Vice Chairman/Vice Chairmen	PL —	Party leader
Min —	Minister	SuprSoviet —	Supreme Soviet

and the continuity of leadership is to be observed." It was a formula offering endless possibilities for evasion. In fact, the Brezhnev period was character-ized by continuity of leadership and no *systematic* replacement of Politburo members. Changes in its composition were effected at plenary meetings of the Central Committee, after these changes had been decided on in the Politburo and the Secretariat, mostly at the instigation of the Secretary-General.

After Brezhnev had died in 1982, it took over two years before the Politburo leadership could bring itself to selecting a young and vigorous leader who was to set things in order. However, although he managed to carry through quite a number of changes in Politburo membership between 1985 and 1990, Gorbachev and his closest associates kept feeling the limitations of collective decision making in the Politburo. The renewal of the Politburo membership body remained a process of co-optation, as it always had been, and thereby subject to the necessity of striking compro-mises between the different wings both in that body and in the membership body of the Central Committee. Moreover, as in the course of 1987 to 1989 more and more leftover leaders of the Brezhnev period lost their main jobs but retained their seats in the Central Committee, the position of the reformist wing led by Gorbachev became precarious. As the number and the bitterness of these so-called *dead souls* grew, so did the danger both to Gorbachev's position and to his ability to implement reform policy. Neither at the 27th Party Congress (1986) nor at the 19th Party Conference in 1988 did he succeed in rejuvenating the Central Committee. Finally, at the plenum of 25 April 1989 he succeed in pressuring 74 members and 24 candidate members of the Central Committee to resign "voluntarily." The many changes intro-duced by Mikhail Gorbachev after that date, and grudgingly approved by the Central Committee, led to the loss of the Communist Party's unique consti-tutional position and to the undoing of the Politburo as the main decision-making body of the land.

PRINCIPAL OFFICES HELD BY MEMBERS

Up to the 28th Party Congress, there was no provision regulating the question whether there would be functionaries who were to have a seat *ex officio* in the Politburo. At the congress, the overlap of membership between the Politburo and top government and state posts that had for decades been actual practice was rejected as a remnant of the past "administrative command system" and at the same time *ex officio* membership of the new Politburo

Table 7.3

Leaders of Party, State and Government,

1917 - 1991

PARTY LEADERS

General Secretary (1934-1953: Secretary)

I. V. Stalin	3 April 1922	- 5 March 1953

First Secretary

N. S. Khrushchev	7 September 1953	- 14 October 1964

General Secretary

L. I. Brezhnev	14 October 1964	- 10 November 1982
Iu. V. Andropov	12 November 1982	- 9 February 1984
K. U. Chernenko	13 February 1984	- 10 March 1985
M. S. Gorbachev	11 March 1985	- 24 August 1991

HEADS OF STATE

Chairman, Russian Central Executive Committee (1917-1922)

L. B. Kamenev	9 - 21 November 1917	
Ia. M. Sverdlov	21 November 1917	- 16 March 1919
(M. F. Vladimirskii	16 - 30 March 1919)	

Chairman, Central Executive Committee of the USSR (1922-1938)

Chairman, Presidium of the USSR Supreme Soviet (1938-1989)

M. I. Kalinin	30 March 1919	- 19 March 1946
N. M. Shvernik	19 March 1946	- 15 March 1953
K. E. Voroshilov	15 March 1953	- 7 May 1960
L. I. Brezhnev	7 May 1960	- 15 July 1964
A. I. Mikoian	15 July 1964	- 9 December 1965
N. V. Podgornyi	9 December 1965	- 16 June 1977
L. I. Brezhnev	16 June 1977	- 10 November 1982
Iu. V. Andropov	16 June 1983	- 9 February 1984
K. U. Chernenko	14 April 1984	- 10 March 1985
A. A. Gromyko	2 July 1985	- 1 October 1988
M. S. Gorbachev	1 October 1988	- 25 May 1989

Chairman, USSR Supreme Soviet (1989-1990)

M. S. Gorbachev	25 May 1989	- 15 March 1990

President of the USSR (1990-1991)

M. S. Gorbachev	15 March 1990	- 25 December 1991

was created: that of the Secretary-General, his deputy and the 15 first secretaries of the republican party organizations. The new party Rules further stated that the Central Committee was to decide on the total number of members of the Politburo and that the Politburo was to present annual reports on its activities to the Central Committee.[1]

Table 7.3 (continued)		
HEADS OF GOVERNMENT		
Council of People's Commissars (1917-1946)		
V. I. Lenin	9 November 1917	- 21 January 1924
A. I. Rykov	2 February 1924	- 19 December 1930
V. M. Molotov	19 December 1930	- 6 May 1941
Council of Ministers of the USSR (1946-1990)		
I. V. Stalin	6 May 1941	- 5 March 1953
G. M. Malenkov	5 March 1953	- 8 February 1955
N. A. Bulganin	8 February 1955	- 27 March 1958
N. S. Khrushchev	27 March 1958	- 15 October 1964
A. N. Kosygin	15 October 1964	- 23 October 1980
N. A. Tikhonov	23 October 1980	- 27 September 1985
N. I. Ryzhkov	27 September 1985	- 26 December 1990
Cabinet of Ministers of the USSR (27 December 1990 - 6 September 1991)		
V. S. Pavlov	14 January 1991	- 22 August 1991

Main Source: Glasnost 1991, No. 2 (January), p. 4.

By comparing the situation at a number of different points in the past, it appears that in practice the incumbents of a number of party and state posts always have had seats in the Politburo (see Table 7.2). These were: the General Secretary of the Communist Party and several other party Secretaries; the Chairman of the Committee for Party Control; the Chairman of the Council of Ministers; and, until the 1980s, several (first) vice chairmen of the Council of Ministers. There have been various pronouncements on the representation of the party Secretariat in the Politburo. At the 9th Party Congress in 1920 Lenin stressed that the implementation of the decisions taken by the Politburo was simplified by the Secretary of the Central Committee having a seat in the Politburo and the Orgburo. In this way, Lenin said, he forms the link between the two organs. At the plenum of 29 November 1919 Krestinsky had become this link, and after this date no further joint meetings of the Politburo and the Orgburo were held until 1921. According to the Soviet historian V. P. Nikolaeva, after that time "the Secretaries of the CC were always members of the Orgburo, and one or more of them were also members of the Politburo, either full members or (after the 10th Party Congress in 1921) candidate members."[2]

The Chairman of the Presidium of the Supreme Soviet also frequently had a seat in the Politburo. In 1951 Nikolai Shvernik held this office; he was then still only a candidate member of the Politburo. On 16 June 1977 Brezhnev became Chairman of the Supreme Soviet Presidium, after the

Central Committee had (on 24 May) decided to combine the posts of General Secretary and Chairman of the Presidium of the Supreme Soviet. This decision, Brezhnev said, "reflected actual practice in our day-to-day work, in the course of which many members of the Politburo have to deal with affairs of state, both at home and abroad. I myself, as General Secretary, have on many occasions ... had to represent our country abroad at negotiations ... Now this practice will receive its logical formalization."[3]

The full history of office-holding by Politburo members is too complex to be dealt with here in detail; it is summarized in the category "positions" in the Background List and in Table 7.2 which brings out clearly enough both the regularities and the main changes since the onset of World War II. The table somewhat understates the frequency with which the leaders of the party organizations in Moscow and Leningrad held full membership. Three related aspects, the overlapping membership and functions of the Politburo with the Council of Ministers, the Defense Council and the Central Committee Secretariat, call for closer attention.

THE POLITBURO AND THE GOVERNMENT

Despite the predictions that Lenin was still making in 1917, the state did not wither away, nor did it become fused with the Communist Party. On the contrary, over the years it became stronger. But within the organs of state and government, the Communist Party played a leading role, as their "guiding nucleus." In the 1930s the NKVD (state security) played an independent role, but over the past decades most if not all organs of state and government served as mere instruments for the implementation of party policy. They were left less and less responsibility for autonomous action. And since the party hierarchy was structured to satisfy the needs and demands of the Moscow leadership, republican and regional state and government organs came to be seen as languid representatives of a federal center that used its power to exploit the peoples of the USSR.

Related to its main function of decision making on all important and, sometimes, unimportant national issues was the Politburo's function of informal administrative jurisdiction: in political and administrative matters the highest party organ was the supreme court of appeal in the land. In the 1920s in particular, appeals were frequently addressed to the Politburo to set aside decisions taken by the Council of People's Commissars. The course followed in such annulment cases was for an individual to give notice of appeal to the Politburo, which then arrived at a decision. This could be to the effect that the annulment was not to be proceeded with, or that the Presidium of the Central Executive Committee (VTsIK) of the Congress of Soviets was charged with setting aside the government decision. By way of an interim solution, an attempt could be made to reach a compromise in the Council of People's Commissars. From the fact that very frequent use was made of the annulment procedure in the first few years of the Soviet regime, Van den Berg has concluded that the most important decision-making body at that time was still the Council of People's Commissars. But decisions of that body were never final until it was certain that the Politburo would not intervene.[4]

This changed after the death of Lenin. Stalin, who was a member of the Politburo and had dominated the party Secretariat since 3 April 1922, did not succeed Lenin as Prime Minister. In February 1924 Aleksei Rykov became the new Chairman of the Council of People's Commissars. Leadership over the party and state was then no longer in the hands of one man. Stalin managed to attract progressively more power to the party's Secretariat and Politburo. The Politburo then took to giving retrospective endorsement to decisions taken by the Council People's Commissars that lost its decision-making functions by roughly 1929. In the 1930s it became the practice to issue joint decisions of the government and the party. The first decision of this type was dated 15 January 1931, a few weeks after Viacheslav Molotov, Stalin's most devoted assistant, had succeeded Rykov as government leader.[5] Molotov gradually assumed the role of a messenger conveying Stalin's will to the Council of People's Commissars. Usually decisions that were published as "joint decisions of the government and the Central Committee" had been finally approved by the Politburo.[6] After the 19th Party Conference in 1988, their number began to decline, and by the summer of 1990 the practice of taking "joint decisions" had "practically ceased."[7]

As was the case with the Supreme Soviet up to 1989, the Council of Ministers—as the government was named after 1946—served principally as the body in whose name decisions were taken by smaller bodies: they had their own "inner circles." In the 1970s, the Council as such met four times a year on average, to listen to long speeches, and perhaps engage in an occasional debate. At these meetings most of the speeches were about the achievement of the economic plan in the previous quarter, and about economic prospects. In general, during the decades preceding Gorbachev's Revolution, more than 100 people had seats in the Council of Ministers. Smaller bodies, in which at least some real discussion and decision making took place, were formed out of the Council and made decisions in its name. One of the most important of these was the *Presidium* of the Council of

Ministers. The Presidium met once a week, or occasionally twice, and dealt mainly with economic matters and other administrative business.

Since the Politburo was first established, the leader of the government and the party leader have always been members. There have been periods during which these functions have even been combined in one person: in Lenin from 1917 to 1922 (although he was not the formal leader of the party), in Stalin from 1941 to 1953 and in Khrushchev from 1958 to 1964. Since 1957 the percentage of members of the inner Council of Ministers (chairman and vice chairmen) with seats on the Politburo has greatly declined, and by October 1980 it had been reduced to one (the new chairman Tikhonov). According to Van den Berg's calculations, however, since the early 1960s, the percentage of members of the Politburo who were simultaneously members of the Council of Ministers itself (not of the inner Council) varied between approximately 20 percent and 40 percent. During these decades, it could be said that the Politburo *governed*—and the government *administered* its decisions.[8]

In the political upheaval of late 1980s, the Council of Ministers was more and more seen as the body obstructing political and economic reform. The Politburo's power to make and break members of the government was weakened when in 1989 the renewed Supreme Soviet asserted its new role by critically evaluating candidates for ministerial posts proposed by the leader of the government; some of them were turned down. And at the time when in the end the Politburo gave way to the new presidency in 1990, the Chairman of the Council of Ministers was under heavy attack; Ryzhkov's government, it was said, had shown itself incapable of providing leadership in the transition to a market economy. In another constitutional change in December 1990, the Council of Ministers was replaced by a Cabinet led by a *"premer-ministr"* and directly responsible to the President.

THE POLITBURO AND THE DEFENSE COUNCIL

A high-level body of considerable importance in decision making on foreign and defense policy, national security, (dis)armament, and the development of military-political strategy was the Defense Council (*Sovet Oborony*) of the USSR.[9] Although this Council was formally affiliated with the USSR Council of Ministers and the appointment of its members needed confirmation of the Presidium of the USSR Supreme Soviet, in practice it operated as a subcommittee of the Politburo, linking that body with the top of the military and defense industry establishments. Such was made possible by a

Table 7.4
Overlapping Membership: Politburo, Secretariat,
Presidia of the Council of Ministers and Supreme Soviet,
November 1980

Politburo	Central Committee Secretariat	Presidium of Council of Ministers	Presidium of Supreme Soviet
Members			
Brezhnev	Brezhnev	—	Brezhnev*
Andropov	—	—	—
Chernenko	Chernenko	—	—
Gorbachev	Gorbachev	—	—
Grishin	—	—	—
Gromyko	—	—	—
Kirilenko	Kirilenko	—	—
Kunaev	—	—	—
Pelshe	—	—	—
Romanov	—	—	Romanov
Shcherbitskii	—	—	Shcherbitskii
Suslov	Suslov	—	—
Tikhonov	—	Tikhonov*	—
Ustinov	—	—	—
Candidates			
Aliev	—	—	—
Demichev	—	—	—
Kiselev	—	—	—
Kuznetsov	—	—	Kuznetsov
Ponomarev	Ponomarev	—	—
Rashidov	—	—	Rashidov
Shevardnadze	—	—	—
Solomentsev	—	—	—
	+ 4 Secretaries	16 members	+ 30 members

* Chairman

considerable overlap in membership between Politburo and Defense Council, and by the fact that the Council was chaired by the *Gensek*. Its membership included the Chairman of the Council of Ministers, the ministers of Defense and Foreign Affairs, the Chairman of Gosplan, officials supervising the defense industry, and the highest commanders of the armed forces. From the moment that he moved from Leningrad to Moscow in 1985, Lev Zaikov had been responsible for defense industry both in the Central Committee Secretariat and in the Defense Council, a position and responsibility that he had retained after he was made First Party Secretary of the Moscow *gorkom* or City Party Committee. In November 1989 he was made First Deputy Chairman of the Defense Council.[10]

The Defense Council was successor to bodies specializing in high-level military coordination and decision making such as the Council of Workers' and Peasants' Defense (1918-'20), and the Council of Labor and Defense (1920-'37). The Defense Committee at the Council of People's Commissars was established in 1937. Its membership of seven was reduced to five in 1941: Voroshilov (chairman), Zhdanov (deputy chairman), Stalin, Timoshenko and Kuznetsov.[11]

In 1976 when Leonid Brezhnev was appointed Marshal of the Soviet Union, the existence of the Council—and the chairmanship of Brezhnev—was disclosed.[12] The Council has been headed by the successive Secretaries-General, and although according to the 1977 Constitution (article 121) it was formed by the Presidium of the USSR Supreme Soviet, decisions concerning the Council were in fact taken by the Politburo.[13] In July 1989 Gorbachev indicated that the Council had not been functioning properly—it had been meeting "episodically and in a formal way"—and was in need of restructuring. In April 1990 he said that the State Committee for Defense, of which the Defense Council had been the "working body," had been abolished "in connection with the introduction of presidential power [the month before] and issues of defense have been devolved to the functions of the President as Commander-in-Chief; but the working body, the Defense Council, operates under the President."[14] In the setup after the constitutional amendments of December 1990, the Defense Council was probably operating under the new Security Council (*Sovet Bezopasnosti*), whose members were appointed by the President in March 1991.

THE POLITBURO AND THE PARTY SECRETARIAT

The main link between the Politburo and its environment was the Secretariat of the Central Committee—the body of around ten party secretaries under the leadership of the Secretary-General—and its *central party apparatus*. The employees of this bureaucracy were housed in the gray building on the west side of Old Square in Moscow, the building from which we have seen Ligachev emerge on his way to a Politburo session in the first paragraph of the introduction to this book. They were engaged in gathering and digesting information for the secretaries and Politburo members, in the preparation of policy documents and decisions to be taken by the Politburo and Secretariat, in daily control over the government and state bureaucracies, in crisis management, in preparing important appointments (and dismissals) to all leading positions in society—the *nomenklatura-*, in supervising the admission of new party members, in the investigation of complaints against officials, and so on.

By 1988 the new party leadership under Gorbachev had concluded that the central party apparatus—and the corresponding party bureaucracies at lower levels—had become the main obstacle to social, economic and political renewal. Since Stalin had created the apparatus, it had increasingly substituted the functions of state and government organs: the soviets and their executive committees. The central problem of the Soviet polity had become that of *podmena*: uncontrolled, closed party bureaucracies secretively (*keleino*) usurping all functions of government. Several campaigns against *podmena* had had no lasting results. The final attack was undertaken by Gorbachev in 1988 and resulted in the partial dismantling of the central party apparatus after the 30 September 1988 Central Committee plenum.[15] Departments of the Central Committee Secretariat concerned with economic affairs were abolished, and six Central Committee Commissions were established: on Party Affairs and Cadres Policy (chaired by Georgii Razumovskii); Ideology (Vadim Medvedev); Social-Economic Policy (Nikolai Sliunkov); Agricultural Policy (Egor Ligachev); International Politics (Alexander Iakovlev); and Legal Policy (Viktor Chebrikov). This withdrawal of the apparatus from day-to-day policy making and implementation went hand in hand with a revaluation of the soviets; in the year ahead the reform of the Soviet polity was given shape in the form of new institutions such as the Congress of People's Deputies, the revived Supreme Soviet, its chairman and, after March 1990, the presidency.

Up to 1988 the "movers and shakers of Soviet society" working in the central party apparatus and the corresponding bureaucracies in the republics, provinces, districts and cities had been subject to periodic reorganizations. Merle Fainsod, who has documented these reorganizations for the period between 1922 and 1962, has shown how these waves of reform oscillated between a functional and an industry-branch emphasis, depending on the needs of the time.[16] During the last decades before the fundamental reform of 1988 to 1990, departments for all sectors of economic activity coexisted with several functional departments; with over 20 departments, the apparatus mushroomed into a giant bureaucracy that suffocated independent initiative.[17]

The most important departments in addition to those that supervised the different sectors of the economy, culture and science were the General Department, the Organizational Party Work Department (cadres policy, *nomenklatura*); the Administrative Organs Department (police, KGB, courts); the International Department, International Information Department, Department for Liaison with Communist and Workers' Parties of Socialist Countries; and the Department for Cadres Abroad. The Main Political Directorate of the Army and Navy, formally in the Ministry of Defense, was in fact the control mechanism of the Secretariat over the armed forces. The Administration of Affairs was in a central place, managing the housekeeping operations of the apparatus and controlling the special facilities and services available to the happy few in leading party positions.[18]

Up to the late 1980s, the Politburo and Secretariat controlled appointments and dismissals for about 15,000 *nomenklatura* positions. This number was reduced to 2,000 positions inside the nationwide party apparatus.[19] The extent of the Secretariat's responsibilities in the field of the implementation of cadre policy was illustrated when in 1990 the number of "confirmations" (*utverzhdeniia*) of cadre appointments and elections given by the Secretariat was disclosed. In a report to the delegates at the 28th Party Congress, the General Department wrote that between March 1986 and 20 June 1990, the Secretariat had "confirmed" 9,756 appointments/elections and 8,266 dismissals; 3,097 and 3,380 of them concerning positions within the CPSU.[20] Thus, on average the Politburo and Secretariat taken together would handle about 170 personnel transfer decisions (60 of them concerning posts in the party) every month.

During the post-Stalin years, the central party apparatus was controlled by the Politburo in two ways. A first and more formal one was through the General Department, which distributed the Politburo's decisions over the Secretariat's other departments. In addition, of course, there was the personal overlap of Politburo and Secretariat members. Each of the members of the Secretariat was responsible for a cluster of departments in the central party apparatus, or headed one of these departments. Thus, through those secretaries who held a seat in the Politburo as well, there was a direct flow of information and policy proposals upward to the Politburo and a flow of decisions down from the Politburo to the bureaucracy. But this overlap also made it possible for the secretaries to sidetrack the other Politburo members. Kirill Mazurov, Politburo member from 1965 to 1978, claimed many years later that Brezhnev "moved the Politburo to the second echelon" and leaned heavily on the Secretariat: "Everything was pre-cooked [*predreshalos*] by a group of secretaries: Suslov, Kirilenko, Kulakov, Ustinov and others. The Secretariat discussed problems before they came in the Politburo. And not seldomly it went like this: we arrive at the [Politburo] meeting and Brezhnev says: 'We already discussed this here, and think that it must be done such and such.' And the voices of the Secretaries again: yes, precisely so, Leonid Ilich. The Politburo members could do nothing but agree." The loners in the Politburo were, in addition to himself, Voronov, Shelepin, Kosygin and Polianskii.[21]

Mazurov's claim that the Brezhnev Secretariat had more or less taken over the Politburo was supported when in February 1989 the proceedings of the October 1987 session of the Central Committee were published and several members and former members of the Secretariat and Politburo reported on the formalism of Politburo meetings under Brezhnev and Chernenko. Nikolai Ryzhkov, later prime minister, had once been at a Politburo session chaired by Brezhnev: "I left feeling crushed, for the meeting lasted fifteen minutes. Yes, I remember how comrade Chernenko led the Politburo, how a speech was read from paper, and that was it... Today we are wet [with perspiration] when we leave the Politburo meeting, it lasts seven to eight hours. Sometimes one question is discussed for seven hours."[22]

The other point of contact between the Politburo and its apparatus was the General Department. This department fulfilled the role of chancellery of the Politburo, the lock-chamber through which all documents to and from the Politburo were to pass. It did duty as the secretariat of the Politburo and dealt with all secret documents sent to the Politburo and emanating from it. It was moreover responsible for issuing and checking party (membership) cards and therefore played a key role during purges. This department was in charge of party archives, dealt with complaints by party members and saw to internal security.[23] Control over the General Department was, of course, essential. When in December 1983 Andropov's economic advisor, Arkadii Volskii, received documents from his hospitalized boss, in which Andropov requested the Central Committee to order Mikhail Gorbachev to stand in for him as leader of the Politburo and Secretariat, he handed those documents to the chief of the General Department, Konstantin Chernenko. Volskii later claimed that in collaboration with Tikhonov and Ustinov, Chernenko made sure that the members of the Central Committee did not get to see the documents.[24]

The General Department had been set up in 1919. Under Stalin it was for a time called the Secret Department and later the Special Sector.[25] From the time of his appointment as General Secretary in April 1922, Stalin used this department as his personal secretariat and as an instrument for manipulating the party apparatus. The notorious Alexander Poskrebyshev was the head of this department between 1928 and the winter of 1952-53. After Stalin's death his successors revived the General Department in 1954, but detached their personal secretariats from it to ensure that its chief never again achieved a position of power such as Poskrebyshev had acquired. Nevertheless, a link between the personal secretariat of the Secretary-General and the General Department remained. Viktor Pribytkov, the personal assistant to Secretary-General Chernenko, wrote in 1990 that he and others had been on the payroll of the General Department. Between 1976 and 1982 when Brezhnev was *Gensek* and Chernenko was chief of the General Department, Secretary of the Central Committee and (since 1977-78) member of the Politburo, Brezhnev's personal assistants came increasingly under Chernenko's influence. Brezhnev became more or less incapacitated, and had Chernenko organize "the business of the Central Committee"—that is, the Secretariat-for him.[26]

The staffing of the central party apparatus increased from 30 in 1919 to 602 in 1921 to several thousand in later decades. In 1990, on the eve of the 28th Party Congress, the central party apparatus numbered 2,352 employees; after the congress it was reduced to the 1921 level.[27] This staff had been divided into a number of different grades. The highest grade consisted of "responsible staff workers." According to information given by Alexander Pravdin, there were more than 900 such workers in 1970 and 1971. Subordinate to these were the "responsible non-staff workers"—specialists who could be called on when required, and the technical staff: female secretaries, guards, messengers, and so on-numbering in all about 2,400. The lowest rank of "responsible staff worker" was that of instructor. These were subordinate to the inspectors.[28] Promotion from instructor to inspector was by interview with one or more secretaries, or in some cases with one of Brezhnev's advisors. The General Secretary himself dealt with only the most important promotions. The powerful position enjoyed by these inspectors could be gauged by the fact that at lower levels, that is to say *na mestakh* ("in the provinces"), they spoke in the name of the Central Committee. They could give instructions to first secretaries of the union republics, or direct the *organy* (state security service) to keep a eye on a particular individual.

CHAIRMAN

Until 1990 the Politburo, like the Communist Party itself and the Central Committee, did not have a formal chairman; it had only a *predsedatelstvuiushchii:* the presiding officer of the meeting. During the first decades of its existence, the meetings were chaired by the successive chairmen of the Council of People's Commissars (Council of Ministers): Lenin, then Rykov, Molotov, and Stalin. In a tradition established under Lenin and continued until Khrushchev's reign, if Politburo members addressed their leader as "chairman," they meant chairman of the government.[29] During the years of Lenin's illness and after his death-when Stalin was already General Secretary-meetings were presided over by Kamenev, who was "mayor" of Moscow and vice chairman of the Council of People's Commissars. According to Voroshilov, he was the one who put all issues into words and formulated the decisions that were reached, which were subsequently written down by secretary Gliasser.[30]

Khrushchev has written that in March 1953, after Stalin's death, it was decided that Malenkov, the new head of government, should preside over the meetings of the Politburo, then renamed Presidium. Khrushchev, who was at that time one of the secretaries of the Central Committee, was to draw up the agenda for the Presidium together with Malenkov.[31] During the year following Khrushchev's election to First Party Secretary at the September 1953 Central Committee meeting, Presidium meetings were still chaired by Malenkov, the head of government, whereas Khrushchev signed all Central Committee documents. This situation of "double power" (*dvoevlastie*) was unsatisfactory to Khrushchev, and during his vacation in the Crimea in August-September 1954 he conspired with Mikoian, Bulganin, Kozlov, Kirichenko, Furtseva and Polianskii and received their support for removing Malenkov from the chair of the Council of Ministers. Malenkov's position had been weakened by what had become known about his role in the so-called Leningrad affair, and although on paper he remained head of government until February 1955, from the autumn of 1954 his governmental functions were in fact executed by Bulganin.[32]

In the meantime, Khrushchev, later accused by Molotov of *"Obkom methods,"* had begun chairing Presidium meetings.[33] Although from 1958 to 1964 Khrushchev was head of government as well, since 1957 it had become custom for the party leader instead of the head of government to chair Politburo sessions. Looking back, it seems likely that this was the moment when the informal position of "Second Secretary of the Central Committee" originated; the task of chairing the sessions of the Secretariat went to this "second-in-command." After Khrushchev was deposed, Brezhnev presided over the meetings. In his absence Suslov or Kirilenko deputized for him. In his reminiscences, Ligachev has written that immediately after Chernenko was elected Secretary-General, Chernenko proposed that Gorbachev chair the Secretariat. In spite of objections by Tikhonov and others, the Politburo agreed: "Obviously, Chernenko understood that [the Secretariat] was in need of an energetic, young and physically strong person."[34] This was in line with what Gromyko had said on 11 March 1985 concerning Gorbachev's "second-in-command" position during the Chernenko interregnum: the Secretary-General chaired Politburo meetings whereas Gorbachev led the Secretariat and chaired the Politburo meetings when Chernenko was absent. After Gorbachev had become Secretary-General, he chaired Politburo meetings, whereas Ligachev was in charge of the meetings of the Secretariat.[35] Nevertheless, Gorbachev assured the Central Committee that he saw all agendas of Secretariat meetings, and that not one decision left the Secretariat "without the Secretary-General seeing it, with the exception of some current affairs."[36] Ligachev said in October 1987 that he chaired Politburo meetings when Gorbachev was absent. In July 1990, article 28 of the new party Rules finally formalized the informal rule that dated from 1957: the chair of the Politburo was reserved for the Secretary-General, that of the Secretariat for his deputy.

RULES OF PROCEDURE AND MINUTES

The apparent lack of a formal rule governing the chairmanship suggests that the Politburo's internal rules of procedure were pretty sketchy. We do know that on 8 December 1922 Lenin dictated by telephone a proposal to the Central Committee for rules of procedure of the Politburo, but history does not relate whether this proposal was adopted. The rules that he proposed were as follows:

> "1. The Politburo meets on Thursday from 11 o'clock until 2 (o'clock) at the latest;
> 2. If questions remain undecided, they are adjourned till Friday or Monday at the same time;

3. The agenda of the Politburo should be circulated not later than Wednesday at 12 o'clock. The (written) documents appertaining to the agenda should be sent out at the same time;

4. Additional points may be handed in on the day of the meeting only under the following conditions:
   a. in cases where deferment is absolutely impossible (particularly diplomatic questions);
   b. only in writing;
   c. only in cases where there is no objection on the part of any member of the Politburo.

The last condition, with reference to the absence of objections to additional agenda items, can be waived only in the case of diplomatic questions which do not admit of any delay whatsoever."[37]

We also know that in December 1945, some months after the abolition of the State Committee for Defense, the rules of procedure obtaining before the war once more came into force in the Politburo, or new rules were adopted.[38] An indication that at least some of these rules remained in force could be found much later when, in 1991, the reminiscences of Egor Ligachev were serialized in the weekly *Argumenty i Fakty*.[39] Ligachev wrote that ever since the days of Lenin, up to the 28th Party Congress, the Politburo had painstakingly kept Thursday, 11 o'clock, as the regular time for its weekly meeting. We will return to the question of the day and frequency of Politburo meetings in the section on frequency of meetings below.

The discussions in the Politburo were not taken down in minutes. From the beginning in 1919, only lists of resolutions (*Protokoly*) were compiled. The Protokol of the first meeting (16 April 1919, see illustration 1 in Chapter 2) shows the format that has been used ever since: on the left side the agenda items are listed, on the right side the decisions taken on each item. From these lists of resolutions, extracts were taken down on specially prepared printed forms, and through the General Department these were sent to the organizations that were to implement them.[40]

QUORUM

One of the most important sections of the rules of procedure must necessarily be the rules governing the quorum. How many members must be present to enable the Politburo to take decisions? It can easily be imagined that these rules are of great importance, particularly at times of tension when there is an acute struggle for power between the various members of the Politburo and when some members want to remove others from certain positions.

In this matter, too, it is almost beyond doubt that the informal rule set by Lenin was honored during the whole period of the Politburo's existence, and became a tradition: there simply was no quorum requirement. Lenin's procedures proposal contained no stipulation regarding a quorum, and nowhere in the many recently published reminiscences is any indication that Politburo members ever made a fuss about quorum requirements.[41] Moreover, in other party and state institutions it was at times customary to hold so-called administrative meetings in addition to the plenary meetings. At plenary meetings of the Central Committee or the Council of Labor and Defense, for instance, an ordinary quorum was required, but for the administrative meetings of the same bodies a lower quorum or none at all was required. At the beginning of the 1920s, if someone present at an administrative meeting of the Council of Labor and Defense objected to a resolution that had been passed, he could lodge a protest, whereupon the issue had to be reconsidered at a plenary meeting. In all other cases the resolution passed by the administrative meeting had the force of a resolution by the Council itself as soon as it had been signed by the Council chairman.

From the middle of the 1920s, chairmen of government bodies started to make decisions on their own in the name of their collective organ.[42] From its inception and particularly in its early years, the Politburo was seen as-and saw itself as-an administrative meeting of the Central Committee that was therefore not in need of a quorum; this was also obvious from the fact that the Politburo's decisions were presented as decisions of the Central Committee. But the center of gravity tended to shift to the Politburo's leader; during three crucial periods—at the end of the rule of Lenin (1919-24), Stalin (1941-53) and Khrushchev (1958-64)—the (informal) leader of the Politburo and the (formal) chairman of the Council of People's Commissars/Ministers were one and the same person; and from 1977 to 1982 the chairman of the Supreme Soviet's Presidium was leader of the Politburo as well. The Politburo became the entourage of leaders who made decisions often on their own or in consultation with only those fellow members whom they cared to confer with.

Could the Politburo meet and make decisions regarding the political fate of the General Secretary in his absence, without his being able subsequently to lodge a protest on formal grounds or to appeal to the Central Committee or the Committee for Party Control? One is tempted to say yes. In both 1957 and 1964 Khrushchev's fellow members met while the First Secretary was absent and confronted him on his return with a *fait accompli*—their decision that he must go. Several authors, including Khrushchev's son Sergei Nikitich, have vividly described the intruiging behind Khrushchev's back that led to his downfall.[43] In palace revolutions of this kind a great deal depended on the way in which the Central Committee was approached. If a majority in the Politburo succeeded in presenting the Central Committee with a draft resolution which indicated that the General Secretary had lost all support, the latter did indeed run the risk of being dismissed by the Central Committee. In 1957 this strategy was not successful, in part because Khrushchev insisted on accompanying the Presidium delegates who went to confer with members of the Central Committee.

AGENDA

In its early years the agenda was very overcrowded, because many minor issues were dragged before the Politburo. In those days, when this body in a very real sense fulfilled the function of the highest (informal) court of appeal in political matters, the Politburo was constantly being called on to arbitrate when people's commissars could not agree among themselves. In the months between March and September 1920, the Politburo dealt with 629 items, while the Central Committee dealt with only 99. One year later, between June and August of 1921, when the Central Committee considered a total of 27 items at five meetings, the Politburo dealt with 264 items at 24 sessions, an average of 11 items per meeting.[44] Boris Bazhanov maintains that in the years from 1923 to 1925, some 80 to 150 items were discussed at a single meeting of the Politburo.[45]

On two occasions, in 1926 and 1928, work schedules for the Politburo were published in the Soviet press. These listed the agenda items to be dealt with in the current year, the month in which they were to come up for consideration and the organizations that had to present reports to the Politburo. The work schedule for 1926 consisted of 40 items, distributed under a number of headings. The schedule for 1928 included only 20 items. Obviously these schedules did not include all the items on the Politburo agenda. Table 7.5 lists the items to be considered in the month of May 1926.

According to Boris Bazhanov, from 1923 to 1925 the agenda was drawn up by Stalin, Zinovev, and Kamenev jointly. In 1925 Stalin abolished the separate meetings held by these three to draft the agenda.[46] In later years the agenda was drawn up under the supervision of the General Secretary by the General Department of the party Secretariat.

Table 7.5
Work Schedule of the Politburo and the Central Committee,
May 1926

- Five Year Plan for industrial development in the various branches and districts. Report by the Supreme Economic Council.
- Report by the Chief Directorate of the Metallurgical Industry (structure, implementation of the work plan).
- Report of the People's Commissariat for Finance on the first half-year(structure, general results), also reports of the Central Control Commission and the Workers' and Peasants' Inspectorate.
- Concerning results achieved and the development of the credit system in the USSR; report by the People's Commissariat for Finance and the State Bank; also reports from the Central Control Commission and the Workers' and Peasants' Inspectorate.
- Results and plan for work among the working people [*rabochee stroitelstvo*]; report of the People's Commissariat for Labor.
- Concerning the simplification, regulation and coordination of the work of the central (state) institutions; report by a commission of the Politburo.
- Concerning the implementation of revolutionary justice with a view to carrying out the party directives; report by the Central Control Commission and the People's Commissariat for Justice, Report by the Orgburo.
- Results of the development of the *sovkhozy* and *kolkhozy*; report by the People's Commissariat for Agriculture and the Agricultural Union; also a report by the Central Control Commission and the Workers' and Peasants' Inspectorate.
- Report by the Moscow Provincial Party Committee on the results of political and economic activities.
- The first, fifth and sixth agenda items shall, after consideration by thePolitburo, be submitted to the Plenum of the Central Committee.

FREQUENCY OF MEETINGS

The first nine months in the existence of the Politburo have been documented extensively, though not exhaustively, in *Izvestia TsK KPSS*.[47] The chronological reports in this journal show a rich variety in types of sessions of the party's top organs: plenary meetings of the Central Committee (four between the first Politburo session of 16 April and 31 December 1919), sessions (*zasedanie*) of the Central Committee (an additional four), meetings of Central Committee members (*soveshchanie chlenov*, one), joint sessions of the Politburo and the Orgburo with all Central Committee members that happened to be in Moscow (one), Joint Politburo-Orgburo meetings (13), and separate Politburo (36) and Orgburo (24) meetings. Once or twice the Politburo and Orgburo met in separate session on the same day.

As is shown in Table 7.6, in the early 1920s roughly seven Politburo meetings were held per month. In those days many members of the Central Committee were at the front and it was not always possible to call together plena of that committee. All members of the Central Committee who were not members of the Politburo or the Orgburo but were present in Moscow were permitted to attend joint meetings of the Politburo and Orgburo. One advantage of such meetings, according to party historian Nikolaeva, was that decisions by the Politburo could be implemented immediately by the Orgburo—their execution no longer met with delays as had frequently been the case previously. The first joint meeting took place on 29 April 1919. There were nine persons present, four of whom were members of the Orgburo. Ten agenda items were dealt with. During the second half of 1919, 18 more joint meetings took place; in 1920 there were none; and in 1921 there were two, on 8 January and 14 February.[48]

The available data on the frequency of meetings in the period after the 1920s is sketchy. Karl Albrecht, who held a high post in the party from 1928 to 1931 and attended a number of Politburo meetings, claimed that the meetings were held "twice or at most three times per week."[49] In the years immediately before World War II meetings were much less frequent. The evidence for this is provided by the serial numbers of three lists of resolutions (*Protokoly*) of the Politburo (one in 1937 and two in 1941), extracts of which were published in 1968 and 1990. The *Protokol* of the Politburo meeting of 17 December 1937 had the serial number 56; that of 19 August 1941, the number 34; and that of the 9 December 1941 meeting, the number 35.[50] Van den Berg has pointed out that in the 1920s the *Protokoly* of the Politburo were numbered from one party congress to the next and that later the same numbering was applied by Bureaus of Central Committees in certain republics. Assuming that this system of numbering was still being applied at the end of the 1930's, the meeting of 17 December 1937 was the 56th after the 17th Party Congress (26 January-10 February 1934), and the meeting of 19 August 1941 was the 34th after the 18th Congress (10-21 March 1939). This would mean that between February 1934 and December 1937—a period

Table 7.6
Number of Reported Politburo Sessions, 1919 - 1990

Period	# sessions	mean # sessions per month
1919	70	8
1920	85	7
1921	110	9
1922	60	5
1923	85	7
Jun 1923 - Dec 1925	92	5
Feb 1934 - Dec 1937	56	1.2
Mar 1939 - Aug 1941	34	1.2
1946	7	0.6
1947	10	0.8
1948	7	0.6
1949	16	1.3
1950	6	0.5
1951	5	0.4
1952	4	0.3
Apr 1971 - Feb 1976	215	3.7
Feb 1976 - Feb 1981	236	3.9
Mar 1986 - Jun 1990	187	3.6

Sources: John Löwenhardt, *The Soviet Politburo*, Edinburgh (Canongate) 1982, p. 97, and by the same author, "*Politburo zasedaet*: Reported and secret meetings of the Politburo of the CPSU", *Nordic Journal of Soviet and East European Studies* Vol. 5, No. 2 (1988), p. 161; *Izvestiia TsK KPSS* 1990, No. 9, pp. 16-34; Iu. S. Aksenov, "Apogei Stalinizma: poslevoennaia piramida vlasti", *Voprosy Istorii KPSS* 1990, No. 11 (November), 90-104 (100).

Table 7.7
7-day Intervals as Percentage of All Intervals
Between Reported Politburo Meetings

Andropov period	86 %
Chernenko period	64 %
Gorbachev period	50 %
1986	59 %
1987	64 %
1988	39 %
1989	16 %

Source: Politbase (database of Politburo meetings, compiled by the author).

of 46 months—56 meetings took place, averaging 14.6 per year. In the period between March 1939 and August 1941, the average was 14.1 per year.

The 35th, and for the time being the last meeting, was held on 9 December 1941. In June Stalin had set up the State Committee of Defense, which took over the functions of both the Politburo and the government. This committee combined within itself the "leadership over the party and the supreme executive power of the Soviet Union."[51] The Politburo met sporadically for the sole purpose of formally ratifying a long list of decisions. The published abstracts of protokols show that at the 34th meeting of the Politburo (19 August 1941), at least 367 decisions were passed, and at least 324 were passed at the following meeting (9 December).

This unique situation—a fusion of the supreme party and state institutions was highly unusual—came to an end at the beginning of September 1945. In December of that year the Politburo decided to meet once every two weeks, but the decision was not implemented. The restoration of collective decision making had to wait for Stalin's death. During the last seven years of his life, the Politburo membership was split up into a number of informal groups ("The Group of Three," "The Group of Five," "The Group of Nine") that were manned, manipulated and played off against each other by the General Secretary as it suited him. In July 1953 Malenkov said that this system had completely replaced Politburo decision making.[52] Stalin decided everything. Sometimes many months passed without a session. During these lean years, many of the country's vital policy issues were never discussed in formal Politburo meetings. With the exception of 1949, it never met more often than ten times a year—with an absolute low of four sessions in 1952—and of the 16 sessions in 1949, more than ten were devoted to repeated discussions of the Leningrad affair.[53]

It is also probable that the Politburo fell short of functioning as a regularly meeting decision-making organ during part of Nikita Khrushchev's rule, specifically between 1958 and 1964. One of the more serious charges leveled by the men who brought about the coup in 1964 was that Khrushchev had developed the habit of making decisions behind their backs and of pillorying them by his public comments. As we have seen, the same tendency emerged in the Brezhnev period.

Since the middle of the 1970s, more information on the frequency of meetings of the Politburo has become available. In 1957 and 1970 it was stated by Khrushchev, and in 1971 and 1973 by Brezhnev, that the "norm" was one meeting per week, but in the absence of precise and official numbers, Western observers could only assume that this "norm" was indeed fulfilled.[54] Information affirming this assumption was released in 1976 for the first time

Figure 7.1
Figure 7.1
Frequency Distribution of Intervals Between Politburo Meetings, in Days

Andropov
9 December 1982 - 9 February 1984: 61 weeks, 52 sessions
days
01-03
04-06
07   **
08-10
11-13
14   ******
15-17
18-20
21
22-24
25-27
28   *
29-34
35-40
>40

Chernenko
13 February 1984 - 10 March 1985: 56 weeks, 45 sessions
days
01-03
04-06 ***
07   ***************************
08-10 **
11-13 *
14   *******
15-17 **
18-20
21   *
22-24
25-27
28
29-34
35-40
>40

Gorbachev pre-27th Congress
11 March 1985 - 25 February 1986: 50 weeks, 39 sessions
days
01-03
04-06 ****
07   *******************
08-10 ****
11-13 ***

Gorbachev pre-27th Congress (continued)
11 March 1985 - 25 February 1986: 50 weeks, 39 sessions
14   *******
15-17
18-20 *
21
22-24
25-27
28
29-34
35-40
>40

Gorbachev 1986-1987
6 March 1986 - 5 December 1987: 95 weeks, 72 sessions
days
01-03 **
04-06 ********
07   *************************************
08-10 *******
11-13 **
14   ********
15-17 ***
18-20 *
21   *
22-24 *
25-27
28   *
29-34
35-40
>40

Gorbachev 1988-1990
6 December 1987 - 14 March 1990: 118 weeks, 56 sessions
days
01-03 *
04-06 *
07   *****************
08-10 ****
11-13 ***
14   **********
15-17 ***
18-20 **
21   *****
22-24 *
25-27 *
28   *
29-34 ***
35-40 *
>40   *
??   **

since the 1920s. In his report to the 25th Party Congress on 24 February 1976, Leonid Brezhnev announced that the Politburo had met 215 times during the five years that had elapsed since the previous congress and the Secretariat, 205 times. Five years later at the 26th Party Congress, Brezhnev reported that in the intermediate period (260 weeks), 236 meetings of the Politburo and 250 Secretariat meetings had been held.[55]

Then, a few weeks after Brezhnev's death, *Pravda*'s 11 December 1982 issue carried a report on a Politburo session held earlier that week, presumably on 9 December. Ever since that date, reports on Politburo sessions have been published in the press, but these reports did not cover all sessions actually held. Ultimate proof of this came in 1990 in the report on the leading organs of the CPSU written in the General Department and distributed to the delegates at the 28th Party Congress. The report mentioned 187 Politburo sessions during the period between 7 March 1986 and 28 June 1990.[56] For the same period, the number of sessions reported in the press had been 131. Thus 56 sessions of Gorbachev's Politburo held between the 27th and 28th party congresses were not reported in *Pravda*. Three out of every ten sessions held during this period were kept secret.

Going by the sessions that were reported in the press-267 since December 1982, 131 between the 27th and the 28th party congresses-the frequency and regularity of Politburo meetings has shown a dramatic decline since the body reluctantly started political reform in 1987. The Andropov period still showed a more or less "ideal-typical" picture of Politburo sessions: almost every Thursday (see Table 7.7 and Figure 7.1). During his reign, 86 percent of the intervals between reported Politburo meetings lasted exactly seven days. There were six 14-day intervals, one 28-day interval and no other intervals. Under Chernenko, the share of seven-day intervals declined to 64 percent, and the Politburo started to meet on other days than the usual Thursday; in addition to seven 14-day intervals and one 21-day interval, there were intervals lasting 6, 8, 10, 11 or 15 days. By the end of 1989, intervals of 20, 30 days became more and more common, and in the first months of 1990 the intervals between reported Politburo sessions lasted 60, 31 and 47 days.

ATTENDANCE BY NONMEMBERS

It would be a mistake to imagine Politburo meetings as entirely closed gatherings. As early as 1919 it was laid down that members of the Central Committee who did not hold seats in the Politburo but who wished to attend a meeting might do so in an advisory capacity. But Politburo meetings were also attended by other officials who were invited to present their case or expertise, or to deliver reports of their institutions that had been ordered by the Politburo (see the Work Schedule, Table 7.5). An early account was given by Boris Bazhanov, who for a short while was secretary to Stalin. Bazhanov wrote that in the years between 1923 and 1925, one official after another attended meetings of the Politburo to present reports, after which the Politburo decided the relevant matter. The room in the Kremlin in which meetings were held was the same as for the Council of People's Commissars, and was the scene of constant coming and going:

> The room next door was as busy as a bee-hive. Who are all these people, jammed in like sardines in a tin?—smoking, gossiping, coming and going to and fro. They are the Soviet ministers, the under-secretaries, the senior dignitaries of the republic. They are not allowed into the room where the Politburo is meeting. They wait patiently for hours till such time as the agenda item for which they have been summoned comes up.

> The secretary of the Politburo rings a bell and his assistant, a female Cerberus who keeps strict watch on the doors of the apartment, gives a signal. "Comrades Menzhinskii and Iagoda!" screams the assistant, her face a picture of zeal and anxiety. Comrades Menzhinskii and Iagoda, the two wizards of the GPU, rise in haste and hurry into the Sanhedrin. Haste is imperative, for the Politburo's time is precious. Menzhinskii and Iagoda are present at the meeting only for the few brief moments required to settle the matter in hand. There are so many problems demanding a solution that only a couple of minutes can be given to each. Comrades Menzhinskii and Iagoda have not had their full say before they are unceremoniously led out and others enter. Here comes Chicherin....[57]

Elsewhere in his book Bazhanov described in his own graphic style how the much feted commander-in-chief of the Red Cavalry, Marshal Budennyi, came to present a report to the Politburo. Bazhanov made no effort to conceal his contempt:

> We were meeting to decide some questions affecting the Red Army and Budennyi was admitted to the meeting for a few minutes. As always, the members of the Politburo were seated in groups, all at one end of the table. At the back of the room a door opens. Budennyi is admitted. He comes in on tiptoe, walking very carefully, but his heavy riding boots make a terrible row nevertheless. His face wears a look of uncertainty. There is a space of at least three metres between the wall and the table, but Budennyi is terrified of losing his balance and bumping into something, making a noise or breaking something.

As usual, Kamenev is in the chair. Budennyi is given a seat between Zinovev and me. His eyes are starting out of his head, he is staring into space and does not appear to have any idea of what is going on round him...

The military item on the agenda has now been dealt with, Budennyi is supposed to take his leave. But he calmly remains seated. At length, Kamenev gives a contemptuous laugh, his eyes like slits: "As the strategic questions have now been dealt with, all military personnel may now leave the meeting!" But Budennyi doesn't move a muscle. He doesn't understand the language used by Kamenev, who finally had to shout out loud: "Comrade Budennyi! Attention! About turn! Forward march!..." With the affable air of a hospitable host, Stalin then said: "You can stay." And so Budennyi sat on for quite a while, with his eyes staring wide, his hands on the table, and his military moustache with the ends turned up...[58]

The habit of inviting lower-level party secretaries, ministers and experts to come and report to the Politburo in session has been preserved ever since.[59]

COMMISSIONS

In 1973 Leonid Brezhnev told an American journalist that if the Politburo could not agree upon a decision, an ad hoc commission of individual members was frequently set up to find a solution to the problem. Brezhnev later revealed that in 1978 two special commissions were appointed by the Politburo: one for the improvement of transport and another for the improvement of information services and propaganda in foreign countries.[60] Many more Politburo commissions have been working since: on the environmental problems of Lake Baikal, on the Chernobyl disaster in 1986, on the Armenian earthquake in 1988 and, most recently, on the Stalin Terror. The findings of the last-mentioned commission *On the Supplementary Study of Materials Related to the Repressions that Took Place in the Period of the 1930's-1940's and the beginning of the 1950's* resulted in the rehabilitation of scores of victims of the Great Terror, and have been published in *Izvestiia TsK KPSS*.[61] Commissions of the Politburo, however, were not new to the 1970s and 1980s: the May 1926 Work Schedule, for example, mentions a Politburo Commission on the coordination of state institutions.

In his speech at the 28th Party Congress, Lev Zaikov disclosed that he had chaired the Politburo Commission on the Military and Technical Aspects of International Politics that operated since 1985-86 and prepared proposals for the talks on arms reductions. Other members were Iakovlev and

Shevardnadze, as well as representatives of the Ministry of Defense, the KGB, the Military-Industrial Commission of the Council of Ministers and other departments. The commission was supported by an interdepartmental working group of experts. Zaikov remained chairman of this commission during the time that he was First Secretary of the Moscow *Gorkom*.[62] On the same occasion, Edvard Shevardnadze disclosed that prior to the withdrawal from Afghanistan, he had chaired a Politburo Commission on Afghanistan, aimed at "getting our lads back from Afghanistan and keeping that country as our friend."[63]

DECISIONS AND DECISION MAKING

Information on the number of decisions taken by the Politburo was published for the first time in 1990 for the period since the 26th Party Congress. These data confirmed (Table 7.8) that the Politburo used to take two different kinds of decisions (*postanovleniia*): decisions reached in sessions of the bureau (averaging about ten per session during the 1980s) and so-called decisions by circulation (*oprosom*). "Decisions by circulation" were circulated among the Politburo members, and had to be initialed by them. In case individual members refused their consent, the issue had to be put on the agenda of the next session. Circulation decisions had been in use for many decades.[64] Since its first issue in January 1989, *Izvestiia TsK KPSS* has been publishing a monthly selection of Politburo decisions. Comparison of the dates of these decisions with the dates of reported Politburo sessions has shown that only a minority have been taken in session.

From the lowest party committees in the cities and districts through the Politburo's of the republics up to the Politburo and the Presidia of the Council of Ministers and the Supreme Soviet of the USSR, the majority of decisions were taken by circulation. During the first six months of 1946, for example, the Politburo of the Ukrainian Party Organization, led by Nikita Khrushchev, took 499 decisions—no less than 486 (97 percent) of them by circulation.[65] Stalin made good use of this technique as a means to circumvent a collective discussion and take formal decisions on removing colleagues from their midst. His invitation to co-sign a draft decision on the removal of a member of the political elite was an offer one could not possibly refuse.

The number of decisions is one thing; the style of decision making, of course, is something else. But the two are related. As is shown in Table 7.8, during the 1980s an average of ten decisions was taken at each meeting. These presumably were the most important and controversial issues,

---

Table 7.8

Number of Decisions Made by the Politburo, 1981-1990

	26-27 Congress 4 March '81 – 6 March '86		27-28 Congress 7 March '86 – 28 June '90	
Decisions taken in Politburo meetings	2,492		1,829	
Mean number per meeting		10.5		9.8
Decisions by circulation*	17,539		9,625	
Mean number per month		292		185
Total number of decisions	20,031		11,454	

Source: *Izvestiia TsK KPSS* 1990, No. 9, p. 21.
* Russian: "*Putem operativnogo golosovaniia (oprosom).*"

---

including draft decisions that individual members had refused to initial in the circulation procedure. An average of ten items per meeting allows for some discussion on each individual issue, and the data on the 1980s therefore seem to confirm the general norm for Politburo decision making that can be distilled from the many reminiscences and testimonies of its former members. That general norm, which was deviated from at different times, was put into words by G. I. Shitarev when, a few months before Khrushchev's fall, he wrote that:

> "differences of opinion are frequently aired at meetings of the Presidium. This is an expression of the desire of the members of the Presidium to study the issue in question from all sides and in the greatest possible depth. As a rule all the members finally agree on a common stand. 'If they do not succeed in agreeing on a united stand on a particular issue,' N. S. Khrushchev has commented, 'that issue is decided by a majority of votes....'[66]

The policy was to reach decisions without having to put motions to the vote-that is, by consensus. Many draft decisions were prepared in the Secretariat under the supervision of the Secretary-General and the other secretaries, and discussed in a secretaries' meeting before they reached the Politburo agenda. In his memoirs, Nikita Khrushchev has written that the Politburo's business was conducted "more or less democratically" until 1939. That is to say that proposals were put forward, discussed, and a collective decision was then arrived at. "But gradually democracy had been giving way to autocracy. Stalin had been barking orders and stifling discussion at [Politburo] meetings ever since the annihilation of the basic staff of the Central Committee which had been elected at the Seventeenth Party Congress [1934]."[67] Khrushchev was exaggerating slightly here. It is true that between the beginning of World War II and the death of Joseph Stalin the Politburo hardly functioned, but from the memoirs of Marshal Zhukov and Minister Zverev, for instance, it appears that there was from time to time effective discussion in the State Committee for Defense and the Bureau of the Council of People's Commissars.

For seven decades, the Politburo kept its doors firmly closed to the uninvited. While its members were engaged in disputes over power and policy, in intrigues and infighting, it presented itself as a solid body of leaders, united in constructive cooperation. Analyses of Sovietologists and journalists on differences of view among different Politburo members were flatly denied. There were no "hawks" and "doves," it was said—they were merely an invention of Kremlinologists paid by the CIA and the infamous military-industrial complex. The Politburo was, had been and always would be united in body and spirit. In earlier chapters we have seen that in some periods such an image was not completely inappropriate. Most recently during the Brezhnev period, the decision-making culture was increasingly hostile to open and businesslike discussion. Ligachev was not the only former leader who testified to this. Discussing the atmosphere at Central Committee meetings, he wrote in his reminiscences that "during the Brezhnev period, those 17 years that I was First Party Secretary of Tomsk province, I did not once succeed in getting the floor at a Central Committee plenum. During the first years I punctually registered to speak, but as the years went by, my hopes faded: it became increasingly clear to me that always the same speakers were allowed to address the Central Committee: those, I think, who knew well what to say, and how to speak..." The sessions of the Politburo itself were short and formal: "During Brezhnev's last years... in an hour or forty minutes the Politburo accepted decisions that had been prepared in advance—and adjourned."[68]

In 1989, when the going got too rough for particular members, the formalism and the monolithic facade started to crumble. The Politburo felt so threatened by the popular success of its former member Boris Eltsin that it decided to publish the verbatim record of the October 1987 session of the Central Committee, documenting for the first time the degree of mutual hatred among Politburo members. At the February 1990 Plenum of the CC, Ligachev and Shevardnadze clashed in the open (speeches from the meeting were promptly published in the press) over decision making on the military intervention in Tbilisi on 8 April 1989. Ligachev claimed that Gorbachev, Ryzhkov, Shevardnadze and Iakovlev were present at a Politburo meeting on 7 April that approved the dispatch of army and MVD troops to Tbilisi. This contradicted the findings of the investigating committee of the Georgian Supreme Soviet, which established earlier that the meeting in question was chaired by Ligachev and attended by Sliunkov, Medvedev, Lukianov, Iazov, Razumovskii and Kriuchkov. Shevardnadze challenged Ligachev's statement and claimed that there had been no such Politburo meeting on the use of troops.[69] By the time this open clash took place, the Politburo had lost most of its authority and power.

INCOME

In an interview taken in the spring of 1989, Mikhail Gorbachev told the correspondent of *Izvestiia TsK KPSS* that Politburo members received a salary of 1,200 rubles per month, irrespective of their main job.[70] Candidate members received 1,100 and secretaries 1,000 rubles. These figures were more or less in line with those provided 15 years earlier by the sociologist and former employee of the Secretariat A. Pravdin. He had valued a secretary at 700 to 800 rubles a month (with a 13th month's pay) in 1970-71.[71] During these years, when the minimum wage for industrial workers in the Soviet Union was 60 rubles and the average wage 125 rubles a month, the *Gensek* was worth 900 rubles. A sinecure-like membership of the Supreme Soviet could bring in another hundred rubles per month, and those who—like Brezhnev and Ustinov—were Marshals of the Soviet Union got 2,000 (maximum) per month extra.[72] Old-age benefits, however, were not always as royal. Khrushchev received about 450 rubles per month after his forced retirement. Ligachev relates in his memoirs that the pensions for party officials depended solely on the whims of Brezhnev, until in 1984 the Council of Ministers took a decision on pensions. On 1 October 1990 the Council of Ministers fixed the pensions for former Politburo and Secretariat members at 500 rubles and that for widows of former secretaries-general at 300 per month.[73]

However high these salaries were, they were almost irrelevant and certainly could not be compared to salaries of political leaders in non-communist countries. In the Soviet Union the elite was rewarded largely in kind. This was so because money alone could not buy very much in an economy where many commodities were scarce, but where prices could not find their

7. Nikita Sergeevich Khrushchev (1894-1971) after his retirement (Ogonek 1990, Nr. 22).

market level. All kinds of scarce goods, beyond the reach of ordinary mortals, were sold in camouflaged shops to a select clientele. For a long time, top political personalities were entitled to the so-called Kremlin ration (*Kremlevskii paek*): every month they received coupons valued at from 240 to 640 rubles, which they could spend in these shops. In addition, special select sanatoria and rest homes dotted the countryside, the mountains and beaches; apartments in the cities and *dachas* in the countryside were made available to them. They had the best possible medical attention inside the Kremlin walls.

There was a Soviet saying, very well known but less popular with the leaders, to the effect that for *them* communism had already dawned. In the end, their royal life-style and the impression that it made on a disgusted population contributed in no small measure to their undoing and to that of the Politburo. The former Politburo members who are still alive will now have to make do with a meager pension of 500 inflated rubles.

CONCLUSION

"Effective government in a large modern state," Harry Rigby wrote in his foreword to the 1982 edition of *The Soviet Politburo*, "*does* require someone to exercise a 'prime-ministerial' (if not a 'presidential') role, and sooner or later a leader emerges who can exercise such a role, but the problem is then how to stop him accumulating 'too much' power once he has 'enough.' Because the Soviet system is essentially a collective dictatorship, anyone who can assert a personal dominance over it is in danger of becoming a personal dicator, as Stalin demonstrated."[74]

The first six chapters of this book have documented the cyclical pattern in the Politburo's history where the obsessions of the Leninist tradition time and again led to a leader establishing his dominance over the Politburo. In this chapter we have gone into more detail concerning the formal and informal rules that governed the operation of the Politburo and its relations with other institutions. The *PB*, as we have come to know it, was and has remained one of several informal "inner circles" through which the chosen few exercised their dictatorship: inner circles of the central party, government and state institutions. With only short interruptions, the Politburo successfully upheld its claim to be the *innermost* circle.

With the onset of serious political reform, however, the Politburo quickly lost ground. The crucial year was 1988, when the Politburo allowed its leader, Mikhail Gorbachev, to introduce, both in words and in deeds, the will of the people as a check on party leadership. It should have known better. Ignoring the basic rule of Leninism that the party (that is, the Politburo or its leader) *always* knows better, Gorbachev was realistic in recognizing that Soviet society of the late 1980s was fundamentally different from that in the beginning of the century; but he underestimated the power of political forces in modern society. His revival of the soviets and his insistence that party leaders receive a mandate from the electorate were forerunners of a profound crisis in party leadership that led to the undoing of the Politburo two years later.

What happened was that Gorbachev broke the traditional cycle in one respect: by establishing his new power position not inside, but outside the Politburo-even though he remained a Politburo member and Secretary General. By the time he had gained sufficient power through the party's Secretariat, the political environment of the Politburo had changed beyond recognition. First of all, the political forces in society had become so strong that old mechanisms of submission were shattered. It was no longer possible to consolidate power in the traditional way in the Politburo, barring an old-style despot who was prepared to throw the Soviet Union back into the Middle Ages. Second, the economic crisis, Gorbachev's domestic and foreign policy, and the weak international position of the Soviet Union made it unlikely that Gorbachev would develop into such a traditional dictator. Gorbachev's respect for the law made it imperative that he consolidate his power outside the Politburo—in a new-style presidency. Even though in this new office he quickly accumulated more and more powers, Gorbachev the supreme leader now was subject to the control of the law and, ultimately perhaps, of the electorate. Once that happened, the Politburo had become redundant.

NOTES TO CHAPTER 7

1. Art. 28 in "Ustav kommunisticheskoi partii...", 1990.
2. Nikolaeva, 1969.
3. *Pravda*, 18 June 1977.
4. Van den Berg, 1984: 75-78.
5. Van den Berg, 1984: 113-124.
6. Such is to be deduced from the fact that the paragraph on joint decisions in the General Department's report to the delegates of the 28th Party Congress was included in the section on the Politburo. See *Izvestiia TsK KPSS* 1990, No. 9: 19.

7. Ibid. On joint decisions, see also Van den Berg, 1985.

8. Van den Berg, 1984: 127-134.

9. Gorbachev during confirmation hearings on Defense Minister Iazov in the Supreme Soviet on 3 July 1989, see *Pervaia Sessiia...*, 1989: 63.

10. Izgarshev, 1989; and Rahr, 1989.

11. *Izvestiia TsK KPSS* 1990, No. 2: 203.

12. See *Vedomosti Verkhovnogo Soveta SSSR* 1976, No. 19, art. 318; *Bolshaia Sovetskaia Entsiklopediia Ezhegodnik* 1976: 68; Garthoff, 1975; and Yasmann, 1989.

13. Gorbachev disclosed on 21 November 1989 that it had been the Politburo that had decided that Lev Zaikov, Politburo member and successor to Boris Eltsin as First Party Secretary of Moscow, was to focus his activities on work in the Central Committee and in the Defense Council. See *Izvestiia*, 22 November 1989.

14. Gorbachev answering questions at the 21st Komsomol Congress; see *BBC SWB* SU/0739 (16 April 1990) B/8. This was confirmed by Lev Zaikov at the 28th Party Congress; see *BBC SWB* SU/0808 C1/11. Different reports on investigations into the April 1989 massacre in Tbilisi have mentioned "the republic's Defense Council," implying that at least Georgia, and possibly other republics, had its own Defense Council in addition to the Defense Council of the USSR. See Fuller, 1989; and the report of the Peoples' Congress Commission Chairman Anatolii Sobchak, 1989.

15. "O demokratizatsii Sovetskogo obshchestva i reforme politicheskoi sistemy", Rezoliutsiia XIX Vsesoiuznoi konferentsii KPSS, 1 iiuliia 1988 g.; "Ob obrazovanii komissii TsK PKSS i reorganizatsii apparata TsK KPSS v svete reshenii XIX Vsesoiuznoi partiinoi konferentsii", Postanovlenie Plenuma Tsentralnogo Komiteta KPSS 30 sentiabria 1988 g., *Spravochnik partiinogo rabotnika 1989*, Moscow 1989, pp. 14-22 and 84-85.

16. Fainsod, 1967: 176-205.

17. On the early history of the Secretariat, see "Kogo izbrali...", 1989.

18. On the activities and role of the International Department, see Schapiro, 1966-67; and Gelman, 1984: 59-63. For the department during the late 1980s, see Kramer, 1990.

19. Shenin, 1990. On Gorbachev's impact on the *nomenklatura* system, see also Hill/Löwenhardt, 1991.

20. *Izvestiia TsK KPSS*, 1990, No. 9: 22-23.

21. Bondarenko, 1989.

22. "Plenum TsK KPSS - Oktiabr 1987 goda...", 1989: 255-56.

23. On the General Department, see a.o. Schapiro, 1975.

24. See Teague, 1990; and the interview with Volskii in *Nedelia* 1990, No. 36.

25. For the history of the Secret Department, see Rosenfeldt, 1978.

26. Pribytkov, 1990.

27. Fainsod, 1967: 180; Rahr, 1990. By October 1990 the staff of the central party apparatus had been reduced to 1,493 and a further reduction of 40 percent was announced.

28. Pravdin, 1974.

29. Interview with Molotov in Chuev, 1990: 53. Nikolaeva, 1969: 40-41 wrote that when Lenin once received a letter addressed to "The Chairman of the Politburo...Comrade Lenin," he struck out the word Chairman and inscribed the note: "does not exist." Going by the notes Zinovev jotted down for a book on Lenin he was preparing to write, Lenin did indeed chair Politburo sessions; see Zinovev, 1989: 174. In his memoirs Khrushchev has told that when in the 1930s he had to present reports at meetings of the Politburo, the chair was always taken by Molotov, premier of the Soviet Union from 1930 to 1941; see Talbott, 1970: 58.

30. Kliment Voroshilov as quoted by Vasetskii, 1988: 623.

31. Talbott, 1970: 325.

32. Barsukov, "Eshche vperedi...", 1989.

33. Molotov interview in Chuev, 1990: 53.

34. Ligachev, "Iz vospominanii", 1991, No. 6.

35. "Plenum TsK KPSS - Oktiabr 1987 goda...", 1989; Tatu/Vernet, 1987; "Die Atomwaffen...", 1987.

36. "Plenum TsK KPSS - Oktiabr 1987 goda...", 1989: 284-85.

37. Lenin, "Predlozhenie plenumu kasaiushcheesia reglamenta Politbiuro", in Lenin, 1970: 327.

38. Petrov, 1968: 389.

39. Ligachev, "Iz vospominanii", 1991, No. 3 and No. 4.

40. Photographic copies of two of these extracts have been reproduced in Petrov, 1968: 389.

41. Medvedev, 1987: 14, discussing the meeting of 10 March 1985 where Gorbachev was nominated to be the new General Secretary, comes to the same conclusion.

42. Van den Berg, 1984: 311-313.

43. See Medvedev/Medvedev, 1977: 173-4; Aksiutin, *Nikita...*, 1989.

44. Schapiro, 1955: 262n.

45. Bajanow, 1931: 92.

46. Bajanow, 1931: 38.

47. See "Deiatelnost Tsentralnogo Komiteta Partii v dokumentakh", *Izvestiia TsK KPSS* 1989, No. 12 to 1990, No. 7.

48. Nikolaeva, 1969: 36-7.

49. Albrecht, 1941: 151.

50. See *Izvestiia*, 19 September 1990: 3 for the text of a secret excerpt from the December 1937 Protokol, and Petrov, 1968: 294, 296 for the other two.

51. Petrov, 1968: 389.

52. See Aksenov, 1990: 103.

53. Aksenov, 1990: 100-101; see also Khrushchev in his 'secret speech' and memoirs, *The Anti-Stalin Campaign...*, 1956: 82; Talbott, 1970: 299.

54. Interview with L. I. Brezhnev, 15 June 1973. See *Radio Free Europe Research, USSR: Party*, 15 June 1973 (1818). *Pravda*, 14 May 1957; G. I. Shitarev in *Voprosy Istorii KPSS* 1964, No. 7, p. 37: at least once weekly; Talbott, 1974: 25; *XXIV S''ezd KPSS, Stenograficheskii Otchet*, t. I, Moscow 1971: 119. On 16 August 1979, Vitali Ruben, then Chairman of the Council for Nationalities of the Supreme Soviet and member of the Central Committee, informed a group including Archie Brown and John Löwenhardt that the Politburo at that time met twice weekly, on Tuesdays and Thursdays. He said that the Party Secretariat met once a week on Wednesdays. See Brown, 1979, and Brown, 1980. In the light of the official figures provided by Brezhnev, Ruben's announcement seemed rather exaggerated unless he meant to say that occasionally, when the Politburo for example did not succeed in concluding its agenda in one weekly meeting, it continued its meeting two days later.

55. *Pravda*, 25 February 1976 and 24 February 1981.

56. "Voprosy, rassmotrennye...", 1990. See also Löwenhardt, 1988, where this author claimed that 24 percent of the Politburo sessions went unreported.

57. Bajanow, 1931: 92, 96.

58. Bajanow, 1931: 46-7.

59. For other illustrations, see a.o. Talbott, 1970: 58-61; Emelianov, 1967: 103-7; Ligachev, 1991, No. 4: 6; and Kaiser, 1976: 378.

60. Shabad, 1973. Brezhnev spoke at the November 1978 Plenum of the Central Committee, see *Pravda*, 28 November 1978.

61. Alexander Iakovlev, the Commission's chairman, later criticized certain aspects of its work, in particular the incomplete investigation of the Kirov assassination. See *Pravda*, 28 January 1991, and Tolz, 1991.

62. *BBC Summary of World Broadcasts* SU/0808 C1/10-11.

63. *BBC Summary of World Broadcasts* SU/0808 C1/15.

64. See Van den Berg, 1984.

65. Aksenov, 1990: 94.

66. Shitarev, 1964: 37.

67. Talbott, 1970: 281, 282.

68. Ligachev, 1991, No. 3: 5.

69. *Report on the USSR*, Vol. 2, No. 7 (16 February 1990), p. 31.

70. "M. S. Gorbachev otvechaet...", 1989.

71. Pravdin, 1974.

72. "O vozmeshchenii...", 1975; Smith, 1976: 28.

73. Ligachev, 1991, No. 5: 5; "Spetsialnym postanovleniem...", 1991.

74. Rigby in Löwenhardt, 1982: 2-3.

Part II

8

The Politburo Dissected

Profile

The Politburo over a period of 856 months was a group of 130 individuals. It wasn't just a commanding height in history and an interesting study in terms of its operations, it was also a specific set of people who varied from each other in many ways. This chapter considers the 130 members from many different perspectives, such as age, nationality, and levels of education, so as to present a multifaceted profile of the group over time. George K. Schueller did this for full members in 1951, as did T. H. Rigby in 1971.[1] This study includes candidate members and uses recent Soviet sources to arrive at the variety of categories highlighted in the tables. All tables include members and candidates.

The raw data on which the tables are based are presented in the Background List (Chapter 10), where the 130 individuals are organized alphabetically according to surname, and the entries below each name normally provide more specific information than that contained in this chapter's tables. For example, a person's first job might be as a worker in the tables but as fitter or machinist in the more complete listing; or agricultural worker in the tables but a shepherd in Chapter 10.

The number of people involved was carefully considered. One man not included, Andrei Bubnov, was omitted because he was appointed only to the October 1917 Politburo. He was never again elected to the Politburo even though he was a member of the Orgburo from 1924 to 1934 and in 1925 served briefly as a member of the Secretariat. He was not included in either this chapter or the Background List. Another person *is* included in both, however, who may not be on many people's Politburo list: E. D. Stasova. In 1919, after the unexpected death of Sverdlov who carried the secretariat in his head, Elena Stasova was named "responsible secretary." She held the Secretariat together by herself until Krestinskii's appointment on 29 November 1919. During that period, specifically from July to September 1919, Stasova functioned as a "temporary" Politburo member, providing liaison between the Secretariat and the Politburo. She was included as a full member.

The data in the following tables have been organized in two basic ways. The first way is to look at the members serving on 1 January every five years beginning with 1920. This method provides 15 data points and clearly shows trends over time. It also shows where trends do not exist as anticipated. The strength of this method is its random time pictures of Politburo individuals, but its unavoidable weakness is the presence of repeaters and the fact that the five-year markers do not capture all the Politburo members. Some 25 of the 130 members (19 percent), all of whom served for short times, are omitted. Thirteen of the 25 were part of the temporary expansion of the Presidium between 16 October 1952 and 6 March 1953. These 13 served only 142 days and did not serve again. The other 12 also served briefly. Overall the average length of tenure for the 25 omitted members was 1.2 years. Six of the ignored group were full members, while 17 were candidates; two of the ignored group were full members for part of the time, and candidate members for part of the time.[2]

The second way in which the data are organized is to consider who the members were at 23 critical dates. These dates pick up a "new" Politburo elected by a "new" Central Committee after a party congress. Some other dates were added to provide a fuller picture (see Background List). A disadvantage of this second method is that repeaters proliferate, even more than in the first method. Voroshilov, for example, is counted nine times, Molotov ten, Stalin 13, and Mikoian 14 times. But very few members are ignored using this method. Only seven of the 130 (5 percent) are omitted: one full member: Nikonov; and six candidates: Bauman, Efremov, Eikhe, Ezhov, Shcherbakov, and Solovev. Between the two methods only three members (2 percent) are left out: Nikonov, Ezhov, and Solovev.

SEX

Despite the ideological rhetoric about gender equality in Soviet socialism, the Politburo for the 71 years studied has been almost entirely masculine in composition. Only three females have ever been members. In 1919, between July and September, by agreement with both the Politburo and the Orgburo, Stasova was accorded a temporary Politburo status. On 29 November

Krestinskii was appointed responsible secretary and Stasova faded out of the Politburo picture. In addition to Stasova, only two women have been members: Ekaterina Furtseva, a candidate member from February 1956 to June 1957 and a full member from June 1957 to October 1961, and Aleksandra Biriukova, who was a candidate member from September 1988 to July 1990. Both women came to prominence during the rule of a "reforming" General Secretary: Khrushchev in one instance and Gorbachev in the other. Three females, with one a "temporary member," in a group of 127 males testifies to the difficulties women have had in reaching high levels in the party apparat.

AGE

The Politburo membership grew older well before the Brezhnev period. Throughout most of the 71-year period under analysis, the Central Committee treated the need for new Politburo members as a matter for the Politburo itself to decide; new members were chosen by existing ones. There thus tended to be a good deal of self-replacement. In addition there was an attempt to tap the pool of people with some revolutionary experience and a tendency to appoint people of similar age to those doing the appointing. The predictable result was a gradual aging. Members in the early years tended to be fairly young, in their thirties and forties, and slowly this age began to creep up. When this was later coupled with the decision to keep as many of the existing Politburo members as possible for as long as possible, as during the Brezhnev years, the word gerontocracy could be correctly used to describe both the Politburo's stagnation and the debacle of three General Secretaries dying within a 28-month period.

Overall, the average age of members increased steadily, with occasional breaks not visible in Table 8.1. For example, there was a break in the aging when Lenin died in 1924, in 1930 when when an older man, Rykov, was replaced by three younger men—Kirov, Kosior, and Ordzhonikidze, and in 1946 when the aged Kalinin died. Nonetheless the table supports an average aging as did the 1951 Schueller and 1971 Rigby studies.

Table 8.1 indicates, for instance, that on 1 January 1920, 50 percent of the total of the eight members were in their thirties and that on that date their average age was 39. The table indicates that the Politburo aged from 1920 through 1980, hitting a high point in the first half of the 1980s, and that this process began to reverse after 1985, revealing the greening effect of younger appointments in the Gorbachev era. The average age, highlighted in Table

Table 8.1
Age Groups
At five-year intervals, percentages

	1920	25	30	35	40	45	50	55	60	65	70	75	80	85	90
30s	50	38	41	14	0	0	0	0	0	0	0	0	0	0	0
40s	50	61	41	57	64	50	17	8	17	24	0	0	4	0	0
50s	0	0	18	29	18	29	58	50	50	41	55	35	13	18	37
60s	0	0	0	0	18	21	17	33	21	29	40	43	39	35	63
70s	0	0	0	0	0	0	8	8	13	6	5	22	39	41	0
80s	0	0	0	0	0	0	0	0	0	0	0	0	4	6	0
AvAge	39	41	42	47	50	52	56	58	58	56	59	63	67	67	60
Total:	8	13	17	14	11	14	12	12	24	17	20	23	23	17	19

Table 8.2
Increases in Average Ages
At five-year intervals, in years

1920	25	30	35	40	45	50	55	60	65	70	75	80	85	90
-	2	1	5	3	2	4	2	0	-2	3	4	4	0	-7

8.2, rose steadily until the plateau from 1955 to 1965, then rose again until 1980. The sharpest decline, as one might expect, occurred after 1985.

Table 8.2 notes that increases were not uniform; that is, they were not the result simply of the same members remaining in place. If that had been true the increments would be evenly spaced and the number in each cell would be five more than the previous number. Some members did remain, but new appointments tapped a similar or even older age group. For a time this small group of bureaucrats acted as though life tenure in their position were normal politics. Comparing the Khrushchev era with the later Brezhnev period is illuminating on this point. Of the men with seats in the 1956 Politburo, 70 percent did not belong five years later. However, those members who were elected to the Politburo on 8 April 1966, after the first party congress under the new Brezhnev regime, were all reelected in 1971 after the 24th Party Congress. As a matter of fact, 12 of the original 19 members elected in April 1966 were still on the Politburo in mid-1980. This is a stultifying retention rate. Twelve of the 23 members with Politburo seats at that date had already been sitting on that body a good 14 years earlier. This excessively high degree of stability—which was a feature of other leading bodies of party and state as well—had not been known in the Politburo previously except for the period when it hardly functioned at all, between 1941 and 1953.

POLITBURO GENERATIONS

These data suggest the possibility of a modest cohort analysis such as that performed on Western nations.[3] Cohort analysis assumes that new generations are reared in a different world from that shared by their parents, and that these differences result in changed values. The differences can be greater access to higher education, new occupational options, or advantages accruing through technological and communication innovations. What the parents have implemented has either succeeded or failed by the time the new generation has reached maturity. Comprehensive reform is more likely following a generational change.

In 1951 Schueller established that all of his group of 27 men had consciously experienced the revolutions of 1917. In 1951, he wrote, nine of the 11 members on the Presidium at that time were born in or before 1901. They had grown up in tsarist Russia, and their political development was in the framework of the struggle against tsarist autocracy. Admittedly these were not the professional revolutionaries of earlier days—the Old Bolsheviks had been decimated by Stalin's purges—but their background was

Table 8.3

Numbers Born in Specific Decades Between 1870 and 1940

At five-year intervals

	1920	25	30	35	40	45	50	55	60	65	70	75	80	85	90
1870s	4	4	3	3	2	2	1	0	0	0	0	0	0	0	0
1880s	4	8	7	6	2	2	2	2	3	1	0	0	0	0	0
1890s	0	1	7	5	7	7	7	5	5	1	1	1	1	0	0
1900s	0	0	0	0	0	3	2	5	12	7	8	9	9	4	0
1910s	0	0	0	0	0	0	0	0	4	8	11	12	9	6	0
1920s	0	0	0	0	0	0	0	0	0	0	0	1	3	6	12
1930s	0	0	0	0	0	0	0	0	0	0	0	0	1	1	7
Total:	8	13	17	14	11	14	12	12	24	17	20	23	23	17	19

Table 8.4
Average Year of Birth
for Selected Dates

Date	Year	Date	Year
25-03-19	1880	16-10-52	1898
05-04-20	1880	06-03-53	1896
16-03-21	1881	27-02-56	1899
03-04-22	1881	29-06-57	1900
26-04-23	1881	31-10-61	1905
02-06-24	1883	08-04-66	1910
01-01-26	1882	09-04-71	1911
19-12-27	1886	05-03-76	1911
13-07-30	1887	03-03-81	1913
10-02-34	1887	06-03-86	1922
22-03-39	1889	02-07-90	1929
01-01-46	1891		

nonetheless very different from that of the generation of leaders that fol-lowed, especially the generation born after 1917 that grew to maturity in the Soviet system.

Looking back at the 71 years of Politburo existence, Schueller's data can be updated. Fifty-three of the 130 members were born before or during 1901. This is 41 percent of the total. In this sense two generations can be discerned: a generation (41 percent) with revolutionary experience followed by a generation (59 percent) of bureaucratic managers. The forward edge of the managerial generation, emerging in the 1980s, suggests the beginnings of a third generation-who might be called the reformers.

The midpoint of the 71 years was 1954-just after the death of Stalin. That 1954 is an arbitrary midpoint is, of course, clear. What may not be so clear is that it may be misleading even to mention a midpoint. Sixty-eight (52 percent) of the members began their Politburo service prior to 1954, but only 48 (37 percent) had completed their service by then. There was, in fact, a considerable overlap by the "revolutionary" generation that went far beyond the arbitrary midpoint. Tables 8.3, 8.4 and 8.5 exhibit this overlap, which did not disappear until almost 1990. The influence of this earlier genera-tion—one unwisely imagined out of the picture—was present on the Polit-buro far in excess of the 41 percent figure just mentioned. People of Schueller's revolutionary generation (those born before or during 1901)

Table 8.5

Members Born During or Before 1901

At five-year intervals

	1920	25	30	35	40	45	50	55	60	65	70	75	80	85	90
	8	13	17	14	11	12	10	8	9	2	1	1	2	1	0
Total	8	13	17	14	11	14	12	12	24	17	20	23	23	17	19

Table 8.6

Slav Percentage of Politburo Membership

At five-year intervals

	1920	25	30	35	40	45	50	55	60	65	70	75	80	85	90
	50	54	71	64	64	71	67	83	79	82	80	87	78	82	89

would be at least 16 years of age during the revolutionary year of 1917. They could be found in the Politburo even in 1985.

JOINING THE PARTY

The average age at which Politburo members joined the Bolshevik faction of the RSDWP or the later communist party was 22. The youngest was Boris Ponomarev, who joined the party in 1919 at the age of 14. The Politburo member who was the oldest to join the Bolsheviks was Trotskii; he was 38 years old in 1917.

There does not seem to be a peak year for joining the party. The years when Politburo members joined the Bolshevik faction or party range from 1903 to 1966, when Masliukov joined at the age of 29. The most popular years for joining were: 1903 and 1904; 1917 and 1919; 1939 and 1940; and 1944. These years are somewhat misleading because one cannot expect many Politburo members to have joined the party after, let us say, the mid-1960s for simple age reasons and because the party as a whole grew in the course of the years. Nevertheless, the dates indicate major events in the life of the party: the founding years of the Bolshevik faction (1903 and 1904); the October revolution and Civil War (1917 and 1919); and victory in World War II (1944). The years 1939 and 1940 are harder to explain. On the negative side, no Politburo member joined the party between 1931 and 1939 except for Sokolov, who joined in 1937. The period from 1931 to 1939 is the widest gap in the years Politburo members joined the party. During these years there was a stop on new memberships for some time. The surge in 1939 may indicate a feeling that the worst of the terror was over, a sense of relief occasioned by the Nazi-Soviet nonaggression pact or relaxed entry requirements.

Additionally, Politburo members took various numbers of years to move from becoming a member of the CPSU to membership on the Politburo. The average length of service prior to Politburo membership was under 28 years, and the range extended from Ponomarev's 53 years to the mere two years of Trotskii.

In terms of age, the youngest members to be elected to the Politburo were Andreev, Bukharin and Mikoian, who were all 30 years old at the time of their first service. The Politburo members who were the oldest at the time of appointment were Tikhonov and Sokolov at age 73. The youngest at the time of release from Politburo service were Syrtsov and Sokolnikov at 37, while the oldest to be released was Kuznetsov at 85 years of age.

Table 8.7
Percentage of Russians in the Politburo
for Selected Dates

Date	%	Date	%
25-03-19	38	16-10-52	78
05-04-20	38	06-03-53	64
16-03-21	50	27-02-56	76
03-04-22	75	29-06-57	67
26-04-23	55	31-10-61	56
02-06-24	46	08-04-66	53
01-01-26	50	09-04-71	57
19-12-27	59	05-03-76	59
13-07-30	53	03-03-81	68
10-02-34	47	06-03-86	74
22-03-39	64	02-07-90	79
01-01-46	69		

GEOGRAPHICAL AND NATIONAL ORIGINS

Slavs have dominated the Politburo. In itself this is to be expected because the majority of the Soviet population is Slav. The three Slav republics (Russia, Belorussia, and the Ukraine) are the most populous. The Slav "weight" in the Politburo increased significantly over time. Table 8.6 depicts the Slav percentage (Russians, Ukrainians, Belorussians, and Poles) of all members over time.

The Slav dominance also included the party Secretariat. However, at lower levels of party organization, other nationalities were better represented. Jerry Hough calculated that for the 139 secretaries of provincial party organizations in June 1966, 47 percent were Russians and 24 percent were Ukrainian, with the remaining 20 percent distributed over 24 nationalities.[4] Such calculations, of course, do not imply non-Slav control in areas where other nationalities have the top position. Often the first secretary of an organization represented the local nationality, while real power lay in the hands of a Slav second secretary.

Table 8.8
Geographical Origin of Politburo Members
At five-year intervals

	1920	25	30	35	40	45	50	55	60	65	70	75	80	85	90
Armenia	0	0	1	1	1	1	1	1	1	1	0	0	0	0	0
Azerbaijan	0	0	0	0	0	0	0	0	0	0	0	0	1	1	0
Belorussia	1	0	0	0	0	0	0	0	1	1	2	2	1	0	1
Finland	0	0	0	0	0	0	0	0	0	0	0	0	0	0	0
Georgia	1	1	1	2	2	2	2	0	1	1	1	0	1	1	1
Kazakhstan	0	0	0	0	0	0	0	0	0	0	1	1	1	1	0
Kirghizia	0	1	0	0	0	0	0	0	0	0	0	0	0	0	0
Latvia	0	1	2	1	0	0	0	0	1	0	1	1	1	0	0
Poland	0	1	1	1	0	0	0	0	0	0	0	0	0	0	0
Russia	5	7	8	4	5	8	6	6	12	9	9	13	15	12	13
Tajikistan	0	0	0	0	0	0	0	0	0	0	0	0	0	0	1
Ukraine	1	2	4	5	3	3	3	5	6	4	5	5	2	2	3
Uzbekistan	0	0	0	0	0	0	0	0	1	1	1	1	1	0	0
Totals	8	13	17	14	11	14	12	12	24	17	20	23	23	17	19

Table 8.9
Nationalities of All Politburo Members
At five-year intervals

	1920	25	30	35	40	45	50	55	60	65	70	75	80	85	90
Armenian	0	0	1	1	1	1	1	1	1	1	0	0	0	0	0
Azerbaijani	0	0	0	0	0	0	0	0	0	0	0	0	1	1	0
Belorussian	0	0	0	0	0	0	0	0	1	1	2	2	1	0	1
Finnish	0	0	0	0	0	0	0	0	1	0	0	0	0	0	0
Georgian	1	1	1	2	2	2	2	0	1	1	1	1	1	0	1
Jewish	3	4	1	1	1	1	1	1	0	0	0	0	0	0	0
Kazakh	0	0	0	0	0	0	0	0	0	0	1	1	1	1	0
Latvian	0	1	2	1	0	0	0	0	0	0	0	0	0	0	1
Polish	0	1	1	1	0	0	0	0	1	0	0	0	0	0	0
Russian	3	6	9	6	7	10	8	8	15	11	11	15	16	13	15
Ukrainian	1	0	2	2	0	0	0	2	3	2	3	3	1	1	1
Uzbek	0	0	0	0	0	0	0	0	1	1	1	1	1	0	0
Totals	8	13	17	14	11	14	12	12	24	17	20	23	23	17	19

Table 8.10
Numbers of Various Nationalities on the Politburo

	Number	Percentage
Armenian	2	2
Azerbaijani	2	2
Belorussian	4	3
Finnish	1	1
Georgian	5	4
Jewish	5	4
Kazakh	1	1
Latvian	6	5
Polish	2	2
Russian	89	68
Ukrainian	11	8
Uzbek	2	2
Total	**130**	**102**

However, it was not simply a Slav presence—it was a Russian dominance, visible in Table 8.7. Except for the first two years of Politburo life and 1924 and 1934, Russians dominated.

Considering the place of birth (the "geographical origin") of Politburo members, it appears that by no means all of the republics have been "represented" in Politburo membership. The majority of members were born in the Russian Federation (RFSFR), while the Ukraine ran a distant second. Other republics were represented sporadically, often by the membership of just one individual, such as the Armenian Mikoian. Some republics did not make the list at all. On the other hand, the inclusion of Finland and Poland may come as a surprise. Finland's brief place was due to Kuusinen, while Poland's was due to Dzerzhinskii and Kosior. Note in Table 8.8 that the trends visible in the beginning continued through 1990 and that there was slightly more diverse "representation" in the first half of the Politburo's life than there was in the second half.

The next two tables refer to the Politburo member's nationality rather than the geographical origin. Again one can see that the overwhelming majority of the members are Russians, while the Ukrainians are again a distant second. There does not appear to have ever been an attempt to correct this imbalance. Rather, the CPSU holding the multinational empire together was staffed and led mainly by Russians. The result is that many of the larger as well as the smaller nationalities have never had a "turn" in the Politburo.

Another striking fact visible in Table 8.9 is the relatively strong presence of Jewish members in the first half of Politburo history and their absence in the second half. This reflects the significance of Jewish socialists in the early years of the 20th century among revolutionary activists. Both Zionism and revolutionary politics were relief valves for Jews oppressed by the anti-Semitic policies of the tsars. The presence of Jews in leadership positions in the early years of Soviet power provides ammunition to right-wing ideologues who seek to blame Soviet misfortunes on the early Jewish presence. The Jewish presence on the Politburo did not last long. Of the five Jewish members, only one overlapped the midpoint of 1954: Lazar Kaganovich, who departed the Politburo in June 1957. The others had disappeared quite early: Kamenev, Sokolnikov, Zinovev and Trotskii were eliminated in the second half of the 1920s and later murdered. After Kaganovich, no Jews have been members of the Politburo.

Georgians appear relatively well represented in Table 8.10. Stalin, Ordzhonikidze and Beriia were the three Georgians in the first half; Ordzhonikidze committed suicide in 1937, and Beriia was executed in 1953. Mzhavanadze, a Georgian candidate member, was ousted in 1972, and Edvard Shevardnadze continued the Georgian representation through 1990.

Tables 8.9 and 8.10 demonstrate that the representation of nationalities other than Russian and Ukrainian was marginal, depending on the success of a very small number of individuals. The Ukrainian representation has been consistent and at times surprisingly large, as in the period 1960 through 1975. Note also that Latvians were present throughout Politburo history, while Estonians and Lithuanians were absent. Kazakhs and Muslims from Central Asia and Azerbaidzhan were not well represented.

CANDIDATE AND FULL MEMBERSHIP

One might imagine that the candidate or nonvoting group was an apprenticeship for later full voting membership, but such was definitely not always the case. Candidate membership on the Soviet Politburo did not necessarily lead to full membership. Of all the candidates serving between 1919 and 1990, 42 never made full membership—nearly one third of the total membership.

Nor should it be imagined that all full members served as candidates. Actually 32 full members (including Stasova) never served in that

Table 8.11
Candidates Who Never Made Full Member

Bagirov	Frunze	Pegov	Shcherbakov
Bauman	Iazov	Petrovskii	Shepilov
Biriukova	Iudin	Ponomarev	Sokolnikov
Demichev	Kabanov	Pospelov	Sokolov
Dolgikh	Kalnberzin	Postyshev	Solovev
Dzerzhinskii	Kiselev	Primakov	Syrtsov
Efremov	Lukianov	Pugo	Talyzin
Eikhe	Masherov	Puzanov	Tevosian
Eltsin	Mzhavanadze	Rashidov	Uglanov
Ezhov	Patolichev	Razumovskii	Vlasov
			Vyshinskii
			Zverev

Table 8.12
Full Members Who Never Served as Candidates

Andrianov	Krestinskii	Medvedev	Shkiriatov
Aristov	Kriuchkov	Mikhailov	Stalin
Beliaev	Kuibyshev	Nikonov	Stasova
Chesnokov	Kulakov	Pelshe	Suslov
Grechko	Kuusinen	Rykov	Tomskii
Gromyko	Lenin	Ryzhkov	Trotskii
Ignatev	Ligachev	Saburov	Voroshilov
Ivashko	Malyshev	Shelepin	Zaikov

Table 8.13
Full Members Who Then Became Candidates

Kamenev	Melnikov
Korotchenko	Pervukhin
Kuznetsov	Ponomarenko

Table 8.14
Size of Birthplace
At five-year intervals, percentages

	1920	25	30	35	40	45	50	55	60	65	70	75	80	85	90
Villages	25	46	76	71	73	64	58	75	75	59	65	70	65	53	53
Cities	75	54	24	29	27	36	42	25	25	41	35	30	35	47	47
Totals	8	13	17	14	11	14	12	12	24	17	20	23	23	17	19

Table 8.15
Father's Job/Education
At five-year intervals, percentages

	1920	25	30	35	40	45	50	55	60	65	70	75	80	85	90
Worker	13	15	47	57	64	57	67	67	67	59	50	39	39	41	42
Peasant	25	23	24	14	18	14	8	8	29	29	35	48	43	35	26
Agric. Worker	0	8	6	7	0	0	0	0	0	0	0	0	0	0	0
Engineer	13	8	0	0	0	0	0	0	0	0	0	0	0	0	0
White Collar	50	46	24	21	18	29	25	25	4	12	15	13	17	24	16
Unknown	0	0	0	0	0	0	0	0	0	0	0	0	0	0	16
Totals	8	13	17	14	11	14	12	12	24	17	20	23	23	17	19

Table 8.16
Father's Job/Education - Total

Category	Number	Percentage
Worker	49	38
Peasant	45	35
Agric. Worker	2	2
Engineer	1	1
White Collar	30	23
Unknown	3	2
Total	**130**	**101**

subordinate position; instead they were appointed to the Politburo without that putative apprenticeship.

Six members were full members first and then became candidate members. Obviously, a clear majority of 80 members out of the total of 130 did not pass through the expected route of candidate membership first and then full or voting status. The remaining 50 members, however, are still the largest group.

TOWN AND COUNTRY ORIGINS

The size of the place of birth of Politburo members is not always easy to establish, for sources vary in the precision with which they indicate that size; often they do not discriminate between the size at the time the person was born and the current size. In support of the analysis of social origins of Politburo members in the next section, it is nevertheless of some importance to know whether they were born in urban or rural environments. The members and candidate members have therefore been classified in two broad categories: those born in cities and those who were born in villages, where the category villages includes so-called settlements (*poselki*). The group as a whole is characterized by a preponderance of persons born in rural settings (59 percent) over those born in an urban environment (41 percent).

Table 8.14 demonstrates that, in terms of birthplace size, the Politburo members did not fall into any anticipated pattern of developing nations. As expected, early members of the Politburo, drawn from the group of

Table 8.17
Member's First Job/Education
At five-year intervals, percentages

	1920	25	30	35	40	45	50	55	60	65	70	75	80	85	90
Worker	13	15	47	57	45	50	33	42	58	59	60	48	43	29	32
Agric. Worker	0	8	6	7	9	7	8	17	13	12	10	13	9	12	0
Soldier	0	0	0	0	0	0	8	0	4	6	5	9	4	6	0
Engineer	0	0	6	0	9	7	8	0	4	6	10	9	13	18	37
White Collar	88	77	41	36	36	36	42	42	21	18	15	22	30	35	32
Totals	8	13	17	14	11	14	12	12	24	17	20	23	23	17	19

Table 8.19
Member's Last Job/Education
At five-year intervals, percentages

	1920	25	30	35	40	45	50	55	60	65	70	75	80	85	90
Worker	13	23	53	64	45	36	33	25	8	6	0	0	0	0	0
Engineer	0	0	0	0	9	14	25	33	33	47	45	39	39	47	53
White Collar	88	77	41	36	45	50	42	33	46	41	45	48	52	41	42
Engin./WhCollr	0	0	6	0	0	0	0	8	13	6	10	13	9	12	5
Totals	8	13	17	14	11	14	12	12	24	17	20	23	23	17	19

Table 8.18
Member's First Job/Education, Total

Category	Number	Percentage
Worker	55	42
Agric. Worker	10	8
Soldier	3	2
Engineer	16	12
White Collar	46	35
Total	130	99

Gorbachev counted as White Collar; Rudzutak and Kirichenko counted as Agricultural Worker in this and previous table.

revolutionary leaders, showed a strong connection to cities. In 1920 six of the eight members were from urban areas; only two (Trotskii and Kalinin) were from villages. But this did not last for long. What is most interesting is that rural backgrounds, after a steep rise during the 1920s, maintain a high percentage up to 1990.

SOCIAL ORIGINS

In this section we analyze the social type of the Politburo members. All members were observed in three stages: their family background, their situation in the initial period of their educational and occupational career, and their educational and occupational achievements before entering the Politburo. The following social types were used and applied to the fathers of the Politburo members and to the members themselves: Agricultural Workers; Workers; Soldiers; Engineers; and other white-collar people, listed as White Collar. This is a sociological approach, merging information on employment and education. For further details the reader is referred to the comments in the Background List.

The strong representation of the rural sector in Politburo membership, noted above, is further illustrated when the occupation of the fathers is considered. Table 8.15 describes the father's social type. Not only do worker and peasant categories dominate, but the numbers do not fit expected patterns. If we imagine the Soviet Union to be an industrializing country after its revolution, we would expect a high level of intelligentsia in the beginning as revolutionary leaders assumed power. This would decline and the peasant

Table 8.20
Member's Last Job/Education, Total

Category	Number	Percentage
Worker	14	11
Agric. Worker	1	1
Engineer	41	32
White Collar	65	50
Engin./WhCollar	9	7
Total	130	101

Table 8.21
Percentage of Members with Manual Work(er) Background

	Fa	Fi	La
25-03-19	38	13	13
05-04-20	38	13	13
16-03-21	38	13	13
03-04-22	50	20	20
26-04-23	55	27	27
02-06-24	46	23	23
01-01-26	64	36	36
19-12-27	76	53	53
13-07-30	74	54	54
10-02-34	73	60	60
22-03-39	82	54	45
01-01-46	69	54	38
16-10-52	83	68	14
06-03-53	79	50	21
27-02-56	83	59	18
29-06-57	91	70	8
31-10-61	94	74	6
08-04-66	84	73	0
09-04-71	86	77	0
05-03-76	90	68	0
03-03-81	81	54	0
06-03-86	84	47	0
02-07-90	82	6	0

category should increase, but by the 1940s and 1950s the peasants should have been replaced by workers. By the 1960s and 1970s we might expect a rise again in intelligensia and white-collar occupations as the new elite began to replicate itself. But this pattern does not emerge from the table. What does emerge is that the share of white-collar background present in the beginning tends to go down rather than up during the life of the Politburo. Since 1930 until the present day the majority of Politburo members come from workers' or peasants' families.

Insofar as the two major categories are concerned, both worker and peasant were "respectable" categories throughout much of the Politburo's life. The large increase in worker backgrounds in the 1960s is expectable, but not the number of peasant backgrounds in 1975 and 1980. Table 8.16 shows the data in lump form rather than stretched out over the years, and underscores the worker/peasant background.

Looking at the Politburo member's first job and/or occupation provides another dimension of the same question. Table 8.17 shows the pattern. The table indicates that, as expected, the first job in many cases was that of a worker, usually a factory worker. It is interesting that this group grows until well into the Brezhnev period. Twenty-one of the 46 white collars were first "employed" as party activists (see Background List). This early significance of party activism as the first employment might have been expected because of the strong influence of the "revolutionary generation." A large number of that group could be said to have devoted their lives to the party. The low significance of the white-collar and the engineering categories is understandable since this table considers only first jobs. As will be visible when education is considered, engineering was a very popular form of education for Politburo members; but, again, first jobs would not necessarily show that strong engineering education. Many Politburo members were educated as working adults. Seeing the data in lump form (Table 8.18) does not change the analysis.

The following two tables (8.19 and 8.20) show the social profile of members before they entered the Politburo. As noted in the comment to the Background List, political-administrative jobs were not taken into account. The tables refer to the highest "nonpolitical" jobs attained by the later Politburo members. Higher education at a party school was taken into account. We noted, while analyzing the family background and initial status in society, that the Politburo remained surprisingly "proletarian" for a long period of its history. In tables 8.19 and 8.20 this conclusion is moderated. In terms of the status that they had reached, the later Politburo members had generally risen above the "lower" strata of society.

Table 8.22
Highest Educational Attainment
At five-year intervals, percentages

	1920	25	30	35	40	45	50	55	60	65	70	75	80	85	90
Higher Educ.	63	54	29	14	18	29	17	17	42	35	45	48	52	41	42
Tech.-Engineer	0	0	6	0	9	14	25	33	33	47	45	39	39	47	53
Tech.-Eng/High	0	0	0	0	0	0	0	8	13	6	10	13	9	12	5
Seminary	13	8	12	14	18	14	17	8	4	6	0	0	0	0	0
Secondary	13	15	0	0	9	7	8	8	0	0	0	0	0	0	0
Technical	0	0	6	14	0	0	0	0	0	0	0	0	0	0	0
Primary	13	23	41	43	36	29	25	17	8	6	0	0	0	0	0
Self-educated	0	0	6	14	9	7	8	8	0	0	0	0	0	0	0
Totals	8	13	17	14	11	14	12	12	24	17	20	23	23	17	19

Table 8.23
Educational Level Attained

	Numbers	Percentages
Higher	56	43
Technical-Engineering	42	32
Technical-Engineering/Higher	8	6
Seminary	2	2
Secondary	5	4
Technical	3	2
Primary	11	8
Self-educated	3	2
Totals	**130**	**99**

The reader is further invited to compare Tables 8.16, 18, and 20 which clarify the upward mobility of the Politburo taken as a collective from 1919 to 1990. The members came from worker and peasant families; they initially became workers or acquired a white-collar status; and they rose to the position of white-collar employees or engineers.

In Table 8.21 this process is further highlighted from a different angle. The categories give percentages of people engaged in manual work or with corresponding educations. The percentage corresponds to the percentage of people of the social type of Peasants, Agricultural Workers, Workers, and Soldiers. "Fa" refers to the father's job/education. "Fi" refers to the first job/education of the member. "La" refers to the last job/education of the member before Politburo membership. For the third category on 2 July 1990 only full members of the Politburo were taken into account.

EDUCATION

The Bolshevik seizure of power in 1917 was largely the work of urbanites, and when educational attainments are considered, it is evident that the early leaders were urban intellectuals. Five of the early group that had studied at a university had also fought with Lenin: Bukharin, Kamenev, Krestinskii, Rykov, and Zinovev. These men were all executed as traitors in the 1930s, which explains the drop in this category during that decade. The changes after the death of Stalin in 1953 led to increases in this category again. It has remained significant, as Table 8.22 demonstrates.

The large increase in technical-engineering backgrounds accurately reflects not only the rapid industrialization process but also the way in which the command economy became an integral part of the ideology. A technical-engineering education was a good background for party advancement. The category takes on its own almost as large a share as all other forms of higher education taken together. In Soviet politics, the technical subjects fulfilled roughly the same traditional function as a law degree in many Western countries. The seminary category includes the Georgian Stalin and the Armenian Mikoian, a background that did not necessarily indicate an interest in theology. In Georgia and Armenia, many seminary students saw the seminary as the only route to higher education. The "secondary only" category is low throughout the period and fades out entirely in 1965. The "primary only" category shows a strong presence until the 1950s, when it begins to fade. The strong primary showing lasted longer than might have been expected, indicative perhaps of Stalin's preference for less educated colleagues.

Schueller in 1951 ascertained that his group of 27 members had a variety of occupations prior to becoming politicians. Ten seemed to have been industrial workers. Others included two lawyers (Lenin and Krestinskii), one tertiary teacher (Voznesenskii), and a shepherd. In 1971 Rigby showed that the number of members who had at one time been manual workers was surprisingly high. Of these the majority had worked in industry; only Polianskii and Shelest had worked on a state farm. Between 1951 and 1971 there was a marked increase in the number of people who had management experience in an enterprise or a ministry connected to the economy. In 1951 there were two, but in 1971 there were ten, eight of whom had fairly long-term managerial experience-three for a period of eight to 12 years and five for a period of three to five years.

CAUSE OF DEATH

In the period March 1919 to July 1990, 86 members (67 percent) died, mostly from natural causes. Of these 86 deaths, 63 (73 percent) were natural deaths while 23 (27 percent) were unnatural in the sense of execution or suicide. These figures need comparison with those of other revolutionary regimes rather than with stable governments.

Table 8.24
Deaths of Politburo Members
in inclusive five-year periods

	1920-1925	26-30	31-35	36-40	41-45	46-50	51-55	56-60	61-65	66-70	71-75	76-80	81-85	86-90	Total
Executed	0	0	1	16	0	1	1	1	0	0	0	0	0	0	20
Suicide	0	0	0	2	0	0	0	0	0	0	0	1	0	0	3
Natural	2	1	1	0	1	2	3	3	2	8	9	8	13	10	63
Totals	2	1	2	18	1	3	4	4	2	8	9	9	13	10	86

The period of the Stalin purges is clearly reflected in the death causes: as Table 8.24 makes clear, the natural deaths peaked near the end of the time span, while the unnatural deaths peaked in the period of 1936 to 1940 at the height of the terror. Prior to 6 March 1953, 28 members (including Stalin) died: eight naturally and 20 unnaturally. After Stalin, beginning with Beriia's execution on 23 December 1953, there were 58 deaths: 55 were natural while three were unnatural (Beriia, Bagirov, and Kulakov).

Natural deaths for Politburo members were thus not unusual. The only five-year span in which none occur is from 1936 to 1940, when the unnatural deaths peaked. The reason fewer natural deaths occurred in the early years was the relative youth of the members. Table 8.24 demonstrates that the watershed for unnatural deaths was not the death of Stalin in 1953, but earlier in the 1936-40 time span. Executions and suicides account for 27 percent of all deaths—too high for a supposedly civilized society, but too low to suggest a permanent purge.

If 1954 is used as a midpoint, the 31 members who died in or before that year were on average 52 years old at the time of their death. For the 55 who died after 1954, the average age was 75 years. The overall average age of death was 67 years. Prior to 1955, or in the first half of Politburo life, there were 19 assassinations or executions, two suicides, and ten natural deaths: 68 percent unnatural, 32 percent natural. The latter half of Politburo life, post-1954, shows but one execution (Bagirov in 1956), one probable suicide (Kulakov in 1978) and 53 natural deaths: 4 percent unnatural, 96 percent natural. Clearly, therefore, the second half was a far less threatening environment than the first half. But a caveat is in order: Table 8.24 indicates that the great divide in terms of unnatural deaths was 13 years before Stalin died, despite the executions of Voznesenksii, Beriia, and Bagirov.

NATURE OF MEMBER'S ACTIVITIES WHILE ON THE POLITBURO

Being a member of the Politburo was a part-time position in the sense that everyone had some other function(s) to perform. Those functions can be summarized as Party, State, Military, Police, or Trade Union. They can also be summarized as being of a central, republic, or local level. Tables 8.25 and 8.26 describe this, measured at important dates in Politburo history. When a person combined two or three types of jobs, each position was then counted as either one half or one third in both tables.

Table 8.25

Percentage of Members According to Branches of Work

	Party	State	Military	Police	Trade Union
25-03-19	19	63	19		
05-04-20	25	63	13		
16-03-21	31	50	19		
03-04-22	28	48	13		10
26-04-23	36	45	9		9
02-06-24	27	46	15	4	8
01-01-26	32	50	7	4	7
19-12-27	47	41	6		6
13-07-30	40	53	7		
10-02-34	33	60	7		
22-03-39	36	36	9	9	9
01-01-46	29	64	2	4	
16-10-52	43	51		3	3
06-03-53	25	71		4	
27-02-56	47	47	6		
29-06-57	71	25	4		
31-10-61	63	31			6
08-04-66	63	32			5
09-04-71	62	29		5	5
05-03-76	64	27	5	5	
03-03-81	66	25	5	5	
06-03-86	53	37	5	5	
02-07-90	39	45	5	5	

It is obvious from Table 8.25 that most Politburo member activity was either involved with party affairs or with state administration. Of the two claims on a member's time, it was usually the state administration that won the toss until 1927. During the early Stalin years the party sometimes gained somewhat, but in the years of high Stalinism the state kept the upper hand. This picture is strengthened if the police and military are added to the state. Police and military officials were people's commissars and ministers-state officials. Beginning in 1956, the party took the lion's share until the point just before the 28th Party Congress in 1990, when once again the state administration surpassed the party in terms of member's time.

Table 8.26 shows that "representatives" of central institutions always had the upper hand in the Politburo. But there was variation. Central institutions

Table 8.26
Level of Work
for selected dates, percentages

	Central	Republic	Local
25-03-19	81	0	19
05-04-20	81	0	19
16-03-21	81	0	19
03-04-22	85	0	15
26-04-23	80	12	7
02-06-24	87	6	6
01-01-26	86	7	7
19-12-27	68	18	15
13-07-30	60	23	16
10-02-34	77	13	10
22-03-39	86	5	9
01-01-46	88	8	4
16-10-52	83	10	7
06-03-53	86	11	4
27-02-56	79	18	3
29-06-57	56	29	15
31-10-61	50	50	0
08-04-66	63	37	0
09-04-71	62	33	5
05-03-76	64	27	9
03-03-81	59	32	9
06-03-86	68	21	11
02-07-90	89	5	0

prevailed strongly until 1957, although during the early Stalin years republic and local organs did a little better. Under Khrushchev and Brezhnev a change is visible-the republic and local share is clearly improved. Under Gorbachev the central institutions regain their former preponderance. Note that there is a parallel between conclusions from tables 8.25 and 8.26. They suggest roughly that there were two periods in the history of the Politburo. Under Lenin, Stalin and Gorbachev, state organs and central institutions did well or even very well. Under Khrushchev and Brezhnev, both the party and republic-local institutions were better represented. These conclusions gain interest when we look back to Table 8.7, which gives the share of Russians in the Politburo. It grew during the period of Stalin and Gorbachev and was (relatively) low under Khrushchev and Brezhnev.

ARMY AND SECURITY POLICE

Army and security police backgrounds became an issue in 1973. The Western press made much of Politburo changes during that year, speculating that the additions of the Minister for Defense and the head of the KGB to the list of top decision makers indicated essential changes in the nature of the Politburo. Iuri Andropov, for example, who had been chairman of the Committee for State Security (KGB) since 1967 and a candidate member of the Politburo since June 1967, was promoted to full membership in April 1973. Ministers of state security and internal affairs Ignatev and Beriia were the last cases, in 1952-53, of comparable officials to earn the status of full Politburo members. Alexander Shelepin had been KGB head between 1958 and 1961, but he did not join the Presidium until November 1964. Shelepin made his political career largely within the communist youth organization, the Komsolmol. One of the more recent full members, Edvard Shevardnadze had been Minister of the Interior of the Georgian republic for seven years before becoming party Secretary for Georgia in 1972, and he did not join the Politburo until November 1978, when he was appointed a candidate member. So Andropov's promotion was different; he was still head of the KGB when appointed to the Politburo.

The other appointment, Andrei Grechko, who was both a military man and the Minister of Defense, seemed less unusual. Earlier, Trotskii (1918-25), Frunze (1925), Voroshilov (1925-40), Stalin (1941-47), Bulganin (1947-49 and 1953-55) and Zhukov (Minister of Defense, 1955-57) had been simultaneously Minister for Defense and Politburo member. But before Grechko only Zhukov had climbed to the top via a military career. Dmitri Ustinov, who succeeded Grechko in 1976 as Minister for Defense, had come up through the defense and armaments industry rather than the military. He was a civilian who represented the military-industrial complex. Ustinov was promoted to full membership in the Politburo just before Grechko's death in 1976. His successor at the Defense Ministry, Sokolov (1984-87), was again a professional soldier.

Many other Politburo members have had military experience. Chubar, Kaganovich, and Zhdanov all served in the tsarist army, but none of them was an officer. Several members of the Politburo took part in the revolution and the Civil War but mostly as political commissars who superintended the

Table 8.27
Stability of Tenure in the Politburo

Date	Value		Date	Value	
1920	0.00		1956	0.23	
1921	0.13		1957	0.53	
1922	0.13		1958	0.07	
1923	0.05		1959	0.00	
1924	0.18		1960	0.06	
1925	0.04		1961	0.31	
1926	0.54		1962	0.06	
1927	0.07		1963	0.06	
1928	0.00		**Average 1953-63**	**0.16**	
Average 1920-28	**0.13**				
			1964	0.14	
1929	0.12		1965	0.06	
1930	0.18		1966	0.16	
1931	0.00		1967	0.03	
1932	0.08		1968	0.00	
1933	0.00		1969	0.00	
1934	0.12		1970	0.00	
1935	0.11		1971	0.05	
1936	0.00		1972	0.05	
Average 1929-36	**0.08**		1973	0.11	
			1974	0.00	
1937	0.10		1975	0.02	
1938	0.18		1976	0.07	
1939	0.18		1977	0.07	
1940	0.00		1978	0.09	
1941	0.14		1979	0.02	
1942	0.00		1980	0.07	
1943	0.00		1981	0.00	
1944	0.00		1982	0.09	
1945	0.04		**Average 1964-82**	**0.05**	
1946	0.12				
1947	0.00		1983	0.13	
1948	0.04		1984	0.05	
1949	0.04		1985	0.24	
1950	0.00		1986	0.18	
1951	0.00		1987	0.16	
1952	0.29		1988	0.29	
Average 1937-52		**0.07**	1989	0.23	
			Average 1983-89	**0.18**	
1953	0.39				
1954	0.00				
1955	0.04		**Average total**		**0.10**

Note: According to Khrushchev, in October 1952 Stalin formed a small Bureau of nine people within the enlarged Presidium: Beriia, Bulganin, Kaganovich, Khrushchev, Malenkov, Pervukhin, Saburov, Stalin, and Voroshilov. For 31 December 1952 these nine have been used rather than the enlarged group.

officers on behalf of the party and politically educated the lower ranks. During World War II Stalin was not only pemier and party leader but also commander-in-chief, Minister for Defense, and chairman of the State Defense Committee. Zhdanov was in charge of the defense of Leningrad, Khrushchev was a political commissar at various fronts and Voroshilov carried out important missions for the supreme command. Kiril Mazurov, a full member of the Politburo from 1965 to 1978, was wounded early in the war and later played a significant role in organizing partisan resistance in Belorussia. Suslov and Kirilenko were members of military front councils. Brezhnev filled a number of political functions. Between 1941 and 1945 he was deputy head of the Political Administration on the Southern Front, then political commissar of the 18th Army and head of the Political Administration on the Fourth Ukrainian Front. Four members (Iazov, Mzhavanadze, Sokolov, and Zhukov) had a military education.

STABILITY OF TENURE

The final profile refers to the stability of tenure for the 130 members, and it is measured in two ways. Table 8.27 lists years next to a number value derived from the formula: $(B+C)/2A$, where A is the number of Politburo members on 31 December of the previous year, B the number of new members added during the respective year, and C the number of members dropped during that same year. The value equals 1 in the hypothetical case when during a year all members were replaced by an identical number of new members. 0.00, of course, indicates no change at all. Numbers approaching 1, therefore, suggest instability, while numbers nearing 0.00 suggest stagnation. Table 8.27 suggests stability bordering on stagnation for much of the Politburo's life.

The second method of measuring stability of tenure on the Politburo is by means of a mathematical model that measures tenures and turnovers. The model anticipates a regular regression, a regular decay of members such as that occurring in any political group, such as the United States Senate or the British House of Commons. The model compares actual tenure length with expected length and indicates how close or how far off the model and the data are. A few years ago, this model was described in *The American Journal of Political Science* and earlier it was applied to the CPSU Central Committee and full members of the Politburo.[6] Here for the first time the model is applied to all 130 Politburo members.[7]

Table 8.28
Continuous Tenures of Politburo Members
(time in months)

Membership	Expectation	Mean	Split
Candidate pre 05-06-53	38.6	39.1	22/22
Candidate post 05-06-53	45.7	52.9	31/29
Candidate whole period	43.0	47.1	54/50
Full pre 05-06-53	82.7	100.5	21/23
Full post 05-06-53	110.8	103.3	24/24
Full whole period	99.4	101.9	47/45
All pre 05-06-53	68.7	87.8	36/35
All post 05-06-53	110.0	107.3	38/37
All whole period	90.3	97.8	75/71

For analytic purposes the tenures are separated into candidate tenures beginning before 5 March 1953, those beginning after that date, and candidate tenures for the entire period 1919 to 1990. The same thing is then done for full members before considering them all together in the third category.

In Table 8.28 the results are expressed in terms of how many months a member could expect to serve. This period is the model's expectation of continuous service, which should correspond closely to the mean derived from actual observation. The split reveals the number of tenures shorter/longer than that which the model predicted. Ideally, the numbers on both sides of the split should be the same.

When looking at Table 8.28, keep in mind that continuous tenures, expressed in months, are being examined, not members. Because some members had more than one continuous tenure (Kosygin had three), the model is measuring 146 continuous tenures for the 130 members, 104 continuous candidate tenures and 92 continuous full member tenures. Both the mean and the split columns suggest that the Politburo follows the model rather well, indicating similarity to Western political institutions.

The difference between the pre- and post-Stalin figures is a real difference, but it is partly due to the presence in the pre-category of the very brief tenures at the end of the period when the Politburo membership was expanded and then contracted again just before the time division in the table. In October 1952 the CC Plenum following the 19th Party Congress appointed 25 full and 11 candidate members to the Politburo. One day after Stalin's death, on 6 March 1953, this membership was reduced to ten full and four candidate members. The difference represents very brief tenures that somewhat distort the data. Before drawing too strong a conclusion about the pre- and post-Stalin categories, these very brief tenures should be removed. The difference then is still significant, but a bit less so. In addition, however, it needs to be recalled that at the end of the period studied, those in Politburo office on 14 July 1990 had their tenures abruptly terminated, either by the Central Committee or, in the case of Gorbachev and Ivashko, by our decision that 14 July 1990 marked the end of the Politburo as we knew it. This slightly increased the short tenures in the second half but does *not* balance the short tenures at the end of the Stalin era. Even with these caveats, however, the latter half of Politburo history shows considerably longer tenure expectations, especially among full members. Part of this is due to stagnation under Brezhnev, part to the lessened impact of unnatural death in the second half.

One last thing that might be kept in mind when considering Table 8.28 is that candidate and full categories are somewhat apples and oranges—they do not compare well. When they are combined in the "All" category, interpretation as to what is being proven should be conservative. Candidate tenure expectations were considerably shorter than those of full members. As a result the category that mixes them is a less reliable indicator than it appears in the table. In addition, there were more candidate tenures (104) than full tenures (92), which slightly weights the shorter candidate tenures.

These then were the individuals who made up the Politburo between 1919 and 1990. A varied group, overwhelmingly males, of different nationalities even though mainly Russian, various places of birth, and wide differences in education. They tended to be engineers as well as politicians, and far more than one might have thought they had peasant or village backgrounds. Almost always they did better than their fathers. Their Politburo career was in most cases not nasty, brutish and short, but tended to be comparable with tenures in Western institutions.

NOTES TO CHAPTER 8

1. Schueller, 1951; Rigby, "The Soviet Politburo...", 1972.
2. Twenty-one of the 25 were Russian, with one each Ukrainian, Belorussian, Latvian and Armenian. The group is made up of Andrianov, Chesnokov,

Eikhe, Eltsin, Ezhov, Ignatev, Iudin, Kabanov, Kiselev, Melnikov, Mikhailov, Nikonov, Patolichev, Pegov, Puzanov, Shepilov, Shkiriatov, Sokolov, Solovev, Talyzin, Tevosian, Uglanov, Vyshinskii, Zhukov, and Zverev.

3. See, for example, Inglehart, 1977.
4. Hough, 1972: 32.
5. Talbott, 1971: 301.
6. Casstevens/Casstevens, 1989. In 1974 the model was used to measure tenure decay in the Central Committee; see Casstevens/Ozinga, 1974. In 1989 the model was applied to all full Politburo members from 1919 to 1987: Ozinga, Casstevens and Casstevens, 1989.
7. For the computerization behind Table 8.28, the authors are indebted to Harold T. Casstevens II of Miller Lake Research Associates.

9

The Politburo: A Complete List of Its Composition at Selected Dates

Under each date three categories are listed, representing: Full Members, Candidate Members, and New Additions before the next date.

25 March 1919/8th Party Congress

Full Members: Kamenev, Krestinskii, Lenin, Stalin, Trotskii.
Candidate Members: Bukharin, Zinovev, Kalinin.
New Addition: Stasova (full from July 1919; until September 1919).

5 April 1920/9th Party Congress

Full Members: Kamenev, Krestinskii, Lenin, Stalin, Trotskii.
Candidate Members: Bukharin, Zinovev, Kalinin.

16 March 1921/10th Party Congress

Full Members: Zinovev, Kamenev, Lenin, Stalin, Trotskii.
Candidate Members: Bukharin, Kalinin, Molotov.

3 April 1922/11th Party Congress

Full Members: Zinovev, Kamenev, Lenin, Rykov, Stalin, Tomskii, Trotskii.
Candidate Members: Bukharin, Kalinin, Molotov.

26 April 1923/12th Party Congress

Full Members: Zinovev, Kamenev, Lenin (death 21 January 1924), Rykov, Stalin, Tomskii, Trotskii.
Candidate Members: Bukharin, Kalinin, Molotov, Rudzutak.

2 June 1924/13th Party Congress

Full Members: Bukharin, Zinovev, Kamenev, Rykov, Stalin, Tomskii, Trotskii.
Candidate Members: Dzerzhinskii, Kalinin, Molotov, Rudzutak, Sokolnikov, Frunze (death 31 October 1925).

1 January 1926/14th Party Congress

Full Members: Bukharin, Voroshilov, Zinovev (until 23 July 1926), Kalinin, Molotov, Rykov, Stalin, Tomskii, Trotskii (until 23 October 1926).
Candidate Members: Dzerzhinskii (death 20 July 1926), Kamenev (until 23 October 1926), Petrovskii, Rudzutak (full from 23 July 1926), Uglanov.
New Additions: Andreev (candidate from 23 July 1926), Kaganovich (candidate from 23 July 1926), Kirov (candidate from 23 July 1926), Mikoian (candidate from 23 July 1926), Ordzhonikidze (candidate from 23 July 1926 until 3 November 1926), Chubar (candidate from 3 November 1926).

19 December 1927/15th Party Congress

Full Members: Bukharin (until 17 November 1929), Voroshilov, Kalinin, Kuibyshev, Molotov, Rykov, Rudzutak, Stalin, Tomskii.
Candidate Members: Andreev, Kaganovich, Kirov, Kosior, Mikoian, Petrovskii, Uglanov (until 29 April 1929), Chubar.
New Additions: Bauman (candidate from 29 April 1929), Syrtsov (candidate from 21 June 1929).

13 July 1930/16th Party Congress

Full Members: Voroshilov, Kaganovich, Kalinin, Kirov, Kosior, Kuibyshev, Molotov, Rudzutak (until 4 February 1932), Rykov (until 21 December 1930), Stalin.

Candidate Members: Andreev (until 21 December 1930; full from 4 February 1932), Mikoian, Petrovskii, Syrtsov (until 1 December 1930), Chubar.

New Addition: Ordzhonikidze (full from 21 December 1930).

10 February 1934/17th Party Congress

Full Members: Andreev, Voroshilov, Kaganovich, Kalinin, Kirov (death 1 December 1934), Kosior (until 1938?), Kuibyshev (death 25 January 1935), Molotov, Ordzhonikidze (death 18 February 1937), Stalin.

Candidate Members: Mikoian (full from 1 February 1935), Petrovskii, Postyshev (until 14 January 1938), Rudzutak (until 26 May 1937), Chubar (full from 1 February 1935; until 16 June 1938).

New Additions: Zhdanov (candidate from 1 February 1935), Eikhe (candidate from 1 February 1935; until 29 April 1938?), Ezhov (candidate from 12 October 1937), Khrushchev (candidate from 14 January 1938).

22 March 1939/18th Party Congress

Full Members: Andreev, Voroshilov, Zhdanov (death 31 August 1948), Kaganovich, Kalinin (death 3 June 1946), Mikoian, Molotov, Stalin, Khrushchev.

Candidate Members: Beriia (full from 18 March 1946); Shvernik.

New Additions: Voznesenskii (candidate from 21 February 1941; full from 26 February 1947; until 7 March 1949), Malenkov (candidate from 21 February 1941; full from 18 March 1946); Shcherbakov (candidate from 21 February 1941; death 10 May 1945), Bulganin (candidate from 18 March 1946; full from 18 February 1948); Kosygin (candidate from 18 March 1946; full from 4 September 1948).

16 October 1952/19th Party Congress

Full Members: Andrianov, Aristov, Beriia, Bulganin, Voroshilov, Ignatev, Kaganovich, Korotchenko, Kuznetsov, Kuusinen, Malenkov, Malyshev, Melnikov, Mikoian, Mikhailov, Molotov, Pervukhin, Ponomarenko, Saburov, Stalin (death 5 March 1953), Suslov, Khrushchev, Chesnokov, Shvernik, Shkiriatov.

Candidate Members: Brezhnev, Vyshinksii, Zverev, Ignatov, Kabanov, Kosygin, Patolichev, Pegov, Puzanov, Tevosian, Iudin.

6 March 1953

Full Members: Beriia (until 7 July 1953), Bulganin, Voroshilov, Kaganovich, Malenkov, Mikoian, Molotov, Pervukhin, Saburov, Khrushchev.

Candidate Members: Bagirov (until 7 July 1953); Melnikov (until 6 June 1953), Ponomarenko, Shvernik.

New Additions: Kirichenko (candidate from 7 July 1953; full from 12 July 1955), Suslov (full from 12 July 1955).

27 February 1956/20th Party Congress

Full Members: Bulganin, Voroshilov, Kaganovich, Kirichenko, Malenkov, Mikoian, Molotov, Pervukhin, Saburov, Suslov, Khrushchev.

Candidate Members: Brezhnev, Zhukov, Mukhitdinov, Furtseva, Shvernik, Shepilov.

New Addition: Kozlov (candidate from 14 February 1957).

29 June 1957

Full Members: Aristov, Beliaev (until 4 May 1960), Brezhnev, Bulganin (until 5 September 1958), Voroshilov (until 16 July 1960), Zhukov (until 29 October 1957), Ignatov, Kirichenko (until 4 May 1960), Kozlov, Kuusinen, Mikoian, Suslov, Furtseva, Khrushchev, Shvernik.

Candidate Members: Kalnberzin, Kirilenko, Korotchenko, Kosygin (full from 4 May 1960), Mazurov, Mzhavanadze, Mukhitdinov (full from 17 December 1957), Pervukhin, Pospelov.

New Additions: Podgornyi (candidate from 18 June 1958; full from 4 May 1960), Polianskii (candidate from 18 June 1958; full from 4 May 1960), Voronov (candidate from 18 January 1961), Grishin (candidate from 18 January 1961).

31 October 1961/22nd Party Congress

Full Members: Brezhnev, Voronov, Kozlov (until 16 November 1964), Kosygin, Kuusinen (death 15 May 1964), Mikoian, Podgornyi, Polianskii, Suslov, Khrushchev (until 14 October 1964), Shvernik.

Candidate Members: Grishin, Mazurov (full from 26 March 1965), Mzhavanadze, Rashidov, Shcherbitskii (until 13 December 1963; candidate from 6 December 1965).

New Additions: Kirilenko (full from 23 April 1962), Efremov (candidate from 23 November 1962), Shelest (candidate from 13 December 1963; full from 16 November 1964), Shelepin (full from 16 November 1964), Demichev (candidate from 16 November 1964), Ustinov (candidate from 26 March 1965).

8 April 1966/23rd Party Congress

Full Members: Brezhnev, Voronov, Kirilenko, Kosygin, Mazurov, Pelshe, Podgornyi, Polianskii, Suslov, Shelepin, Shelest.

Candidate Members: Grishin, Demichev, Kunaev, Masherov, Mzhavanadze, Rashidov, Ustinov, Shcherbitskii.

New Addition: Andropov (candidate from 21 June 1967).

9 April 1971/24th Party Congress

Full Members: Brezhnev, Voronov (until 27 April 1973), Grishin, Kirilenko, Kosygin, Kulakov, Kunaev, Mazurov, Pelshe, Podgornyi, Polianskii, Suslov, Shelepin (until 16 April 1975), Shelest (until 27 April 1973), Shcherbitskii.

Candidate Members: Andropov (full from 27 April 1973), Demichev, Masherov, Mzhavanadze (until 18 December 1972), Rashidov, Ustinov.

New Additions: Solomentsev (candidate from 23 November 1971), Ponomarev (candidate from 19 May 1972), Grechko (full from 27 April 1973), Gromyko (full from 27 April 1973), Romanov (candidate from 27 April 1973).

5 March 1976/25th Party Congress

Full Members: Andropov, Brezhnev, Grechko (death 26 April 1976), Grishin, Gromyko, Kirilenko, Kosygin (until 21 October 1980), Kulakov (death 17 July 1978), Kunaev, Mazurov (until 27 November 1978), Pelshe, Podgornyi (until 24 May 1977), Romanov, Suslov, Ustinov, Shcherbitskii.

Candidate Members: Aliev, Demichev, Masherov (death 4 October 1980), Ponomarev, Rashidov, Solomentsev.

New Additions: Kuznetsov (candidate from 3 October 1977), Chernenko (candidate from 3 October 1977; full from 27 November 1978), Tikhonov (candidate from 27 November 1978; full from 27 November 1979), Shevardnadze (candidate from 27 November 1978). Gorbachev (candidate from 27 November 1979; full from 21 October 1980), Kiselev (candidate from 21 October 1980).

3 March 1981/26th Party Congress

Full Members: Andropov (death 9 February 1984), Brezhnev (death 10 November 1982), Gorbachev, Grishin (until 18 February 1986), Gromyko, Kirilenko (until 22 November 1982), Kunaev, Pelshe (death 29 May 1983), Romanov (until 1 July 1985), Suslov (death 25 January 1982), Tikhonov (until 15 October 1985), Ustinov (death 20 December 1984), Chernenko (death 10 March 1985), Shcherbitskii.

Candidate Members: Aliev (full from 22 November 1982), Demichev, Kiselev (death 11 January 1983), Kuznetsov, Ponomarev, Rashidov (death 31 October 1983), Solomentsev (full from 26 December 1983), Shevardnadze (full from 1 July 1985).

New Additions: Dolgikh (candidate from 24 May 1982), Vorotnikov (candidate from 15 June 1983; member from 26 December 1983); Chebrikov (candidate from 26 October 1983; full from 23 April 1985), Ligachev (full from 23 April 1985), Ryzhkov (full from 23 April 1985), Sokolov (candidate from 23 April 1985), Talyzin (candidate from 15 October 1985), Eltsin (candidate from 18 February 1986).

6 March 1986/27th Party Congress

Full Members: Aliev (until 21 October 1987), Vorotnikov, Gorbachev, Gromyko (until 30 September 1988), Zaikov, Kunaev (until 28 January 1987), Ligachev, Ryzhkov, Solomentsev (until 30 September 1988), Chebrikov (until 20 September 1989), Shevardnadze, Shcherbitskii (until 20 September 1989).

Candidate Members: Demichev (until 30 September 1988), Dolgikh (until 30 September 1988), Eltsin (until 18 February 1988), Sliunkov (full from 26 June 1987), Sokolov (until 26 June 1987), Solovev (until 20 September 1989), Talyzin (until 20 September 1989).

New Additions: Iakovlev (candidate from 28 January 1987; full from 26 June 1987), Nikonov (full from 26 June 1987; until 20 September 1989), Iazov (candidate from 26 June 1987), Masliukov (candidate from 18 February 1988; full from 20 September 1989); Razumovskii (candidate from 18 February 1988), Medvedev (full from 30 September 1988), Biriukova (candidate from 30 September 1988), Vlasov (candidate from 30 September 1988), Lukianov (candidate from 30 September 1988), Kriuchkov (full from 20 September 1989), Primakov (candidate from 20 September 1989), Pugo (candidate from 20 September 1989), Ivashko (full from 9 December 1989).

14 July 1990/28th Party Congress

Full Members: Gorbachev, Ivashko, Burokiavichus, Gumbaridze (until 31 January 1991), Gurenko, Dzasokhov, Karimov, Luchinskii, Masaliev (until 25 April 1991), Makhkamov, Movsisian (until 11 December 1990), Mutalibov, Nazarbaev, Niiazov, Polozkov, Prokofev, Rubiks, Semenova, Sillari, Sokolov (until 11 December 1990), Stroev, Frolov, Shenin, Ianaev (until 31 January 1991).

Candidate Members: none.

New Additions: Malofeev (full from 11 December 1990), Pogosian (full from 11 December 1990), Annus (full from 31 January 1991), Amanbaev (full from 25 April 1991), Eremei (full from 25 April 1991), Surkov (full from 25 April 1991).

Note: With the exception of Gorbachev and Ivashko, both of whom had been a member before, these persons have not been included in the Politburo Background List (Chapter 10) because of the fundamental change in the Politburo's character after the 28th Party Congress.

10

Politburo Background List 1919 - 1990

The Politburo Background List includes all members and candidate members of the Politburo up to the 28th Party Congress in July 1990; the 22 new members who on the 14th of that month were elected to the Politburo New Style are not included. The list summarizes the raw data on which the analysis in this book is based in 16 different categories. Several of them require some explanation.

Birth

Date of birth according to the Gregorian calendar; see also the note on dates on one of the first pages of this book.

Death

Date and cause of death. Causes of death:
N - Natural;
E - Executed; also includes death in a prison or camp, or murdered;
S - Suicide.

Party

Year in which the person became a member of the bolshevik faction of the RSDWP, or later communist party. This date is never earlier than 1903 even though many early Politburo members became members of the RSDWP between 1898 and 1903.

Nationality

One source described Ignatev and Polianskii as Ukrainians, other sources as Russians. Kirilina et al. was taken as authoritative, and both men are considered as Russians born in the Ukraine.

Birthplace

gub. = guberniia; obl. = oblast (both: province). If applicable and if known, the name of the location at time of birth is followed by the present name in brackets.

Size

Size of the birthplace at time of birth. "Village" is used for both villages and "poselki," settlements.

Job/education

The categories *Last job/education*, *First job/education*, and *Father's job/education* provide a social type of the person (in two stages) and of his or her family background. Each of these three categories merges information on employment and education into one social characterization. To give an example: if the first job of a person is unknown, but if he is known to have studied at a *tekhnikum* to become a fitter, he has been listed as Worker in the category *First job/education*.

The category *Last job/education* concerns the last occupation / education of the person before Politburo membership. Often, people in this phase of their career were students at an institute or university and had no job. In such cases, of course, our categorization could be based only on their education. Party and administrative positions such as First Secretary or People's Commissar are not counted, but a higher education at a party school is taken into account if it occurred (as it generally did) before entry into the Politburo. This means that the many ministerial and party positions that future members had before they entered the Politburo are not included in our list. The reason is that all members had such high government, state or party positions before they entered the Politburo.

Agricultural workers include "*batraki*," hired hands in the fields, workers on *kolkhozy* and *sovkhozy* and those who studied at agricultural technical schools (*tekhnikumy*) but without further education; *Workers* include artisans, fishermen and those who studied at *rabfaki* (workers' faculties) and *tekhnikumy* (but with no further education), even if they afterward performed engineering jobs; *Soldiers* are rank-and-file soldiers; *Engineers* include those who studied at (technological) *instituty* (including in the agronomical sphere), even if they afterward performed work of skilled workers. *White collar* is a broad category covering those with various forms of secondary and higher education or occupations, but excluding engineers. It includes such people as teachers, clerical workers, army officers, businessmen, medical personnel, shop workers, landowners and nobility. Whether an education was completed has been disregarded. Note: The occupations of the fathers of A. V. Vlasov, A. I. Lukianov and G. P. Razumovskii are unknown.

In the category *Last job/education* the final educational level attained by a person has been noted in a systematic way and divided into types: *Self-educated, Primary,*

Secondary, Technical, Seminary, Technical-engineering and *Higher. Technical* education includes *rabfaki* and *tekhnikumy* (the training to be a medical orderly has also been included in this category). *Technical-engineering* education includes higher technological education (mainly at *instituty*). *Higher* education includes all other forms of higher education, including higher vocational trainings of various kinds (commercial, military, administrative, economic, nontechnological departments of polytechnical schools, etc.). The categories do not assume completion of the education.

Position(s)

This category refers to offices held while the individual was serving on the Politburo/Presidium. The information given is the type of job held on the dates that mark a new Politburo/Presidium selected by a new Central Committee immediately after a party congress. The period covers the congresses from the 8th in 1919 to the 27th in 1986. We added 1 January 1946 as a date of measurement between the 18th and 19th congresses because of the very long time between them. In March 1953 and June 1957 the Presidium was so drastically changed that it was useful to add these events as separate dates. No new Presidium was elected after the 21st Party Congress in 1959. The situation just before the 28th Party Congress was also added. Thus, the dates are:

25 March 1919	13 July 1930	31 October 1961
5 April 1920	10 February 1934	8 April 1966
16 March 1921	22 March 1939	9 April 1971
3 April 1922	1 January 1946	5 March 1976
26 April 1923	16 October 1952	3 March 1981
2 June 1924	6 March 1953	6 March 1986
1 January 1926	27 February 1956	2 July 1990
19 December 1927	29 June 1957	

Positions have been characterized as *C*entral, *R*epublic or *L*ocal; and as *P*arty, *S*tate, *M*ilitary, *P*olice, or *Tr*ade Union. Only the main positions were considered. Membership on the Orgburo, Presidential Council, and Defense Council was not included. Local jobs include positions at the levels of *oblasti, krai,* and cities. The Council for Labor and Defense was considered a state rather than military organ. The Bureau of the Central Committee for the Russian Federation and the Central Asian Bureau of the Central Committee were treated as republic rather than central positions. The North Western Bureau of the Central Committee was treated as a local position. Voroshilov, Pervukhin and Saburov had no official positions on 6 March 1953, but were placed in the category of St/Ce on the basis of the positions they occupied from 15 March onward. Vlasov was without a specific position on 2 July 1990. Seven members' Politburo service did not cross one of the date markers and are marked with an asterisk (*).

Sources

The main sources used for the compilation of this list have been A. A. Kirilina, et al., *Politbiuro, Orgbiuro, Sekretariat TsK RKP(b) - VKP(b) - KPSS. Spravochnik.* Moscow (Politizdat) 1990; and "Sostav rukovodiashchikh organov Tsentralnogo Komiteta Partii - Politbiuro (Prezidiuma), Orgbiuro, Sekretariata TsK (1919-1990)", *Izvestiia TsK KPSS* 1990, No. 7, 69-136. A variety of other sources, listed in the bibliography, was used to complete the picture.

Name	**Aliev, Geidar Alievich**
Birth	10-05-1923
Death	
Party	1945
Full on	22-11-82
Full off	21-10-87
Candidate on	05-03-76
Candidate off	22-11-82
Nationality	Azerbaijani
Birthplace	Nakhichevan
Size	City
Last job/education	White Collar (Higher)
First job/education	White Collar (pedagogical tekhnikum/Post in Nakhichevan NKVD)
Father's job/education	Worker
Positions	5-3-76: Pa/Re; 3-3-81: Pa/Re; 6-3-86: St/Ce

Name	**Andreev, Andrei Andreevich**
Birth	30-10-1895
Death	05-12-1971; N
Party	1914
Full on	04-02-32
Full off	05-10-52
Candidate on	23-07-26
Candidate off	21-12-30
Nationality	Russian
Birthplace	Kuznetsovo, Sychevsk uezd, Smolensk gub.
Size	Village
Last job/education	Worker (primary)
First job/education	Worker (factory/primary)
Father's job/education	Worker
Positions	19-12-27: Pa/Lo; 13-07-30: Pa?/Lo?; 10-02-34: St/Ce; 22-03-39: Pa/Ce; 1-1-46: Pa+St/Ce

Name	**Andrianov, Vasilii Mikhailovich**
Birth	??-03-1902
Death	03-10-1978; N
Party	1926
Full on	16-10-52
Full off	06-03-53
Nationality	Russian
Birthplace	Village later named Krasnyi Oktiabr, Briansk gub. (Kaluga obl.)
Size	Village
Last job/education	White Collar (higher/Moscow State University)
First job/education	Worker (railroad/tailor/rabfak of an institute)
Father's job/education	Peasant
Position	16-10-52: Pa/Lo

Name	**Andropov, Iurii Vladimirovich**
Birth	15-06-1914
Death	09-02-1984; N
Party	1939
Full on	27-04-73
Full off	09-02-84
Candidate on	21-06-67
Candidate off	27-04-73
Nationality	Russian
Birthplace	Nagutskaia Station, Stavropol krai
Size	Village
Last job/education	White Collar (higher/university/higher party school)
First job/education	Worker (telegraph/sailor/tekhnikum)
Father's job/education	Worker (railroad)
Positions	9-4-71: Po/Ce; 5-3-76: Po/Ce; 3-3-81: Po/Ce

Name	**Aristov, Averkii Borisovich**
Birth	04-11-1903
Death	11-07-1973; N
Party	1921
Full on	16-10-52, 29-06-57
Full off	06-03-53, 17-10-61
Nationality	Russian
Birthplace	Krasnyi Iar, Astrakhan gub.
Size	City
Last job/education	Technical-engineering (polytechnical institute, engineer)
First job/education	Worker (fishing industry)
Father's job/education	Worker (fisherman)
Positions	16-10-52: Pa/Ce; 29-6-57: Pa/Ce+Re

Name	**Bagirov, Mir Dzhafar Abbasovich**
Birth	17-09-1895
Death	26-05-1956; E
Party	1917
Candidate on	06-03-53
Candidate off	07-07-53
Nationality	Azerbaijani
Birthplace	Kuba, Baku gub.
Size	City
Last job/education	White Collar (higher/marxism-leninism courses)
First job/education	White Collar (teacher village school/ pedagogical courses)
Father's job/education	Peasant
Position	6-3-53: Pa/Re+Lo

Name	**Bauman, Karl Ianovich**
Birth	29-08-1892
Death	14-10-1937; E
Party	1907
Candidate on	29-04-29
Candidate off	26-06-30
Nationality	Latvian
Birthplace	Vilkia volost, Latvia
Size	Village
Last job/education	White Collar (higher)
First job/education	White Collar (clerk at bank/Kiev Commercial Institute)
Father's job/education	Peasant
Positions	*

Name	**Beliaev, Nikolai Ilich**
Birth	01-02-1903
Death	28-10-1966; N
Party	1921
Full on	29-06-57
Full off	04-05-60
Nationality	Russian
Birthplace	Kuterem, Birsk uezd, Ufa gub. (Bashkiria)
Size	Village
Last job/education	White Collar (higher/economical institute/manager)
First job/education	White Collar (party activist/higher primary school)
Father's job/education	Peasant
Position	29-6-57: Pa/Ce+Re

Name	**Beriia, Lavrentii Pavlovich**
Birth	29-03-1899
Death	23-12-1953; E
Party	1919
Full on	18-03-46
Full off	07-07-53
Candidate on	22-03-39
Candidate off	18-03-46
Nationality	Georgian
Birthplace	Merkhauli, Sukhumi raion, Abkhazia
Size	Village
Last job/education	Engineer (technical-engineering)
First job/education	Engineer (office clerk, mailman/higher technical education)
Father's job/education	Peasant
Positions	22-3-39: Po/Ce; 1-1-46: St+Po/Ce; 16-10-52:St/Ce; 6-3-53: St+Po/Ce

Name	**Biriukova, Aleksandra Pavlovna**
Birth	25-02-1929
Death	
Party	1956
Candidate on	30-09-88
Candidate off	14-07-90
Nationality	Russian
Birthplace	Russkaia Zhuravka, Verkhnemamonsk raion, Voronezh obl.
Size	Village
Last job/education	Engineer (technical-engineering)
First job/education	Engineer (textile institute/supervisor in fabric works)
Father's job/education	Peasant
Position	2-7-90: St/Ce

Name	**Brezhnev, Leonid Ilich**
Birth	19-12-1906
Death	10-11-1982; N
Party	1931
Full on	29-06-57
Full off	10-11-82
Candidate on	16-10-52, 27-02-56
Candidate off	06-03-53, 29-06-57
Nationality	Russian
Birthplace	Kamenskoe (Dneprodzerzhinsk)
Size	Village
Last job/education	Engineer (technical-engineering)
First job/education	Worker (land reclamation)
Father's job/education	Worker
Positions	16-10-52: Pa/Ce; 27-2-56: Pa/Ce+Re; 29-6-57; Pa/Ce; 31-10-61: Pa+St/Ce+Re; 8-4-66: Pa/Ce; 9-4-71:Pa/Ce; 5-3-76: Pa/Ce; 3-3-81: Pa+St/Ce

Name	**Bukharin, Nikolai Ivanovich**
Birth	09-10-1888
Death	15-03-1938; E
Party	1906
Full on	02-06-24
Full off	17-11-29
Candidate on	25-03-19
Candidate off	02-06-24
Nationality	Russian
Birthplace	Moscow
Size	City
Last job/education	White Collar (higher/party activist)
First job/education	White Collar (party activist/university education)
Father's job/education	White Collar (teacher)
Positions	25-3-19: Pa/Ce; 5-4-20: Pa/Ce; 16-3-21: Pa/Ce; 3-4-22: Pa/Ce; 26-4-23: Pa/Ce; 2-6-24: Pa/Ce; 1-1-26: Pa/Ce; 19-12-27: Pa/Ce

Name	**Bulganin, Nikolai Aleksandrovich**
Birth	11-06-1895
Death	24-02-1975; N
Party	1917
Full on	18-02-48
Full off	05-09-58
Candidate on	18-03-46
Candidate off	18-02-48
Nationality	Russian
Birthplace	Nizhnii Novgorod
Size	City
Last job/education	White Collar (secondary)
First job/education	White Collar (post in Cheka/secondary education)
Father's job/education	White Collar (clerk)
Positions	16-10-52: St/Ce; 6-3-53: St/Ce; 27-2-56: St/Ce; 29-6-57: St/Ce

Name	**Chebrikov, Viktor Mikhailovich**
Birth	27-04-1923
Death	
Party	1944
Full on	23-04-85
Full off	20-09-89
Candidate on	26-12-83
Candidate off	23-04-85
Nationality	Russian
Birthplace	Dnepropetrovsk
Size	City
Last job/education	Engineer (technical-engineering)
First job/education	Soldier
Father's job/education	Worker
Position	6-3-86: Po/Ce

Name	**Chernenko, Konstantin Ustinovich**
Birth	24-09-1911
Death	10-03-1985; N
Party	1931
Full on	27-11-78
Full off	10-03-85
Candidate on	03-10-77
Candidate off	27-11-78
Nationality	Russian
Birthplace	Bolshaia Tes (Novoselov raion, Krasnoiarsk krai)
Size	Village
Last job/education	White Collar (higher/pedagogical institute)
First job/education	Agricultural Worker (farm hand)
Father's job/education	Peasant
Position	3-3-81: Pa/Ce

Name	**Chesnokov, Dmitrii Ivanovich**
Birth	07-11-1910
Death	17-09-1973; N
Party	1939
Full on	16-10-52
Full off	06-03-53
Nationality	Russian
Birthplace	Kaplino, Staro-Oskolskii raion, Kursk (Belgorod) obl.
Size	Village
Last job/education	White Collar (higher/doctor of philosophy/ journalist)
First job/education	White Collar (pedagogical institute/teacher)
Father's job/education	Peasant
Position	16-10-52: Pa/Ce

Name	**Chubar, Vlas Iakovlevich**
Birth	22-02-1891
Death	26-02-1939; E
Party	1907
Full on	01-02-35
Full off	16-06-38
Candidate on	03-11-26
Candidate off	01-02-35
Nationality	Ukrainian
Birthplace	Fedorovka, Ekaterinoslav gub. (Dnepropetrovsk obl.)
Size	Village
Last job/education	Worker (technical)
First job/education	Worker
Father's job/education	Peasant
Positions	19-12-27: St/Re; 13-7-30: St/Re; 10-2-34: St/Ce

Name	**Demichev, Petr Nilovich**
Birth	03-01-1918
Death	
Party	1939
Candidate on	16-11-64
Candidate off	30-09-88
Nationality	Russian
Birthplace	Pesochnaia (Kirov, Kaluga obl.)
Size	Village
Last job/education	Engineer (technical-engineering/chemistry teacher)
First job/education	Worker (tekhnikum)
Father's job/education	Worker
Positions	8-4-66: Pa/Ce; 9-4-71: Pa/Ce; 5-3-76: St/Ce; 3-3-81: St/Ce; 6-3-86: St/Ce

Name	**Dolgikh, Vladimir Ivanovich**
Birth	05-12-1924
Death	
Party	1942
Candidate on	24-05-82
Candidate off	30-09-88
Nationality	Russian
Birthplace	Ilanskii (Krasnoiarsk krai)
Size	City
Last job/education	Engineer (technical-engineering/managing director)
First job/education	White Collar (officer Soviet army)
Father's job/education	Worker (railroad)
Position	6-3-86: Pa/Ce

Name	**Dzerzhinskii, Feliks Edmundovich**
Birth	11-09-1877
Death	20-07-1926; N
Party	1903
Candidate on	02-06-24
Candidate off	20-07-26
Nationality	Polish
Birthplace	Dzerzhinovo Estate, Oshmianskii uezd, Vilensk gub. (Minsk obl.)
Size	Village
Last job/education	White Collar (secondary/party activist)
First job/education	White Collar (party activist/secondary education)
Father's job/education	White Collar (Polish gentry)
Positions	2-6-24: St+Po/Ce; 1-1-26: St+Po/Ce

Name	**Efremov, Leonid Nikolaevich**
Birth	07-06-1912
Death	
Party	1941
Candidate on	23-11-62
Candidate off	29-03-66
Nationality	Russian
Birthplace	Voronezh
Size	City
Last job/education	Engineer (technical-engineering)
First job/education	Engineer (head of tractor repair shop/agricultural institute)
Father's job/education	Worker
Positions	*

Name	**Eikhe, Robert Indrikovich**
Birth	12-08-1890
Death	04-02-1940; E
Party	1905
Candidate on	01-02-35
Candidate off	29-04-38
Nationality	Latvian
Birthplace	Avotyn Farmstead, Doblensk uezd, Kurland gub. (Latvia)
Size	Village
Last job/education	Worker (blacksmith/primary)
First job/education	Agricultural Worker (primary)
Father's job/education	Agricultural Worker
Positions	*

Name	**Eltsin, Boris Nikolaevich**
Birth	01-02-1931
Death	
Party	1961
Candidate on	18-02-86
Candidate off	18-02-88
Nationality	Russian
Birthplace	Butka, Talitskii raion, Sverdlovsk obl.
Size	Village
Last job/education	Engineer (technical-engineering/managing director)
First job/education	Engineer (polytechnical institute)
Father's job/education	Peasant
Position	6-3-86: Pa/Lo

Name	**Ezhov, Nikolai Ivanovich**
Birth	??-04-1895
Death	04-02-1940; E
Party	1917
Candidate on	12-10-37
Candidate off	10-03-39
Nationality	Russian
Birthplace	St. Petersburg
Size	City
Last job/education	Worker (self-educated)
First job/education	Worker
Father's job/education	Worker
Positions	*

Name	**Frunze, Mikhail Vasilevich**
Birth	02-02-1885
Death	31-10-1925; N?
Party	1904
Candidate on	02-06-24
Candidate off	31-10-25
Nationality	Russian (mother Russian, father 'Moldavian')
Birthplace	Pishpek (Frunze), Kirgizia
Size	City
Last job/education	White Collar (higher/party activist)
First job/education	White Collar (party activist/economic dept. polytechnical institute)
Father's job/education	White Collar (military medical orderly)
Position	2-6-24: Mi/Ce

Name	**Furtseva, Ekaterina Alekseevna**
Birth	07-12-1910
Death	24-10-1974; N
Party	1930
Full on	29-06-57
Full off	17-10-61
Candidate on	27-02-56
Candidate off	29-06-57
Nationality	Russian
Birthplace	Vishnii Volochek, Tver gub.
Size	City
Last job/education	Engineer/White Collar (technical-engineering [chemical institute]/higher [party school])
First job/education	Worker (weaver)
Father's job/education	Worker
Positions	27-2-56: Pa/Ce+Lo; 29-6-57: Pa/Ce+Lo

Name	**Gorbachev, Mikhail Sergeevich**
Birth	02-03-1931
Death	
Party	1952
Full on	21-10-80
Full off	August 1991 (Central Committee dissolved)
Candidate on	27-11-79
Candidate off	21-10-80
Nationality	Russian
Birthplace	Privolnoe, Krasnogvardeisk raion, Stavropol krai
Size	Village
Last job/education	White Collar (higher/lawyer/economic department)
First job/education	White Collar/Agricultural Worker (Machine Tractor Station/secondary)
Father's job/education	Peasant
Positions	3-3-81: Pa/Ce; 6-3-86: Pa/Ce; 2-7-90: Pa+St/Ce

Name	**Grechko, Andrei Antonovich**
Birth	17-10-1903
Death	26-04-1976; N
Party	1928
Full on	27-04-73
Full off	26-04-76
Nationality	Ukrainian
Birthplace	Golodaevka (Kuibyshevo, Rostov obl.)
Size	Village
Last job/education	White Collar (higher/army officer)
First job/education	Soldier
Father's job/education	Peasant
Position	5-3-76: Mi/Ce

Name	Grishin, Viktor Vasilevich
Birth	18-09-1914
Death	
Party	1939
Full on	09-04-71
Full off	18-02-86
Candidate on	18-01-61
Candidate off	09-04-71
Nationality	Russian
Birthplace	Serpukhov, Moscow gub.
Size	City
Last·job/education	White Collar (higher/higher party school)
First job/education	Worker (railroad/tekhnikum)
Father's job/education	Worker (railroad)
Positions	31-10-61: Tr/Ce; 8-4-66: Tr/Ce; 9-4-71: Pa/Lo; 5-3-76: Pa/Lo; 3-3-81: Pa/Lo

Name	Gromyko, Andrei Andreevich
Birth	18-07-1909
Death	02-07-1989; N
Party	1931
Full on	27-04-73
Full off	30-09-88
Nationality	Russian
Birthplace	Starye Gromyki (Viatkovsk raion, Gomel obl.)
Size	Village
Last job/education	White Collar (higher/doctor of economic sciences/scientific secretary)
First job/education	White Collar (clerk in archives of local newspaper/economical institute)
Father's job/education	Peasant
Positions	5-3-76: St/Ce; 3-3-81: St/Ce; 6-3-86: St/Ce

Name	**Iakovlev, Aleksandr Nikolaevich**
Birth	02-12-1923
Death	
Party	1944
Full on	26-06-87
Full off	14-07-90
Candidate on	28-01-87
Candidate off	26-06-87
Nationality	Russian
Birthplace	Korolevo (Iaroslavl raion, Iaroslavl obl.)
Size	Village
Last job/education	White Collar (higher/doctor of history)
First job/education	White Collar (army officer)
Father's job/education	Peasant
Position	1-7-90: Pa/Ce

Name	**Iazov, Dmitrii Timofeevich**
Birth	08-11-1923
Death	
Party	1944
Candidate on	26-06-87
Candidate off	14-07-90
Nationality	Russian
Birthplace	Iazovo (Okoneshnikovo raion, Omsk obl.)
Size	Village
Last job/education	White Collar (higher/military academy)
First job/education	White Collar (army officer)
Father's job/education	Peasant
Position	1-7-90: Mi/Ce

Name	**Ignatev, Semen Denisovich**
Birth	14-09-1904
Death	27-11-1983; N
Party	1926
Full on	16-10-52
Full off	06-03-53
Nationality	Russian
Birthplace	Karlovka, Elizavetgrad uezd, Kherson gub.
Size	Village
Last job/education	White Collar (higher/industrial academy)
First job/education	Worker
Father's job/education	Peasant
Position	16-10-52: Po?/Ce

Name	**Ignatov, Nikolai Grigorevich**
Birth	16-05-1901
Death	14-11-1966; N
Party	1924
Full on	29-06-57
Full off	17-10-61
Candidate on	16-10-52
Candidate off	06-03-53
Nationality	Russian
Birthplace	Stanitsa Tishanskaia (Nekhaev raion, Volgograd obl.)
Size	Village
Last job/education	White Collar (higher/marxism-leninism courses)
First job/education	Worker (carpenter)
Father's job/education	Worker
Positions	16-10-52: Pa/Ce; 29-6-57: Pa/Lo

Name	**Iudin, Pavel Fedorovich**
Birth	07-09-1899
Death	10-04-1968; N
Party	1918
Candidate on	16-10-52
Candidate off	06-03-53
Nationality	Russian
Birthplace	Apraksino, Nizhegorod gub. (Gorkii obl.)
Size	Village
Last job/education	White Collar (higher/doctor of philosophy)
First job/education	Worker (lathe operator)
Father's job/education	Peasant
Position	16-10-52: Pa?/Ce

Name	**Ivashko, Vladimir Antonovich**
Birth	28-10-1932
Death	
Party	1960
Full on	09-12-89
Full off	August 1991 (Central Committee dissolved)
Nationality	Ukrainian
Birthplace	Poltava
Size	City
Last job/education	Engineer (technical-engineering/teacher at mining institute)
First job/education	Engineer (mining institute)
Father's job	Worker
Position	2-7-90: St/Re

Name	**Kabanov, Ivan Grigorevich**
Birth	03-02-1898
Death	02-07-1972; N
Party	1917
Candidate on	16-10-52
Candidate off	06-03-53
Nationality	Russian
Birthplace	Usole (Perm obl.)
Size	Village
Last job/education	Engineer (technical-engineering)
First job/education	Worker
Father's job/education	Worker
Position	16-10-52: St/Ce

Name	**Kaganovich, Lazar Moiseevich**
Birth	22-11-1893
Death	25-07-1991; N
Party	1911
Full on	13-07-30
Full off	29-06-57
Candidate on	23-07-26
Candidate off	13-07-30
Nationality	Jewish
Birthplace	Kabany, Chernobyl uezd, Kiev gub.
Size	Village
Last job/education	Worker (self-educated)
First job/education	Worker (shoe factory)
Father's job/education	Worker
Positions	19-12-27: Pa/Re; 13-7-30: Pa/Ce+Lo; 10-2-34: Pa/Ce+Lo; 22-3-39: St/Ce; 1-1-46: St/Ce; 16-10-52: St/Ce; 6-3-53: St/Ce; 27-2-56: St/Ce

Name	**Kalinin, Mikhail Ivanovich**
Birth	19-11-1875
Death	03-06-1946; N
Party	1903
Full on	01-01-26
Full off	03-06-46
Candidate on	25-03-19
Candidate off	01-01-26
Nationality	Russian
Birthplace	Verkhniaia Troitsa, Korchev uezd, Tver gub.
Size	Village
Last job/education	Worker (primary)
First job/education	Worker (lathe operator)
Father's job/education	Peasant
Positions	25-3-19: St/Ce; 5-4-20: St/Ce; 16-3-21: St/Ce; 3-4-22: St/Ce; 26-4-23: St/Ce; 2-6-24: St/Ce; 1-1-26: St/Ce; 19-12-27: St/Ce; 13-7-30: St/Ce; 10-2-34: St/Ce; 22-3-39: St/Ce; 1-1-46: St/Ce

Name	**Kalnberzin(sh), Ian Edvardovich**
Birth	17-09-1893
Death	04-02-1986; N
Party	1917
Candidate on	29-06-57
Candidate off	17-10-61
Nationality	Latvian
Birthplace	Katlakalna volost, Riga uezd, Latvia
Size	Village
Last job/education	White Collar (higher/Institute of Red Professors)
First job/education	Worker (Riga docks)
Father's job/education	Worker
Position	29-6-57: Pa/Re

Name	**Kamenev (Rozenfeld), Lev Borisovich**
Birth	18-07-1883
Death	25-08-1936; E
Party	1903
Full on	25-03-19
Full off	18-12-25
Candidate on	01-01-26
Candidate off	23-10-26
Nationality	Jewish
Birthplace	Moscow
Size	City
Last job/education	White Collar (higher/party activist)
First job/education	White Collar (party activist/university)
Father's job/education	Engineer
Positions	25-3-19: St/Lo; 5-4-20: St/Lo; 16-3-21: St/Lo; 3-4-22: St/Lo; 26-4-23: St/Ce+Re+Lo; 2-6-24: St/Ce+Re+Lo; 1-1-26: St/Ce

Name	**Khrushchev, Nikita Sergeevich**
Birth	17-04-1894
Death	11-09-1971; N
Party	1918
Full on	22-03-39
Full off	14-10-64
Candidate on	14-01-38
Candidate off	22-03-39
Nationality	Russian
Birthplace	Kalinovka, Kursk gub.
Size	Village
Last job/education	White Collar (higher/industrial academy)
First job/education	Agricultural Worker (shepherd)
Father's job/education	Worker (miner)
Positions	22-3-39: Pa/Re+Lo; 1-1-46: Pa/Re+Lo; 16-10-52: Pa/Ce+Lo; 6-3-53: Pa/Ce; 27-2-56: Pa/Ce+Re; 29-6-57: Pa/Ce+Re; 31-10-61: Pa+St/Ce+Re

Name	**Kirichenko, Aleksei Illarionovich**
Birth	25-02-1908
Death	28-12-1975; N
Party	1930
Full on	12-07-55
Full off	04-05-60
Candidate on	07-07-53
Candidate off	12-07-55
Nationality	Ukrainian
Birthplace	Chernobaevka (Belozersk raion, Kherson obl.)
Size	Village
Last job/education	Engineer (technical-engineering/agronomy)
First job/education	Agricultural Worker/Worker (farm hand/railroad)
Father's job/education	Worker
Positions	27-2-56: Pa/Re; 29-6-57: Pa/Re

Name	**Kirilenko, Andrei Pavlovich**
Birth	08-09-1906
Death	12-05-1990; N
Party	1931
Full on	23-04-62
Full off	22-11-82
Candidate on	29-06-57
Candidate off	17-10-61
Nationality	Russian
Birthplace	Alekseevka, Voronezh gub. (Belgorod obl.)
Size	Village
Last job/education	Engineer (technical-engineering)
First job/education	Worker (fitter and electrician/miner)
Father's job/education	Worker
Positions	29-6-57: Pa/Lo; 8-4-66: Pa/Ce; 9-4-71: Pa/Ce; 5-3-76: Pa/Ce; 3-3-81: Pa/Ce

Name	**Kirov (Kostrikov), Sergei Mironovich**
Birth	27-03-1886
Death	01-12-1934; E
Party	1904
Full on	13-07-30
Full off	01-12-34
Candidate on	23-07-26
Candidate off	13-07-30
Nationality	Russian
Birthplace	Urzhum, Viatka gub. (Kirov obl.)
Size	Village
Last job/education	Engineer/White Collar (technical-engineering/ journalist)
First job/education	Engineer (draftsman)
Father's job/education	White Collar
Positions	19-12-27: Pa/Lo; 13-7-30: Pa/Lo; 10-2-34: Pa/Ce+Lo

Name	**Kiselev, Tikhon Iakovlevich**
Birth	12-08-1917
Death	11-01-1983; N
Party	1940
Candidate on	21-10-80
Candidate off	11-01-83
Nationality	Belorussian
Birthplace	Ogorodnia (Dobrushan raion, Gomel obl.)
Size	Village
Last job/education	White Collar (higher/party school/school director)
First job/education	White Collar (teacher)
Father's job/education	Peasant
Position	3-3-81: Pa/Re

Name	**Korotchenko, Demian Sergeevich**
Birth	29-11-1894
Death	07-04-1969; N
Party	1918
Full on	16-10-52
Full off	06-03-53
Candidate on	29-06-57
Candidate off	17-10-61
Nationality	Ukrainian
Birthplace	Pogrebki (Shostka raion, Sumy obl.)
Size	Village
Last job/education	White Collar (higher/marxism-leninism courses)
First job/education	Worker (railroad)
Father's job/education	Peasant
Positions	16-10-52: St/Re; 29-6-57: St/Ce+Re

Name	**Kosior, Stanislav Vikentevich**
Birth	18-11-1889
Death	26-02-1939; E
Party	1907
Full on	13-07-30
Full off	??-??-38
Candidate on	19-12-27
Candidate off	13-07-30
Nationality	Polish
Birthplace	Wegrow (Poland)
Size	Village
Last job/education	Worker (primary)
First job/education	Worker (fitter)
Father's job/education	Worker
Positions	19-12-27: Pa/Ce; 13-7-30: Pa/Re; 10-2-34: Pa/Re

Name	**Kosygin, Aleksei Nikolaevich**
Birth	21-02-1904
Death	18-12-1980; N
Party	1927
Full on	04-09-48, 04-05-60
Full off	05-10-52, 21-10-80
Candidate on	18-03-46, 16-10-52, 29-06-57
Candidate off	04-09-48, 06-03-53, 04-05-60
Nationality	Russian
Birthplace	St. Petersburg
Size	City
Last job/education	Engineer (technical-engineering/textile institute)
First job/education	Soldier
Father's job/education	Worker
Positions	16-10-52: St/Ce; 29-6-57: St/Ce; 31-10-61: St/Ce; 8-4-66: St/Ce; 9-4-71: St/Ce; 5-3-76: St/Ce

Name	**Kozlov, Frol Romanovich**
Birth	18-08-1908
Death	30-01-1965; N
Party	1926
Full on	29-06-57
Full off	16-11-64
Candidate on	14-02-57
Candidate off	29-06-57
Nationality	Russian
Birthplace	Loshchinino (Kasimov raion, Riazan obl.)
Size	Village
Last job/education	Engineer (technical-engineering/polytechnical institute)
First job/education	Worker (textile mill)
Father's job/education	Peasant
Positions	29-6-57: Pa/Lo; 31-10-61: Pa/Ce

Name	**Krestinskii, Nikolai Nikolaevich**
Birth	25-10-1883
Death	15-03-1938; E
Party	1903
Full on	25-03-19
Full off	08-03-21
Nationality	Ukrainian
Birthplace	Mogilev
Size	City
Last job/education	White Collar (higher/party activist)
First job/education	White Collar (party activist/lawyer)
Father's job/education	Teacher
Positions	25-3-19: St/Ce; 5-4-20: Pa+St/Ce

Name	**Kriuchkov, Vladimir Aleksandrovich**
Birth	29-02-1924
Death	
Party	1944
Full on	20-09-89
Full off	14-07-90
Nationality	Russian
Birthplace	Tsaritsyn (Volgograd)
Size	City
Last job/education	White Collar (higher/juridical-diplomatic)
First job/education	Worker
Father's job/education	Worker
Position	2-7-90: Po/Ce

Name	**Kuibyshev, Valerian Vladimirovich**
Birth	06-06-1888
Death	25-01-1935; N?
Party	1904
Full on	19-12-27
Full off	25-01-35
Nationality	Russian
Birthplace	Omsk
Size	City
Last job/education	White Collar (higher/party activist)
First job/education	White Collar (party activist/military medical academy)
Father's job/education	White Collar (army officer)
Positions	19-12-27: St/Ce; 13-7-30: St/Ce; 10-2-34: St/Ce

Name	**Kulakov, Fedor Davydovich**
Birth	04-02-1918
Death	17-07-1978; S?
Party	1940
Full on	09-04-71
Full off	17-07-78
Nationality	Russian
Birthplace	Fitizh (Lgov raion, Kursk obl.)
Size	Village
Last job/education	Engineer (technical-engineering/agricultural institute)
First job/education	Agricultural Worker (agricultural tekhnikum)
Father's job/education	Peasant
Positions	9-4-71: Pa/Ce; 5-3-76: Pa/Ce

Name	**Kunaev, Dinmukhamed Akhmedovich**
Birth	12-01-1912
Death	
Party	1939
Full on	09-04-71
Full off	28-01-87
Candidate on	08-04-66
Candidate off	09-04-71
Nationality	Kazakh
Birthplace	Vernyi (Alma Alta)
Size	City
Last job/education	Engineer (technical-engineering/doctor of technical sciences)
First job/education	Engineer (factory foreman/metallurgical institute)
Father's job/education	White Collar (clerk)
Positions	8-4-66: Pa/Re; 9-4-71: Pa/Re; 5-3-76: Pa/Re; 3-3-81: Pa/Re; 6-3-86: Pa/Re

Name	**Kuusinen, Otto Vilgelmovich**
Birth	04-10-1881
Death	17-05-1964; N
Party	1904
Full on	16-10-52, 29-06-57
Full off	06-03-53, 17-05-64
Nationality	Finnish
Birthplace	Lauka (Finland)
Size	Village
Last job/education	White Collar (higher)
First job/education	White Collar (editor Finnish journal/university)
Father's job/education	Worker (tailor)
Positions	16-10-52: St/Ce+Re; 29-6-57: Pa/Ce; 31-10-61: Pa/Ce

Name	**Kuznetsov, Vasilii Vasilevich**
Birth	13-02-1901
Death	05-06-1990; N
Party	1927
Full on	16-10-52
Full off	06-03-53
Candidate on	03-10-77
Candidate off	25-02-86
Nationality	Russian
Birthplace	Sofilovka, Kostroma gub. (Gorkii obl.)
Size	Village
Last job/education	Engineer (technical-engineering/candidate of technical sciences)
First job/education	Engineer (polytechnical institute)
Father's job/education	Peasant
Positions	16-10-52: Tr/Ce; 3-3-81: St/Ce

Name	**Lenin (Ulianov), Vladimir Ilich**
Birth	22-04-1870
Death	21-01-1924; N
Party	1903
Full on	25-03-19
Full off	21-01-24
Nationality	Russian
Birthplace	Simbirsk (Ulianovsk)
Size	City
Last job/education	White Collar (higher/party activist)
First job/education	White Collar (party activist/lawyer)
Father's job/education	White Collar (school inspector)
Positions	25-3-19: St/Ce; 5-4-20: St/Ce; 16-3-21: St/Ce; 3-4-22: St/Ce; 26-4-23: St/Ce

Name	**Ligachev, Egor Kuzmich**
Birth	29-11-1920
Death	
Party	1944
Full on	23-04-85
Full off	14-07-90
Nationality	Russian
Birthplace	Dubinkino, Chulym raion, Novosibirsk obl.
Size	Village
Last job/education	Engineer/White Collar (technical-engineering/ higher [party school])
First job/education	Engineer (aviation institute)
Father's job/education	Worker
Positions	6-3-86: Pa/Ce; 2-7-90: Pa/Ce

Name	**Lukianov, Anatolii Ivanovich**
Birth	07-05-1930
Death	
Party	1955
Candidate on	30-09-88
Candidate off	14-07-90
Nationality	Russian
Birthplace	Smolensk
Size	City
Last job/education	White Collar (higher/lawyer)
First job/education	Worker
Father's job/education	Unknown
Position	2-7-90: St/Ce

Name	**Malenkov, Georgii Maksimilianovich**
Birth	08-01-1902
Death	14-01-1988; N
Party	1920
Full on	18-03-46
Full off	29-06-57
Candidate on	21-02-41
Candidate off	18-03-46
Nationality	Russian
Birthplace	Orenburg
Size	City
Last job/education	Engineer (technical-engineering)
First job/education	White Collar (secondary/clerk in army)
Father's job/education	White Collar (clerk)
Positions	1-1-46: Pa/Ce; 16-10-52: Pa+St/Ce; 6-3-53: St+Pa/Ce; 27-2-56: St/Ce

Name	**Malyshev, Viacheslav Aleksandrovich**
Birth	16-12-1902
Death	20-02-1957; N
Party	1926
Full on	16-10-52
Full off	06-03-53
Nationality	Russian
Birthplace	Ust-Sysolsk (Syktyvkar, Komi ASSR)
Size	City
Last job/education	Engineer (technical-engineering)
First job/education	Worker (fitter)
Father's job/education	White Collar (teacher)
Position	16-10-52: St/Ce

Name	**Masherov, Petr Mironovich**
Birth	26-02-1918
Death	04-10-1980; N
Party	1943
Candidate on	08-04-66
Candidate off	04-10-80
Nationality	Belorussian
Birthplace	Shirki (Senno raion, Vitebsk obl.)
Size	Village
Last job/education	White Collar (higher/teacher)
First job/education	White Collar (teacher/pedagogical institute)
Father's job/education	Peasant
Positions	8-4-66: Pa/Re; 9-4-71: Pa/Re; 5-3-76: Pa/Re

Name	**Masliukov, Iurii Dmitrievich**
Birth	30-09-1937
Death	
Party	1966
Full on	20-09-89
Full off	14-07-90
Candidate on	18-02-88
Candidate off	20-09-89
Nationality	Russian
Birthplace	Khodzhent (Leninabad), Tadzhikstan
Size	City
Last job/education	Engineer (technical-engineering)
First job/education	Engineer (mechanical institute)
Father's job/education	Worker
Position	2-7-90: St/Ce

Name	**Mazurov, Kirill Trofimovich**
Birth	07-04-1914
Death	19-12-1989; N
Party	1940
Full on	26-03-65
Full off	27-11-78
Candidate on	29-06-57
Candidate off	26-03-65
Nationality	Belorussian
Birthplace	Rudnia-Pribytkovskaia (Gomel raion, Gomel obl.)
Size	Village
Last job/education	White Collar (higher [party school])
First job/education	Worker (supervisor of local road building/ tekhnikum)
Father's job/education	Peasant
Positions	29-6-57: Pa/Re; 31-10-61: Pa/Re; 8-4-66: St/Ce; 9-4-71: St/Ce; 5-3-76: St/Ce

Name	**Medvedev, Vadim Andreevich**
Birth	29-03-1929
Death	
Party	1952
Full on	30-09-88
Full off	14-07-90
Nationality	Russian
Birthplace	Mokhonkovo, Danilov raion, Iaroslavl obl.
Size	Village
Last job/education	White Collar (higher/doctor of economic sciences/ lecturer)
First job/education	White Collar (lecturer Leningrad State University)
Father's job/education	Peasant
Position	2-7-90: Pa/Ce

Name	**Melnikov, Leonid Georgievich**
Birth	31-05-1906
Death	16-04-1981; N
Party	1928
Full on	16-10-52
Full off	06-03-53
Candidate on	06-03-53
Candidate off	06-06-53
Nationality	Russian
Birthplace	Degtiarevka (Briansk obl.)
Size	Village
Last job/education	Engineer (technical-engineering/industrial institute)
First job/education	Worker (sugar refinery)
Father's job/education	Peasant
Position	16-10-52: Pa/Re

Name	**Mikhailov, Nikolai Aleksandrovich**
Birth	10-10-1906
Death	25-05-1982; N
Party	1930
Full on	16-10-52
Full off	06-03-53
Nationality	Russian
Birthplace	Moscow
Size	City
Last job/education	White Collar (higher/journalist)
First job/education	Worker (steel mill)
Father's job/education	Worker
Position	16-10-52: Pa/Ce

Name	**Mikoian, Anastas Ivanovich**
Birth	25-11-1895
Death	21-10-1978; N
Party	1915
Full on	01-02-35
Full off	29-03-66
Candidate on	23-07-26
Candidate off	01-02-35
Nationality	Armenian
Birthplace	Sanain, Tiflis gub. (Tumanian raion, Armenia)
Size	Village
Last job/education	White Collar (seminary/theological academy; party activist)
First job/education	White Collar (party activist/seminary)
Father's job/education	Worker (carpenter)
Positions	19-12-27: St/Ce; 13-7-30: St/Ce; 10-2-34: St/Ce; 22-3-39: St/Ce; 1-1-46: St/Ce; 16-10-52: St/Ce; 6-3-53: St/Ce; 27-2-56: St/Ce; 29-6-57: St/Ce; 31-10-61: St/Ce

Name	**Molotov (Skriabin), Viacheslav Mikhailovich**
Birth	09-03-1890
Death	08-11-1986; N
Party	1906
Full on	01-01-26
Full off	29-06-57
Candidate on	16-03-21
Candidate off	01-01-26
Nationality	Russian
Birthplace	Kukarka, Viatka gub. (Sovetsk, Kirov obl.)
Size	Village
Last job/education	White Collar (higher/party activist)
First job/education	White Collar (party activist/economic dept. polytechnical institute)
Father's job/education	White Collar
Positions	16-3-21: Pa/Ce; 3-4-22: Pa/Ce; 26-4-23: Pa/Ce; 2-6-24: Pa/Ce; 1-1-26: Pa/Ce; 19-12-27: Pa/Ce; 13-7-30: Pa/Ce; 10-2-34: St/Ce; 22-3-39: St/Ce; 1-1-46: St/Ce; 16-10-52: St/Ce; 6-3-53: St/Ce; 27-2-56: St/Ce

Name	**Mukhitdinov, Nuritdin Akramovich**
Birth	19-11-1917
Death	
Party	1942
Full on	17-12-57
Full off	17-10-61
Candidate on	12-02-56
Candidate off	17-12-57
Nationality	Uzbek
Birthplace	Tashkent suburb
Size	City
Last job/education	White Collar (higher/teacher)
First job/education	White Collar (teacher/pedagogical education)
Father's job/education	Peasant
Positions	27-2-56: Pa/Re; 29-6-57: Pa/Re

Name	**Mzhavanadze, Vasilii Pavlovich**
Birth	20-09-1902
Death	31-08-1988; N
Party	1927
Candidate on	29-06-57
Candidate off	18-12-72
Nationality	Georgian
Birthplace	Kutaisi
Size	City
Last job/education	White Collar (higher/military academy)
First job/education	Worker
Father's job/education	Worker
Positions	29-6-57: Pa/Re; 31-10-61: Pa/Re; 8-4-66: Pa/Re; 9-4-71: Pa/Re

Name	**Nikonov, Viktor Petrovich**
Birth	28-02-1929
Death	
Party	1954
Full on	26-06-87
Full off	20-09-89
Nationality	Russian
Birthplace	Belogorka, Veshensk raion, Rostov obl.
Size	Village
Last job/education	Engineer (technical-engineering)
First job/education	Engineer (agricultural institute)
Father's job/education	Peasant
Positions	*

Name	**Ordzhonikidze, Grigorii Konstantinovich**
Birth	24-10-1886
Death	18-02-1937; S
Party	1903
Full on	21-12-30
Full off	18-02-37
Candidate on	23-07-26
Candidate off	03-11-26
Nationality	Georgian
Birthplace	Goresha, Kutaisi gub. (Georgia)
Size	Village
Last job/education	White Collar (technical/party activist)
First job/education	White Collar (party activist/military medical orderly)
Father's job/education	White Collar (gentry)
Position	10-2-34: St/Ce

Name	**Patolichev, Nikolai Semenovich**
Birth	23-09-1908
Death	01-12-1989; N
Party	1928
Candidate on	16-10-52
Candidate off	06-03-53
Nationality	Russian
Birthplace	Zolino (Gorokhovetsk raion, Vladimir obl.)
Size	Village
Last job/education	Engineer (technical-engineering/chemical institute)
First job/education	Worker (factory)
Father's job/education	Peasant
Position	16-10-52: Pa/Re

Name	**Pegov, Nikolai Mikhailovich**
Birth	16-04-1905
Death	
Party	1930
Candidate on	16-10-52
Candidate off	06-03-53
Nationality	Russian
Birthplace	Moscow
Size	City
Last job/education	White Collar (higher/industrial academy)
First job/education	Worker (factory)
Father's job/education	White Collar (clerk)
Position	16-10-52: Pa/Ce

Name	**Pelshe, Arvid Ianovich**
Birth	07-02-1899
Death	29-05-1983; N
Party	1915
Full on	08-04-66
Full off	29-05-83
Nationality	Latvian
Birthplace	Mazais, Griunvald volost (Latvia)
Size	Village
Last job/education	White collar (higher/teacher)
First job/education	Worker
Father's job/education	Peasant
Positions	8-4-66: Pa/Ce; 9-4-71: Pa/Ce; 5-3-76: Pa/Ce; 3-3-81: Pa/Ce

Name	**Pervukhin, Mikhail Georgievich**
Birth	14-10-1904
Death	22-07-1978; N
Party	1919
Full on	16-10-52
Full off	29-06-57
Candidate on	29-06-57
Candidate off	17-10-61
Nationality	Russian
Birthplace	Iuriuzan (Cheliabinsk obl.)
Size	Village
Last job/education	Engineer (technical-engineering)
First job/education	White Collar (party activist / secondary)
Father's job/education	Worker (smith)
Positions	16-10-52: St/Ce; 6-3-53: St/Ce; 27-2-56: St/Ce; 29-6-57: St/Ce

Name	**Petrovskii, Grigorii Ivanovich**
Birth	04-02-1878
Death	09-01-1958; N
Party	1903
Candidate on	01-01-26
Candidate off	10-03-39
Nationality	Ukrainian
Birthplace	Kharkov
Size	City
Last job/education	Worker (primary)
First job/education	Worker (fitter/primary)
Father's job/education	Worker (tailor)
Positions	1-1-26: St/Ce+Re; 19-12-27: St/Ce+Re; 13-7-30: St/Ce+Re; 10-2-34: St/Ce+Re

Name	**Podgornii, Nikolai Viktorovich**
Birth	18-02-1903
Death	11-01-1983; N
Party	1930
Full on	04-05-60
Full off	24-05-77
Candidate on	18-06-58
Candidate off	04-05-60
Nationality	Ukrainian
Birthplace	Karlovka (Poltava obl.)
Size	Village
Last job/education	Engineer (technical-engineering)
First job/education	Worker
Father's job/education	Worker
Positions	13-10-61: Pa/Re; 8-4-66: St/Ce; 9-4-71: St/Ce; 5-3-76: St/Ce

Name	**Polianskii, Dmitrii Stepanovich**
Birth	07-11-1917
Death	
Party	1939
Full on	04-05-60
Full off	24-02-76
Candidate on	18-06-58
Candidate off	04-05-60
Nationality	Russian
Birthplace	Slavianoserbsk, Lugansk obl.
Size	Village
Last job/education	Engineer/White Collar (technical-engineering/ higher [party school])
First job/education	Agricultural Worker
Father's job/education	Peasant
Positions	31-10-61: St/Re; 8-4-66: St/Ce; 9-4-71: St/Ce

Name	**Ponomarenko, Panteleimon Kondratevich**
Birth	09-08-1902
Death	18-01-1984; N
Party	1925
Full on	16-10-52
Full off	06-03-53
Candidate on	06-03-53
Candidate off	14-02-56
Nationality	Ukrainian
Birthplace	Shelkovskii (Belorechensk raion, Krasnodar krai)
Size	Village
Last job/education	Engineer (technical-engineering/transport engineer)
First job/education	Worker (fitter)
Father's job/education	Peasant
Positions	16-10-52: Pa+St/Ce; 6-3-53: St/Ce

Name	**Ponomarev, Boris Nikolaevich**
Birth	17-01-1905
Death	
Party	1919
Candidate on	19-05-72
Candidate off	25-02-86
Nationality	Russian
Birthplace	Zaraisk (Moscow obl.)
Size	City
Last job/education	White Collar (higher/university professor)
First job/education	White Collar (university professor)
Father's job/education	White Collar (clerk)
Positions	5-3-76: Pa/Ce; 3-3-81: Pa/Ce

Name	**Pospelov, Petr Nikolaevich**
Birth	20-06-1898
Death	21-04-1979; N
Party	1916
Candidate on	29-06-57
Candidate off	17-10-61
Nationality	Russian
Birthplace	Konakovo, Tver gub.
Size	Village
Last job/education	Engineer/White Collar (higher/technical engineering/doctor of historical sciences/agricultural institute)
First job/education	Engineer (professor/agricultural institute)
Father's job/education	White Collar (clerk)
Position	29-6-57: Pa/Ce

Name	**Postyshev, Pavel Petrovich**
Birth	18-09-1887
Death	26-02-1939; E
Party	1904
Candidate on	10-02-34
Candidate off	14-01-38
Nationality	Russian
Birthplace	Ivanovo-Voznesensk
Size	City
Last job/education	Worker (self-educated/electrician)
First job/education	Worker (electrician/self-educated)
Father's job/education	Worker (weaver)
Position	10-2-34: Pa/Re+Lo

Name	**Primakov, Evgenii Maksimovich**
Birth	29-10-1929
Death	
Party	1959
Candidate on	20-09-89
Candidate off	14-07-90
Nationality	Russian
Birthplace	Kiev
Size	City
Last job/education	White Collar (higher/doctor of economic sciences)
First job/education	White Collar (university/journalist)
Father's job/education	White Collar (clerk)
Position	2-7-90: St/Ce

Name	**Pugo, Boris Karlovich**
Birth	19-02-1937
Death	22?-08-1991; S
Party	1963
Candidate on	20-09-89
Candidate off	14-07-90
Nationality	Latvian
Birthplace	Kalinin (Tver)
Size	City
Last job/education	Engineer (technical-engineering)
First job/education	Engineer (polytechnical institute)
Father's job/education	White Collar (party activist)
Position	2-7-90: Pa/Ce

Name	**Puzanov, Aleksandr Mikhailovich**
Birth	25-10-1906
Death	
Party	1925
Candidate on	16-10-52
Candidate off	06-03-53
Nationality	Russian
Birthplace	Lezhkovka (Puchezh raion, Ivanovo obl.)
Size	Village
Last job/education	Agricultural Worker (technical)
First job/education	Agricultural Worker (agricultural tekhnikum)
Father's job/education	Peasant
Position	16-10-52: Pa/Lo

Name	**Rashidov, Sharaf Rashidovich**
Birth	06-11-1917
Death	31-10-1983; N?
Party	1939
Candidate on	31-10-61
Candidate off	31-10-83
Nationality	Uzbek
Birthplace	Dzhizak
Size	City
Last job/education	White Collar (higher/journalist)
First job/education	White Collar (teacher/pedagogical tekhnikum)
Father's job/education	Peasant
Positions	31-10-61: Pa/Re; 8-4-66: Pa/Re; 9-4-71: Pa/Re; 5-3-76: Pa/Re; 3-3-81: Pa/Re

Name	**Razumovskii, Georgii Petrovich**
Birth	19-01-1936
Death	
Party	1961
Candidate on	18-02-88
Candidate off	14-07-90
Nationality	Russian
Birthplace	Krasnodar
Size	City
Last job/education	Engineer (technical-engineering)
First job/education	Engineer (agronomist/agricultural institute)
Father's job/education	Unknown
Position	2-7-90: Pa/Ce

Name	**Romanov, Grigorii Vasilevich**
Birth	07-02-1923
Death	
Party	1944
Full on	05-03-76
Full off	01-07-85
Candidate on	27-04-73
Candidate off	05-03-76
Nationality	Russian
Birthplace	Zikhnovo, Borovichi raion, Novgorod obl.
Size	Village
Last job/education	Engineer (technical-engineering)
First job/education	Worker (designer/tekhnikum)
Father's job/education	Peasant
Positions	5-3-76: Pa/Lo; 3-3-81: Pa/Lo

Name	**Rudzutak, Ian Ernestovich**
Birth	15-08-1887
Death	29-07-1938; E
Party	1905
Full on	23-07-26
Full off	04-02-32
Candidate on	26-04-23, 10-02-34
Candidate off	23-07-26, 29-07-38
Nationality	Latvian
Birthplace	Tsauni, Kurland gub. (Latvia)
Size	Village
Last job/education	Worker (primary)
First job/education	Agricultural Worker/Worker (shepherd/primary)
Father's job/education	Agricultural Worker (farmhand)
Positions	26-4-23: Pa/Ce+Re; 2-6-24: St/Ce; 1-1-26: St/Ce; 19-12-27: St/Ce; 13-7-30: St/Ce; 10-2-34: St/Ce

Name	**Rykov, Aleksei Ivanovich**
Birth	13-02-1881
Death	15-03-1938; E
Party	1903
Full on	03-04-22
Full off	21-12-30
Nationality	Russian
Birthplace	Saratov
Size	City
Last job/education	White Collar (higher/party activist)
First job/education	White Collar (party activist/university)
Father's job/education	Peasant
Positions	3-4-22: St/Ce; 26-4-23: St/Ce+Re; 2-6-24: St/Ce+Re; 1-1-26: St/Ce+Re; 19-12-27: St/Ce+Re; 13-7-30: St/Ce

Name	**Ryzhkov, Nikolai Ivanovich**
Birth	28-09-1929
Death	
Party	1956
Full on	23-04-85
Full off	14-07-90
Nationality	Russian
Birthplace	Dyleevka, Dzerzhinsk raion, Donetsk obl.
Size	Village
Last job/education	Engineer (technical-engineering)
First job/education	Worker (mining foreman/tekhnikum)
Father's job/education	Worker
Positions	6-3-86: St/Ce; 2-7-90: St/Ce

Name	**Saburov, Maksim Zakharovich**
Birth	19-02-1900
Death	24-03-1977; N
Party	1920
Full on	16-10-52
Full off	29-06-57
Nationality	Russian
Birthplace	Druzhkovka (Donetsk obl.)
Size	Village
Last job/education	White Collar/Engineer (technical-enineering/higher/communist university)
First job/education	Worker (railroad)
Father's job/education	Worker
Positions	16-10-52: St/Ce; 6-3-53: St/Ce; 27-2-56: St/Ce

Name	**Shcherbakov, Aleksandr Sergeevich**
Birth	10-10-1901
Death	10-05-1945; N
Party	1918
Candidate on	21-02-41
Candidate off	10-05-45
Nationality	Russian
Birthplace	Ruza (Moscow obl.)
Size	City
Last job/education	White Collar (higher/institute of red professors)
First job/education	Worker (printing shop)
Father's job/education	Worker
Positions	*

Name	**Shcherbitskii, Vladimir Vasilevich**
Birth	17-02-1918
Death	16-02-1990; N
Party	1941
Full on	09-04-71
Full off	20-09-89
Candidate on	31-10-61, 06-12-65
Candidate off	13-12-63, 09-04-71
Nationality	Ukrainian
Birthplace	Verkhnedneprovsk (Dnepropetrovsk obl.)
Size	Village
Last job/education	Engineer/White Collar (technical-engineering/higher/ military academy)
First job/education	Engineer (chemical-technical institute)
Father's job/education	Worker
Positions	31-10-61: St/Re; 8-4-66: St/Re; 9-4-71: St/Re; 5-3-76: Pa/Re; 3-3-81: Pa/Re; 6-3-86: Pa/Re

Name	**Shelepin, Aleksandr Nikolaevich**
Birth	18-08-1918
Death	
Party	1940
Full on	16-11-64
Full off	16-04-75
Nationality	Russian
Birthplace	Voronezh
Size	City
Last job/education	White Collar (higher/philosophy)
First job/education	White Collar (party activist/institute of philosophy)
Father's job/education	White Collar (railroad clerk)
Positions	8-4-66: Pa/Ce; 9-4-71: Tr/Ce

Name	**Shelest, Petr Efimovich**
Birth	14-02-1908
Death	
Party	1928
Full on	16-11-64
Full off	27-04-73
Candidate on	13-12-63
Candidate off	16-11-64
Nationality	Ukrainian
Birthplace	Andreevka (Balakleia raion, Kharkov obl.)
Size	Village
Last job/education	Engineer (technical-engineering/metallurgical institute)
First job/education	Agricultural Worker
Father's job/education	Peasant
Positions	8-4-66: Pa/Re; 9-4-71: Pa/Re

Name	**Shepilov, Dmitrii Trofimovich**
Birth	05-11-1905
Death	
Party	1926
Candidate on	27-02-56
Candidate off	29-06-57
Nationality	Russian
Birthplace	Ashkhabad
Size	City
Last job/education	White Collar (higher/institute of red professors)
First job/education	White Collar (university/judiciary work)
Father's job/education	Worker
Position	27-2-56: Pa/Ce

Name	**Shevardnadze, Edvard Amvrosievich**
Birth	25-01-1928
Death	
Party	1948
Full on	01-07-85
Full off	14-07-90
Candidate on	27-11-78
Candidate off	01-07-85
Nationality	Georgian
Birthplace	Mamati, Lanchkhut raion, Georgia
Size	Village
Last job/education	White Collar (higher/teacher)
First job/education	White Collar (teacher in party school/pedagogical institute)
Father's job/education	Teacher
Positions	3-3-81: Pa/Re; 6-3-86: St/Ce; 2-7-90: St/Ce

Name	**Shkiriatov, Matvei Fedorovich**
Birth	15-08-1883
Death	18-01-1954; N
Party	1906
Full on	16-10-52
Full off	06-03-53
Nationality	Russian
Birthplace	Vishniakovo, Tula gub.
Size	Village
Last job/education	Worker (primary)
First job/education	Worker (tailor/primary)
Father's job/education	Peasant
Position	16-10-52: Pa/Ce

Name	**Shvernik, Nikolai Mikhailovich**
Birth	19-05-1888
Death	24-12-1970; N
Party	1905
Full on	16-10-52, 29-06-57
Full off	06-03-53, 29-03-66
Candidate on	22-03-39, 06-03-53
Candidate off	05-10-52, 29-06-57
Nationality	Russian
Birthplace	St. Petersburg
Size	City
Last job/education	Worker (primary/lathe operator)
First job/education	Worker (lathe operator/primary)
Father's job/education	Worker
Positions	22-03-39: Tr/Ce; 1-1-46: St/Ce+Re; 16-10-52: St/Ce; 6-3-53: St/Ce; 27-2-56: Pa/Ce; 29-6-57: Pa/Ce; 31-10-61: Pa/Ce

Name	**Sliunkov, Nikolai Nikitovich**
Birth	26-04-1929
Death	
Party	1954
Full on	26-06-87
Full off	14-07-90
Candidate on	06-03-86
Candidate off	26-06-87
Nationality	Belorussian
Birthplace	Gorodets, Rogachev raion, Gomel obl.
Size	Village
Last job/education	Engineer (technical-engineering/agricultural institute)
First job/education	Worker (assistant foreman/tekhnikum)
Father's job/education	Worker
Positions	6-3-86: Pa/Re; 2-7-90: Pa/Ce

Name	Sokolnikov (Brilliant), Grigorii lakovlevich
Birth	15-08-1888
Death	21-05-1939; E
Party	1905
Candidate on	02-06-24
Candidate off	18-12-25
Nationality	Jewish
Birthplace	Romny, Poltava gub.
Size	City
Last job/education	White Collar (higher/party activist)
First job/education	White Collar (party activist/lawyer)
Father's job/education	White Collar (doctor and lawyer)
Position	2-6-24: St/Ce

Name	Sokolov, Sergei Leonidovich
Birth	01-07-1911
Death	
Party	1937
Candidate on	23-04-85
Candidate off	26-06-87
Nationality	Russian
Birthplace	Evpatoria (Crimea obl.)
Size	City
Last job/education	White Collar (higher/military academy/army officer)
First job/education	Worker (packer)
Father's job/education	White Collar (clerk)
Position	6-3-86: Mi/Ce

Name	Solomentsev, Mikhail Sergeevich
Birth	07-11-1913
Death	
Party	1940
Full on	26-12-83
Full off	30-09-88
Candidate on	23-11-71
Candidate off	26-12-83
Nationality	Russian
Birthplace	Erilovka (Eletsk raion, Lipetsk obl.)
Size	Village
Last job/education	White Collar/Engineer (technical-engineering/higher/ military academy)
First job/education	Agricultural Worker
Father's job/education	Peasant
Positions	5-3-76: St/Re; 3-3-81: St/Re; 6-3-86: Pa/Ce

Name	**Solovev, Iurii Filippovich**
Birth	20-08-1925
Death	
Party	1955
Candidate on	06-03-86
Candidate off	20-09-89
Nationality	Russian
Birthplace	Bogatoe Station, Bogatov raion, Kuibyshev obl.
Size	Village
Last job/education	Engineer (technical-engineering)
First job/education	White Collar (teacher)
Father's job/education	Peasant
Position	6-3-86: Pa/Lo

Name	**Stalin (Dzhugashvili), Iosif Vissarionovich**
Birth	18-12-1878
Death	05-03-53; N
Party	1903
Full on	25-03-19
Full off	05-03-53
Nationality	Georgian
Birthplace	Gori, Tiflis gub.
Size	City
Last job/education	White Collar (seminary/party activist)
First job/education	White Collar (party activist/employee at meteorological observatory/seminary)
Father's job/education	Worker (cobbler)
Positions	25-3-19: St+Mi/Ce; 5-4-20: St+Mi/Ce; 16-3-21: St+Mi/Ce; 3-4-22: Pa+St+Mi/Ce; 26-4-23: Pa+St/Ce; 2-6-24: Pa/Ce; 1-1-26: Pa/Ce; 19-12-27: Pa/Ce; 13-7-30: Pa/Ce; 10-2-34: Pa/Ce; 22-3-39: Pa/Ce; 1-1-46: Pa+St+Mi/Ce; 16-10-52: Pa+St/Ce

Name	**Stasova, Elena Dmitrievna**
Birth	15-10-1873
Death	31-12-1966; N
Party	1903
Full on	??-07-19
Full off	??-09-19
Nationality	Russian
Birthplace	St. Petersburg
Size	City
Last job/education	White Collar (secondary/teacher/party activist)
First job/education	White Collar (party activist/teacher/secondary)
Father's job/education	White Collar (lawyer)
Positions	*

Name	**Suslov, Mikhail Andreevich**
Birth	21-11-1902
Death	25-01-1982; N
Party	1921
Full on	16-10-52, 12-07-55
Full off	06-03-53, 25-01-82
Nationality	Russian
Birthplace	Shakhovskoe (Pavlovka raion, Ulianovsk obl.)
Size	Village
Last job/education	White Collar (higher/economical institute/teacher/ institute of red professors)
First job/education	Worker (poverty relief committee/worker's faculty)
Father's job/education	Peasant
Positions	16-10-52: Pa/Ce; 27-2-56: Pa/Ce; 29-6-57: Pa/Ce; 31-10-61: Pa/Ce; 8-4-66: Pa/Ce; 9-4-71: Pa/Ce; 5-3-76: Pa/Ce; 3-3-81: Pa/Ce

Name	**Syrtsov, Sergei Ivanovich**
Birth	17-07-1893
Death	10-09-1937; E
Party	1913
Candidate on	21-06-29
Candidate off	01-12-30
Nationality	Russian
Birthplace	Slavgorod, Ekaterinoslav gub. (Dnepropetrovsk obl.)
Size	Village
Last job/education	White Collar (higher/polytechnical institute/party activist)
First job/education	White Collar (party activist/commercial school)
Father's job/education	White Collar (clerk)
Position	13-7-30: St/Re

Name	**Talyzin, Nikolai Vladimirovich**
Birth	28-01-1929
Death	23-01-1991; N
Party	1960
Candidate on	15-10-85
Candidate off	20-09-89
Nationality	Russian
Birthplace	Moscow
Size	City
Last job/education	Engineer (technical-engineering/doctor of technical sciences)
First job/education	Worker
Father's job/education	Worker
Position	6-3-86: St/Ce

Name	**Tevosian, Ivan Fedorovich**
Birth	04-01-1902
Death	30-03-1958; N
Party	1918
Candidate on	16-10-52
Candidate off	06-03-53
Nationality	Armenian
Birthplace	Shusha, Nagornyi Karabakh
Size	City
Last job/education	White Collar/Engineer (technical-engineering/higher/ mining academy)
First job/education	White Collar (bookkeeper/commercial school)
Father's job/education	Worker (tailor)
Position	16-10-52: St/Ce

Name	**Tikhonov, Nikolai Aleksandrovich**
Birth	14-05-1905
Death	
Party	1940
Full on	27-11-79
Full off	15-10-85
Candidate on	27-11-78
Candidate off	27-11-79
Nationality	Russian
Birthplace	Kharkov
Size	City
Last job/education	Engineer (technical-engineering/metallurgical institute/doctor of technical sciences)
First job/education	Worker (railroad)
Father's job/education	White Collar (clerk)
Position	3-3-81: St/Ce

Name	**Tomskii (Efremov), Mikhail Pavlovich**
Birth	31-10-1880
Death	22-08-1936; S
Party	1904
Full on	03-04-22
Full off	26-06-30
Nationality	Russian
Birthplace	Kolpino, St. Petersburg gub.
Size	Village
Last job/education	Worker (primary)
First job/education	Worker (factory/primary)
Father's job/education	Worker
Positions	3-4-22: Tr/Ce; 26-4-23: Tr/Ce; 2-6-24: Tr/Ce; 1-1-26: Tr/Ce; 19-12-27: Tr/Ce

Name	**Trotskii (Bronshtein), Lev Davidovich**
Birth	07-11-1879
Death	20-08-1940; E
Party	1917
Full on	25-03-19
Full off	23-10-26
Nationality	Jewish
Birthplace	Ianovka, Elizavetgrad uezd, Kherson gub.
Size	Village
Last job/education	White Collar (secondary/party activist)
First job/education	White Collar (party activist/secondary)
Father's job/education	Peasant
Positions	25-3-19: Mi/Ce; 5-4-20: St+Mi/Ce; 16-3-21: Mi/Ce; 3-4-22: Mi/Ce; 26-4-23: Mi/Ce; 2-6-24: Mi/Ce; 1-1-26: St/Ce

Name	**Uglanov, Nikolai Aleksandrovich**
Birth	17-12-1886
Death	31-05-1937; E
Party	1907
Candidate on	01-01-26
Candidate off	29-04-29
Nationality	Russian
Birthplace	Feodoritskii, Rybinsk uezd, Iaroslavl gub.
Size	Village
Last job/education	White Collar (primary/clerk)
First job/education	White Collar (clerk/primary)
Father's job/education	Peasant
Positions	1-1-26: Pa/Ce+Lo; 19-12-27: Pa/Ce+Lo

Name	**Ustinov, Dmitrii Fedorovich**
Birth	30-10-1908
Death	20-12-1984; N
Party	1927
Full on	05-03-76
Full off	20-12-84
Candidate on	26-03-65
Candidate off	05-03-76
Nationality	Russian
Birthplace	Samara (Kuibyshev)
Size	City
Last job/education	Engineer (technical-engineering)
First job/education	Worker (fitter, machinist)
Father's job/education	Worker
Positions	8-4-66: Pa/Ce; 9-4-71: Pa/Ce; 5-3-76: Pa/Ce; 3-3-81: Mi/Ce

Name	**Vlasov, Aleksandr Vladimirovich**
Birth	20-01-1932
Death	
Party	1956
Candidate on	30-09-88
Candidate off	14-07-90
Nationality	Russian
Birthplace	Mysovsk (Babushkin, Buriatia)
Size	Village
Last job/education	Engineer (technical-engineering)
First job/education	Engineer (shift foreman/mining metallurgical institute)
Father's job/education	Unknown
Position	No position held 2-7-90

Name	**Voronov, Gennadii Ivanovich**
Birth	31-08-1910
Death	
Party	1931
Full on	31-10-61
Full off	27-04-73
Candidate on	18-01-61
Candidate off	31-10-61
Nationality	Russian
Birthplace	Rameshki, Tver gub.
Size	Village
Last job/education	Engineer (technical-engineering/industrial institute)
First job/education	Worker (factory)
Father's job/education	White Collar (teacher)
Positions	31-10-61: Pa/Re; 8-4-66: St/Re; 9-4-71: St/Re

Name	**Voroshilov, Kliment Efremovich**
Birth	04-02-1881
Death	02-12-1969; N
Party	1903
Full on	01-01-26
Full off	16-07-60
Nationality	Russian
Birthplace	Verkhnee, Bakhmutovo uezd, Ekaterinoslav gub.
Size	Village
Last job/education	Worker (primary)
First job/education	Worker (steel plant/primary)
Father's job/education	Worker
Positions	1-1-26: Mi/Ce; 19-12-27: Mi/Ce; 13-7-30: Mi/Ce; 10-2-34: Mi/Ce; 22-3-39: Mi/Ce; 1-1-46: St/Ce; 16-10-52: St/Ce; 6-3-53: St/Ce; 27-2-56: St/Ce; 29-6-57: St/Ce

Name	Vorotnikov, Vitalii Ivanovich
Birth	20-01-1926
Death	
Party	1947
Full on	26-12-83
Full off	14-07-90
Candidate on	15-06-83
Candidate off	26-12-83
Nationality	Russian
Birthplace	Voronezh
Size	City
Last job/education	Engineer (technical-engineering/aviation institute)
First job/education	Worker (fitter/tekhnikum)
Father's job/education	Worker
Positions	6-3-86: St/Re; 2-7-90: St/Ce

Name	Voznesenskii, Nikolai Alekseevich
Birth	01-12-1903
Death	01-10-1950; E
Party	1919
Full on	26-02-47
Full off	07-03-49
Candidate on	21-02-41
Candidate off	26-02-47
Nationality	Russian
Birthplace	Teploe, Tula gub.
Size	Village
Last job/education	White Collar (higher/doctor of economic sciences/ institute of red professors)
First job/education	Worker (fitter)
Father's job/education	White Collar (clerk)
Position	1-1-46: St/Ce

Name	**Vyshinskii, Andrei Ianuarevich**
Birth	10-12-1883
Death	22-11-1954; N
Party	1920
Candidate on	16-10-52
Candidate off	06-03-53
Nationality	Russian
Birthplace	Odessa
Size	City
Last job/education	White Collar (higher/lawyer)
First job/education	White Collar (lawyer)
Father's job/education	White Collar (pharmaceutical chemist)
Position	16-10-52: St/Ce

Name	**Zaikov, Lev Nikolaevich**
Birth	03-04-1923
Death	
Party	1957
Full on	06-03-86
Full off	14-07-90
Nationality	Russian
Birthplace	Tula
Size	City
Last job/education	Engineer (technical-engineering)
First job/education	Worker (fitter)
Father's job/education	Worker
Positions	6-3-86: Pa/Ce; 2-7-90: Pa/Ce

Name	**Zhdanov, Andrei Aleksandrovich**
Birth	26-02-1896
Death	31-08-1948; N
Party	1915
Full on	22-03-39
Full off	31-08-48
Candidate on	01-02-35
Candidate off	22-03-39
Nationality	Russian
Birthplace	Mariupol
Size	City
Last job/education	White Collar (secondary/party activist)
First job/education	White Collar (party activist/secondary)
Father's job/education	White Collar (school inspector)
Positions	22-3-39: Pa/Ce+Lo; 1-1-46: Pa/Ce

Name	Zhukov, Georgii Konstantinovich
Birth	01-12-1896
Death	18-06-1974; N
Party	1919
Full on	29-06-57
Full off	29-10-57
Candidate on	27-02-56
Candidate off	29-06-57
Nationality	Russian
Birthplace	Strelkovka (Ugodsk-Zavod raion, Kaluga obl.)
Size	Village
Last job/education	White Collar (higher/military academy)
First job/education	Worker
Father's job/education	Peasant
Positions	27-2-56: Mi/Ce; 29-6-57: Mi/Ce

Name	Zinovev (Radomyslskii), Grigorii Evseevich
Birth	20-09-1883
Death	25-08-1936; E
Party	1903
Full on	16-03-21
Full off	23-07-26
Candidate on	25-03-19
Candidate off	16-03-21
Nationality	Jewish
Birthplace	Elizavetgrad (Kirovgrad), Kherson gub.
Size	City
Last job/education	White Collar (higher/party activist)
First job/education	White Collar (party activist/university)
Father's job/education	White Collar (entrepreneur)
Positions	25-3-19: Pa+St/Ce+Lo; 5-4-20: Pa+St/Ce+Lo; 16-3-21: Pa+St/Ce+Lo; 3-4-22: Pa+St/Ce+Lo; 26-4-23: Pa+St/Ce+Lo; 2-6-24: Pa+St/Ce+Lo; 1-1-26: Pa+St/Ce+Lo

Name	**Zverev, Arsenii Grigorevich**
Birth	02-03-1900
Death	27-07-1969; N
Party	1919
Candidate on	16-10-52
Candidate off	06-03-53
Nationality	Russian
Birthplace	Tikhomirovo (Klin raion, Moscow obl.)
Size	Village
Last job/education	White Collar (higher/financial-economic institute/ doctor of economic sciences)
First job/education	Worker (factory)
Father's job/education	Worker
Position	16-10-52: St/Ce

BIBLIOGRAPHY

BIOGRAPHICAL REFERENCE WORKS—All Languages

Bolshaia Sovetskaia Entsiklopediia 2-e izd. Moscow (BSE) 1949-1958.

Bolshaia Sovetskaia Entsiklopediia 3-e izd. Moscow (Sovetskaia Entsiklopediia) 1970-1981.

CROWLEY, EDWARD L., et al., eds., *Party and Government Officials of the Soviet Union 1917-1967.* Metuchen NJ (The Scarecrow Press) 1969.

Directory of Soviet Officials: National Organizations. A Reference Aid. Washington DC (CIA) 1984, 1986, 1987.

Directory of Soviet Officials: Republic Organizations. A Reference Aid. Washington DC (CIA) 1985, 1987, 1988.

HODNETT, GREY, and VAL OGAREFF, *Leaders of the Soviet Republics 1955-1972. A Guide to Posts and Occupants.* Canberra (The Australian National University) 1973.

KIRILINA, A. A., et al., *Politbiuro, Orgbiuro, Sekretariat TsK RKP(b) - VKP(b) - KPSS.* Spravochnik, Moscow (Politizdat) 1990.

OGAREFF, VAL, *Leaders of the Soviet Republics 1971-1980. A Guide to Posts and Occupants.* Canberra (The Australian National University) 1980.

PRAVDA, ALEX, et al., eds., *The Tauris Soviet Directory. The Elite of the USSR Today.* London (Tauris) 1989.

RAHR, ALEXANDER, ed., *A Biographic Directory of 100 Leading Soviet Officials.* Munich (Radio Liberty Research) 1988.

SCHULZ, HEINRICH E., et al., eds., *Who Was Who in the USSR. A Biographic Directory Containing 5,015 Biographies of Prominent Soviet Historical Personalities.* Metuchen NJ (The Scarecrow Press) 1972.

"Sostav rukovodiashchikh organov Tsentralnogo Komiteta Partii - Politbiuro (Prezidiuma), Orgbiuro, Sekretariata TsK (1919-1990)", *Izvestiia TsK KPSS* 1990, No. 7, 69-136.

"Sostavy Politbiuro (Prezidiuma v 1952-1966 gg.) Tsentralnogo Komiteta Kommunisticheskoi partii", in V. I. Kuptsov (Ed.), *Stranitsy istorii KPSS. Fakty, Problemy, Uroki.* Moscow (Vysshaia shkola) 1988, 684-699.

Sovetskaia Voennaia Entsiklopediia. Moscow (Voenizdat) 1976-1979.

Ukrainskaia Sovetskaia Entsiklopediia. Kiev 1978-1985.

VRONSKAYA, JEAN, and VLADIMIR CHUGUEV, *A Biographical Dictionary of the Soviet Union, 1917-1988.* London (Saur) 1989.

WIECZYNSKI, JOSEPH L., ed., *The Modern Encyclopedia of Russian and Soviet History.* Gulf Breeze (Academic International Press) 1976-1989.

DOCUMENTS—All Languages

"Deiatelnost Tsentralnogo Komiteta Partii v dokumentakh", *Izvestiia TsK KPSS* 1989, No. 1 to 1990, No. 7.

Desiatyi s''ezd RKP(b). Mart 1921 goda. Stenograficheskii otchet. Moscow (Politizdat) 1963.

GILL, GREAME, *The Rules of the Communist Party of the Soviet Union.* Houndmills etc. (Macmillan) 1988.

GRULIOW, LEO, ed., *Current Soviet Policies. II. The Documentary Record of the 20th Communist Party Congress and Its Aftermath.* New York (Praeger) 1957.

"K 70-letiiu Politbiuro TsK partii. Protokol pervogo zasedaniia Politbiuro TsK RKP(b) 16 aprelia 1919 g.", *Izvestiia TsK KPSS* 1989, No. 3, 116-121.

KHRUSHCHEV, N. S., "O kulte lichnosti i ego posledstviiakh", *Izvestiia TsK KPSS* 1989, No. 3, 128-70.

Konstitutsiia i zakony Soiuza SSR. Moscow (Izvestiia sovetov narodnykh deputatov SSSR) 1983.

KPSS v rezoliutsiiakh i resheniiakh s''ezdov, konferentsii i plenumov TsK, Vol. 1 (Moscow, Politizdat, 1970) - Vol. 14 (Moscow, Politizdat, 1982); Chast I. 1898-1925 (Moscow, Politizdat, 1953); Chast II. 1925-1953 (Moscow, Politizdat, 1953).

V. I. Lenin i VChK. Sbornik dokumentov (1917-1922 gg.). Moscow 1975.

Materialy XXVIII sezda kommunisticheskoi partii Sovetskogo Soiuza. Moscow (Politizdat) 1990.

"O dele tak nazyvaemogo 'Soiuza marksistov-lenintsev'", *Izvestiia TsK KPSS* 1989, No. 6, 103-15.

"O demokratizatsii Sovetskogo obshchestva i reforme politicheskoi sistemy", Rezoliutsiia XIX Vsesoiuznoi konferentsii KPSS, 1 iiuliia 1988 g.; "Ob obrazovanii komissii TsK PKSS i reorganizatsii apparata TsK KPSS v svete reshenii XIX Vsesoiuznoi partiinoi konferentsii", Postanovlenie Plenuma Tsentralnogo Komiteta KPSS 30 sentiabria 1988 g., *Spravochnik partiinogo rabotnika 1989,* Moscow 1989, 14-22 and 84-85.

"O partiinosti lits, prokhodivshikh po delu tak nazyvaemogo 'antisovetskogo pravotrotskistskogo bloka'", *Izvestiia TsK KPSSu* 1989, No. 5, 69-85.

"O tak nazyvaemom 'antipartiinoi kontrrevoliutsionnoi gruppirovke Eismonta, Tolmacheva i drugikh'", *Izvestiia TsK KPSS* 1990, No. 11, 63-74.

"O tak nazyvaemom 'dele evreiskogo antifashistskogo komiteta'", *Izvestiia TsK KPSS* 1989, No. 12, 35-40.

"O tak nazyvaemom 'Leningradskom dele'", *Izvestiia TsK KPSS* 1989, No. 2, 126-137.

"O vozmeshchenii deputatam raskhodov, sviazannykh s vypolneniem deputatskikh obiazannostei, Zakon ot 17 ianvaria 1938 g.", *Sbornik Zakonov SSR i Ukazov Prezidiuma Verkhovnoga Soveta SSR 1938-1975,* tom 1., Moscow 1975, 350

"Ob obrazovanii Rossiiskogo Biuro TsK KPSS. Postanovlenie TsK KPSS ot 9 dekabria 1989 goda", *Pravda,* 10 December 1989.

Odinnadtsatyi s''ezd RKP(b). Mart-aprel 1922 goda. Stenograficheskii otchet. Moscow (Politizdat) 1961.

"Otvet chlenov Politbiuro TsK RKP(b) na pismo L. D. Trotskogo ot 8 oktiabria 1923g. 19 oktiabria 1923g.", *Izvestiia TsK KPSS* 1990, No. 7, 176-90.

"Pervaia Sessiia Verkhovnogo Soveta SSSR", *Biulletin* No. 9, Moscow 1989.

Piatnadtsatyi s''ezd VKP(b). Dekabr 1927 goda. Stenograficheskii otchet I. Moscow (Politizdat) 1961.

"Plan raboty Politbiuro TsK i Plenuma TsK na 1926 god", *Pravda*, 13 April 1926, later published in *Plenum TsK VKP (b) 6-9 1926 g.*, 103-5.

"Plenum TsK KPSS. Iul 1953 goda. Stenograficheskii otchet", *Izvestiia TsK KPSS* 1991, No. 1, 140-214; and 1991, No. 2, 141-208.

"Plenum TsK KPSS. Oktiabr 1987 goda. Stenograficheskii otchet", *Izvestiia TsK KPSS* 1989, No. 2, 209-287.

"Proekt platformy TsK KPSS k XXVIII s''ezdu partii (s predlozheniiami redaktsionnoi komissii Plenuma", *Izvestiia TsK KPSS* 1990, No. 3, 94-115.

"Protokol zasedaniia Politicheskogo biuro TsK [RKP(b)]. 16 aprelia 1919g.", *Izvestiia TsK KPSS* 1989, No. 3, 117-21.

"Protokoly i rezoliutsii Biuro TsK RSDRP(b) (mart 1917g.)", *Voprosy Istorii KPSS* 1962, No. 3, 134-57.

Protokoly Tsentralnogo Komiteta RSDRP(b), Avgust 1917-Fevral 1918. Moscow 1958.

Sbornik Zakonov SSR i Ukazov Prezidiuma Verkhovnoga Soveta SSR 1938-1975, tom 1. Moscow 1975.

XIV s''ezd Vsesoiuznoi kommunisticheskoi partii (b). 18-31 dekabria 1925g. Stenograficheskii otchet. Moscow-Leningrad (Gosizdat) 1926.

XVI s''ezd Vsesoiuznoi kommunisticheskoi partii (b). 26 iiunia-13 iiulia 1930g. Stenograficheskii otchet. Moscow-Leningrad (Gosizdat) 1930.

XVII s''ezd Vsesoiuznoi kommunisticheskoi partii (b). 26 ianvaria-10 fevralia 1934g. Stenograficheskii otchet. Nendeln-Liechtenstein (Kraus Reprint) 1975 (1934).

XX s''ezd Kommunisticheskoi partii Sovetskogo Soiuza. 14-25 fevralia 1956 goda. Stenograficheskii otchet. I. Moscow (Politizdat) 1956.

XXII s''ezd Kommunisticheskoi partii Sovetskogo Soiuza. 17-31 oktiabria 1961 goda. Stenograficheskii otchet III. Moscow (Politizdat) 1962.

XXIII s''ezd Kommunisticheskoi partii Sovetskogo Soiuza. 29 marta-8 aprelia 1966 goda. Stenograficheskii otchet II. Moscow (Politizdat) 1966.

XXVII s''ezd Kommunisticheskoi partii Sovetskogo Soiuza. 25 fevralia-6 marta 1986 goda. Stenograficheskii otchet 1. Moscow (Politizdat) 1986.

Spravochnik partiinogo rabotnika t. 1-t. 29. Moscow 1957-1989.

"Ustav kommunisticheskoi partii Sovetskogo Soiuza. Utverzhden XXVIII s''ezdom KPSS", in *Materialy XXVIII s''ezda kommunisticheskoi partii Sovetskogo Soiuza.* Moscow (Politizdat) 1990, 108-124.

"Voprosy, rassmotrennye na plenumakh TsK KPSS, zasedaniiakh ego rukovodiashchikh organov i komissii v period mezhdu XXVII i XXVIII sezdami KPSS", *Izvestiia TsK KPSS* 1990, No. 9, 16-34.

Vosmoi s''ezd RKP(b), mart 1919 goda. Protokoly. Moscow 1959.

XIX vsesoiuznaia konferentsiia Kommunisticheskoi Partii Sovetskogo Soiuza. 28 iiunia-1 iiulia 1988 goda. Stenograficheskii otchet. V dvukh tomakh. Moscow (Politizdat) 1988, 2 vols.

"'Zaiavlenie 46-ti' v Politbiuro TsK RKP(b). 15 oktiabria 1923 g.", *Izvestiia TsK KPSS* 1990, No. 6, 189-94.

BOOKS AND ARTICLES in Russian

ADZHUBEI, ALEKSEI, "Po sledam odnogo iubileia", *Ogonek* 1989, No. 41 (October), 7-10.

AFANASEV, IU. N., ed., *Inogo ne dano. Perestroika: glasnost, demokratiia, sotsializm.* Moscow (Progress) 1988.

AKSENOV, IU. S., "Apogei Stalinizma: poslevoennaia piramida vlasti", *Voprosy Istorii KPSS* 1990, No. 11 (November), 90-104.

AKSIUTIN, IU. V., ed., *Nikita Sergeevich Khrushchev. Materialy k biografii.* Moscow (Politizdat) 1989.

AKSIUTIN, IU., "N. S. Khrushchev: nado skazat pravdu o kulte lichnosti", *Sovety narodnykh deputatov* 1989, No. 5, 105-113.

ALLILUEVA, SVETLANA, *Dvadtsat pisem k drugu.* London (Hutchinson) 1967.

ARBATOV, GEORGII, "Iz nedavnego proshlogo", *Znamia* 1990 (September), 201-22.

———, "Iz nedavnego proshlogo. Okonchanie", *Znamia* 1990 (October), 197-227.

AVTORKHANOV, ABDURAKHMAN, *Proiskhozhdenie partokratii. Tom pervyi. TsK i Lenin.* Frankfurt a.M. (Posev) 1981 (1973). *Tom vtoroi. TsK i Stalin.* Frankfurt a.M. (Posev) 1983 (1973).

BARDIN, S., "'Leningradskoe delo' glazami ochevidtsev", *Nedelia* 1988, No. 40 (3-9 October), 10-11.

BARSUKOV, N., "Mart 1953-go", *Pravda*, 27 October 1989.

———, "Na puti k XX s''ezdu", *Pravda*, 10 November 1989.

———, "Eshche vperedi XX s''ezd...", *Pravda*, 17 November 1989.

"Bolsheviki o samikh sebe", *Sotsialisticheskii Vestnik* 1929, No. 6 (22 March), 10-11.

BONDARENKO, TATIANA, "Kirill Mazurov: Ia govoriu ne tolko o sebe" [interview K. Mazurov], *Sovetskaia Rossiia*, 19 February 1989.

BORDIUGOV, G., and V. KOZLOV, "Nikolai Bukharin. Epizody politicheskoi biografii", *Kommunist* 1988, No. 13 (September), 91-109.

BORDIUGOV, G.A., and V.A. KOZLOV, "Povorot 1929 goda i alternativa Bukharina", *Voprosy Istorii KPSS* 1988, No. 8 (August), 15-33.

BORDIUGOV, G., and V. KOZLOV, "Vremia trudnykh voprosov. Istoriia 20-30-kh godov i sovremennaia obshchestvennaia mysl", *Pravda*, 3 October 1988.

BURLATSKII, FEDOR, *Vozhdi i sovetniki. O Khrushcheve, Andropove i ne tolko o nikh.* Moscow (Politizdat) 1990.

"Chelovek", *Dialog* 1990, No. 17, 90-103.

"Chelovek i simvol", *Komsomolskaia pravda*, 2 April 1988.

CHIZHOVA, L. M., "Kto vinovat v politicheskoi diskreditatsii N. A. Uglanova", *Voprosy Istorii KPSS* 1990, No. 8, 77-87.

CHUEV, F., "Iz besed c V. M. Molotovym", in G. V. Ivanova (ed.), *Ot ottepeli do zastoia*, Moscow (Sovetskaia Rossiia) 1990, 36-77.

ELTSIN, BORIS, *Ispoved na zadannuiu temu*. Moscow (Sovetsko-Britanskaia Tvorcheskaia Assotsiatsiia, "Ogonek"-Variant) 1990.

EMELIANOV, V., "O vremeni, o tovarishchakh, o sebe", *Novyi Mir* 1967, No. 2, 61-141.

ERENBURG, ILIA, "Moi drug Nikolai Bukharin", *Nedelia* 1988, No. 20 (May), 10.

GAVRILIUK, ALEKSANDR, "Zabytyi iubilei", *Selskaia molodezh* 1990, No. 12, 22-28.

GDLIAN, T., and N. IVANOV, "Protivostoianie", *Ogonek* 1988, No. 26 (June), 27-29.

GERASIMOV, I. A., "Revoliutsioner po prizvaniiu, bolshevik po ubezhdeniiu [K 100-letiiu so dnia rozhdeniia V. V. Kuibysheva]", *Voprosy Istorii KPSS* 1988, No. 6 (June), 142-47.

GNEDIN, EVGENII, *Katastrofa i vtoroe rozhdenie. Memuarnye zapiski*. Amsterdam (Fond imeni Gertsena) 1977.

GOLOVKOV, ANATOLII, "Vechnyi isk", *Ogonek* 1988, No. 18 (April), 28-31.

"M. S. Gorbachev otvechaet na voprosy korrespondenta 'Izvestii TsK KPSS'", *Izvestiia TsK KPSS* 1989, No. 5, 57-60.

GORCHAKOV, O. A., "Dokumenty general-leitenanta T. A. Strokacha o podgotovke Beriei zagovora v 1953 g.", *Novaia i Noveishaia Istoriia* 1989, No. 3, 166-176.

GRIGOREV, LEONID, "Do upadu. Vozmozhno li priostonovit polet v ekonomicheskuiu propast?", *Moskovskie Novosti* 1991, No. 15 (April), 7.

GRISHIN, V.V., "Ligachev i Ko", *Sobesednik* 1991, No. 14 (April), 7.

GROMYKO, A. A., *Pamiatnoe*. Moscow (Politizdat) 1988, 2 vols.

"'Ia vsegda byl protivnikom liberalizma'", *Nashe delo* 1990, No. 4 (7), 2-12.

IAKOVLEV, ALEKSANDR, "O dekabrskoi tragedii 1934 goda", *Pravda*, 28 January 1991.

IAKOVLEV, A. S., *Tsel zhizni. Zapiski aviakonstruktora*. Moscow (Politizdat) 1966.

ILISHEV, G. SH., "Bashkirskaia partorganizatsiia v seredine 1930-kh godov", *Voprosy Istorii* 1988, No. 9, 126-31.

IVANOVA, G. V., ed., *Ot ottepeli do zastoia*. Moscow (Sovetskaia Rossiia) 1990.

"Iz istorii obrazovaniia SSSR", *Izvestiia TsK KPSS* 1989, No. 9, 191-218.

IZGARSHEV, V., "Na Sovete Oborony..." [interview L. N. Zaikov], *Pravda*, 27 November 1989.

KABAKOV, A., "Izgnanie prokurora respubliki" [on Geidar Aliev], *Moskovskie Novosti* 1989, No. 48 (November), 27.

KARAULOV, A., "Brezhnevu ia tak i skazal: 'Ty plokho konchish...'" [interview Petr Shelest], *Moskovskie Novosti* 1989, No. 37 (September).

KHLEVNIUK, O., "1937 god: protivodeistvie repressiiam", *Kommunist* 1989, No. 18 (December), 98-109.

KITAEV, M. A., *Partiinoe stroitelstvo v gody grazhdanskoi voiny*. Moscow 1975.

"Kogo izbrali sekretariami TsK partii v 1917-1922 gg.?", *Izvestiia TsK KPSS* 1989, No. 8, 135-136.

KOSTIKOV, V., "Blesk i nishcheta Nomenklatury", *Ogonek* 1989, No. 1, 12-15.

"Kriuchkov, Vladimir Aleksandrovich" [interview], *Pravitelstvennyi Vestnik* 1989, No. 14-15 (July), 23-24.

KUPTSOV, V. I., ed., *Stranitsy istorii KPSS. Fakty, Problemy, Uroki*. Moscow (Vysshaia shkola) 1988.

KUTUZOV, V. A., "Tak nazyvaemoe 'leningradskoe delo'", *Voprosy Istorii KPSS* 1989, No. 3, 53-67.

"Lazar Kaganovich zagovoril...", *Sovetskaia Latviia*, 11 October 1990.

LENIN, V. I., "Shag vpered, dva shaga nazad (krizis v nashei partii)", *Polnoe sobranie sochinenii*. Izd. piatoe. Tom 8. Vtoraia polovina sentiabria 1903-iiul 1904. Moscow (Politizdat) 1959, 185-414.

———, *Polnoe sobranie sochinenii*. Izd. piatoe. Tom 45. Mart 1922-mart 1923. Moscow (Politizdat) 1964 & 1970.

LIGACHEV, E., "Iz vospominanii", *Argumenty i Fakty* 1991, No. 3, 5-6; No. 4, 5-6; No. 5, 5-6; No. 6, 6.

LIKHANOV, DMITRII, "Koma", *Ogonek* 1989, No. 1, 27-30; No. 2, 25-29; No. 3, 28-30; No. 4, 18-22.

LYNEV, R., "Ot ottepeli do zastoia. Beseda s personalnym pensionerom, byvshim chlenom Politbiuro TsK KPSS" [interview G. I. Voronov], *Izvestiia*, 18 November 1988.

MEDVEDEV, ROI, "Konets 'sladkoi zhizni' dlia Galiny Brezhnevoi", *Sovershenno Sekretno* 1990, No. 2, 11-13.

MIKHAILOV, NIKOLAI, "'Tainoe' golosovanie. Skolko delegatov XVII s''ezda partii golosovalo protiv Stalina?", *Dialog* 1991, No. 1 (January), 79-87.

MIKHAILOV, N., and V. NAUMOV, "Skolko delegatov XVII S''ezda partii golosovalo protiv Stalina?", *Izvestiia TsK KPSS* 1989, No. 7, 114-121.

MIKOIAN, A. I., "V Nizhnem Novgorode (Prodolzhenie)", *Novyi Mir* 1972, No. 11 (November), 176-208.

———, "V pervyi raz bez Lenina", *Ogonek* 1987, No. 50 (December), 5-7.

NEBOGIN, O. B., and M. D. SLANSKAIA, "...Nelzia ostavit v riadakh partii" [on Lazar Kaganovich], *Voprosy Istorii KPSS* 1989, No. 5, 91-102.

NEKRASOV, V. F. (ed.), *Beriia: konets karery*. Moscow 1991.

NIKOLAEVA, V. P., "V. I Lenin i Organizatsionnoe biuro TsK RKP(b) 1919-1922 gg.", *Voprosy Istorii KPSS* 1969, No. 9, 34-41.

NOVIKOV, V. N., "V gody rukovodstva N. S. Khrushcheva", *Voprosy Istorii* 1989, No. 1, 105-117; No. 2, 103-117.

"O Khrushcheve, Brezhneve i drugikh" [interview P. Shelest], *Argumenty i Fakty* 1989, No. 2, 5-6.

"O sudbe chlenov i kandidatov v chleny TsK VKP(b), izbrannogo XVII s''ezdom partii", *Izvestiia TsK KPSS* 1989, No. 12 (December), 82-113.

PAVLENKO, N., "G. K. Zhukov. Iz neopublikovannykh vospominanii", *Kommunist* 1988, No. 14 (September), 87-101.

"Perevorot nevozmozhen" [interview Boris Eltsin], *Argumenty i Fakty* 1989, No. 27, 4-5.

PETROV, Iu. P., *Stroitel'stvo politorganov, partiinykh i komsololskikh organizatsii armii i flota (1918-1968).* Moscow 1968.

Politicheskii dnevnik 1964-1970 (No.3,...). Amsterdam (Fond imeni Gertsena) 1972.

POSPELOV, P. N., et al., eds., *Istoriia kommunisticheskoi partii Sovetskogo Soiuza.*
Tom 1. *Sozdanie bolshevistskoi partii. 1883-1903gg.* Moscow (Politizdat) 1964;
Tom 2. *Partiia bolshevikov v borbe za sverzhenie tsarizma. 1904-fevral 1917 goda.* Moscow (Politizdat) 1966.
Tom 3. *Kommunisticheskaia partiia-organizator pobedy velikoi oktiabrskoi sotsialisticheskoi revoliutsii i oborony sovetskoi respubliki. Mart 1917-1920g. Kniga pervaia (Mart 1917-mart 1918g.).* Moscow (Politizdat) 1967.
Tom 3. *Kommunisticheskaia partiia-organizator pobedy velikoi oktiabrskoi sotsialiticheskoi revoliutsii i oborony sovetskoi respubliki. Mart 1917-1920g. Kniga vtoraia (Mart 1918-1920g.).* Moscow (Politizdat) 1968.
Tom 4. *Kommunisticheskaia partiia v borbe za postroenie sotsializma v SSSR. 1921-1937gg. Kniga pervaia (1921-1929gg.).* Moscow (Politizdat) 1970.
Tom 5. *Kommunisticheskaia partiia nakanune i v gody Velikoi otechestvennoi voiny, v period uprocheniia i razvitiia sotsialisticheskogo obshchestva. 1938-1958gg. Kniga pervaia (1938-1945gg.).* Moscow (Politizdat) 1970.

PRIBYTKOV, VIKTOR, "Pomoshchnik Genseka", *Sovershenno Sekretno* 1990, No. 7 (14), 16-18.

"Problemy istorii i sovremennost", *Voprosy Istorii KPSS* 1989, No. 2 (February), 47-67.

"Pugo, Boris Karlovich", *Izvestiia TsK KPSS* 1989, No. 10 (October), 11.

RIUTIN, MARTEMIAN, "'Prochitav, peredai drugomu!'", *Iunost* 1988, No. 11, 22-26.

RODIONOV, P. A., "Kak nachinalsia zastoi? Zametki istorika partii", *Znamia* 1989, No. 8, 182-210.

ROMANOV, A., "Chastnoe rassledovanie", *Moskovskie Novosti* 1989, No. 37 (September), 13.

ROMANOV, G., "Pismo v redaktsiiu", *Pravda*, 15 September 1989.

RYBIN, A. T., "Riadom s I.V. Stalinym", *Sotsiologicheskie Issledovaniia* 1988, No. 3, 84-94.

SARASKINA, L. I., "O Staline i Stalinizme. Beseda s D. A. Volkogonovym i R. A. Medvedevym" [interview Dmitri Volkogonov and Roi Medvedev], *Istoriia SSSR* 1989, No. 4 (July-August), 89-108.

SHATUNOVSKAIA, O., "Falsifikatsiia", *Argumenty i Fakty* 1990, No. 22, 6-7.

SHATUNOVSKII, ILIA, "Chelovek v futliare. Sub''ektivnye zametki o M. A. Suslove" [on Mikhail Suslov], *Ogonek* 1989, No. 4 (January), 26-28.

SHENIN, OLEG, "Prislushivatsia k pulsu strany i partii", *Izvestiia TsK KPSS* 1990, No. 10, 3-7.

SHITAREV, G. I., "Vosstanovlenie i razvitie leninskogo printsipa kollektivnosti partiinogo rukovodstva (1953-1963)", *Voprosy Istorii KPSS* 1964, No. 7, 29-42.

SIMONOV, KONSTANTIN, "Glazami cheloveka moego pokoleniia (Razmyshleniia o I. V. Stalina; Prodolzhenie)", *Znamia* 1988, April, 49-121.

SOBCHAK, ANATOLII, "O sobytiiakh v g. Tbilisi", *Izvestiia*, 29 December 1989.

SOBOLEV, N., and A. CHERNEV, "Na vysshikh postakh", *Glasnost* 1991, No. 2 (January), 4.

"Spetsialnym postanovleniem...", *Argumenty i Fakty* 1991, No. 16 (April), 3.

STALIN, I. V., *Sochineniia*.
    Tom 5. 1921-1923. Moscow (Politizdat) 1947.
    Tom 6. 1924. Moscow (Politizdat) 1947.
    Tom 11. 1928-mart 1929. Moscow (Politizdat) 1949.

STASOVA, E. D., *Stranitsy zhizni i borby*. Moscow 1988.

SVETITSKII, K., and S. SOKOLOV, "'Ia by spravilsia s liuboi raboi'" [interview Vladimir Semichastnyi], *Ogonek* 1989, No. 24 (June), 24-26.

SVIRIDOCHKIN, I. I., ed., *Mikhail Vasilevich Frunze. Sbornik*. Moscow (Voenizdat) 1965.

TEPTSOV, N. V., "A. I. Rykov-partiinyi i gosudarstvennyi deiatel leninskoi shkoly", *Voprosy Istorii KPSS* 1989, No. 6, 117-128.

"Treugolnik s dvumia uglami?", *Literaturnaia Gazeta* 1990, No. 27 (4 July), 2.

TROTSKII, N. [= L. D.], *Nashi politicheskiia zadachi (takticheskie i organizatsionnye voprosy)*. Geneva (Tipografiia partii) 1904.

———, "Pismo L. D. Trotskogo chlenam TsK i TsKK RKP(b). 8 oktiabria 1923g.", *Izvestiia TsK KPSS* 1990, No. 5, 165-75.

TSELMS, GEORGII, "Ubiistvo Kirova: poslednii svidetel", *Literaturnaia Gazeta*, 27 June 1990, 12-13.

VASETSKII, N., "Stalin: borba za liderstvo v partii" in V. I. Kuptsov (ed.), *Stranitsy istorii KPSS. Fakty. Problemy. Uroki*. Moscow (Vysshaia shkola) 1988, 621-635.

VIKTOROV, BORIS, "'Zagovor' v Krasnoi Armii", *Pravda*, 29 April 1988.

"Vokrug ubiistva Kirova", *Pravda*, 4 November 1990.

VOLKOGONOV, DMITRII, *Triumf i tragediia. Politicheskii portret I. V. Stalina v 2-kh knigakh. Kniga I. Chast 1 & 2; Kniga II. Chast 1*. Moscow (Novosti) 1989.

"V verkh po lestnitse, vedushchei vniz", *Literaturnaia Gazeta* 1991, No. 4 (30 January), 3.

ZINOVEV, G. E., "O zhizni i deiatelnosti V. I. Lenina", *Izvestiia TsK KPSS* 1989, No. 7, 166-185

BOOKS AND ARTICLES in Other Languages

ALBRECHT, KARL I., *Der verratene Sozialismus*. Berlin & Leipzig, 1941.

ALLILUYEVA, SVETLANA, "Two last conversations", *Moscow News* 1990, No. 42 (October-November), 8-9.

The Anti-Stalin Campaign and International Communism. New York (Russian Institute, Columbia University) 1956.

BAJANOV, BORIS, *Stalin, der rote Diktator; von seinem ehemaligen Privatsekretär*. Berlin 1931.

BASCHANOW, BORIS, *Ich war Stalins Sekretär*. Frankfurt a.M. (Ullstein) 1977.

BELITSKY, SERGEI, "Authors of USSR's Afghan War Policy", *Report on the USSR*, 28 April 1989, 11-12.

BENVENUTI, FRANCESCO, *The Bolsheviks and the Red Army, 1918-1922*. Cambridge (Cambridge University Press) 1988.

BOROVIK, ARTYOM, *The Hidden War. A Russian Journalist's Account of the Soviet War in Afghanistan*. New York (The Atlantic Monthly Press) 1990.

BRESLAUER, GEORGE W., *Khrushchev and Brezhnev as Leaders: Building Authority in Soviet Politics*. London etc. (Allen & Unwin) 1982.

BROWN, ARCHIE, "Governing the USSR", *Problems of Communism* Vol. 28 (September-December 1979), 103-8.

————, "The Power of the General Secretary of the CPSU", in T. H. Rigby, Archie Brown and Peter Reddaway (eds.), *Authority, Power and Policy in the USSR. Essays dedicated to Leonard Schapiro*. London (Macmillan) 1980, 135-157.

CARR, E.H., *The Interregnum 1923-24*. Harmondsworth (Penguin) 1969 (1954).

CASSTEVENS, THOMAS W. and HAROLD T. CASSTEVENS II, "The Circulation of Elites. A Review and Critique of a Class of Models", *American Journal of Political Science* Vol. 33, No. 1 (February 1989), 294-317.

CASSTEVENS, THOMAS W. and JAMES R. OZINGA, "The Soviet Central Committee Since Stalin", *American Journal of Political Science* Vol. 18, No. 3 (August 1974), 559-568.

CHROESJTSJOV, SERGEJ, *Herinneringen aan mijn vader. Kroniek van zijn laatste zeven jaren*. Utrecht (Bruna) 1990 (Dutch translation of: *Pensioner soiuznogo znacheniia*).

CONQUEST, ROBERT, *Power and Policy in the USSR, The Study of Soviet Dynastics*. London (Macmillan) 1961.

————, *Stalin and the Kirov Murder*. London (Hutchinson) 1989.

————, *The Great Terror. A Reassessment*. London (Hutchinson) 1990.

"Die Atomwaffen sind Teufelsdinger" [interview with V. Falin], *Der Spiegel* 1987, No. 51, 109-113.

DZHIRKVELOV, ILYA, *Secret Servant. My life with the KGB & the Soviet Elite*. New York etc. (Simon & Schuster) 1989 (1987).

FAINSOD, MERLE, *How Russia is Ruled. Revised Edition*. Cambridge Mass. (Harvard University Press) 1967.

FULLER, ELIZABETH, "Official and Unofficial Investigations into Tbilisi Massacre Yield Contradictory Results", *Report on the USSR* Vol. 1, No. 44 (3 November 1989), 26-29;

GARTHOFF, R. L., "SALT and the Soviet Military", *Problems of Communism* 1975, Nr. 1, 29.

GELMAN, HARRY, *The Brezhnev Politburo and the Decline of Detente*, Ithaca & London (Cornell University Press) 1984.

GEVORKYAN, NATALYA, "Corruption. The exception or the rule?", *Moscow News* 1989, No. 34, 10.

HILL, RONALD J., and JOHN LöWENHARDT, "*Nomenklatura* and *Perestroika*", *Government and Opposition* Vol. 26, No. 2 (Spring 1991), 229-243.

HOUGH, JERRY, "The Soviet System, Petrification or Pluralism", *Problems of Communism* 1972, No. 2, 25-45.

HOUGH, JERRY F., and MERLE FAINSOD, *How the Soviet Union is Governed.* Cambridge Mass.-London (Harvard University Press) 1979.

INGLEHART, RONALD, *The Silent Revolution: Changing Values and Political Styles Among Western Publics.* Princeton N.J. (Princeton University Press) 1977.

KAISER, ROBERT G., *Russia, the People & the Power.* London 1976.

———, *Why Gorbachev Happened. His Triumphs and His Failure.* New York etc. (Simon & Schuster) 1991.

KELLER, BILL, "In Moscow, a Glimpse of Dynamics at Party's Core", *International Herald Tribune,* 5 July 1988.

KHOKHRYAKOV, GENNADY, "The shadow economy and the administrative-command system", *Moscow News* 1988, No. 46, 12.

KOSTIUK, HRYHORY, *Stalinist Rule in the Ukraine. A Study of the Decade of Mass Terror (1929-39).* London (Stevens & Sons) 1960.

KRAMER, MARK, "The role of the CPSU International Department in Soviet Foreign Relations and National Security Policy", *Soviet Studies* Vol. 42, No. 3 (July 1990), 429-466.

LAIRD, ROY, *The Politburo, Demographic Trends, Gorbachev, and the Future.* Boulder Colo.-London (Westview) 1986.

LEWIN, MOSHE, *Lenin's Last Struggle.* London (Faber & Faber) 1969.

LOSHAK, VIKTOR, "'Up against the mafia'", *Moscow News* 1988, No. 14, 13.

LöWENHARDT, JOHN, *Het Russische Politburo. Geschiedenis, profiel en werkwijze.* Assen (Van Gorcum) 1978.

———, *The Soviet Politburo.* Translated by Dymphna Clark. Edinburgh (Canongate) and New York (St. Martin's Press) 1982.

———, "*Politburo zasedaet*: Reported and secret meetings of the Politburo of the CPSU", *Nordic Journal of Soviet and East European Studies* Vol. 5, No. 2 (1988), 157-174.

MEDVEDEV, ROY, "Advantages of mediocrity. Leonid Brezhnev: a political profile", *Moscow News* 1988, No. 37 (11 September), 8-9.

———, *All Stalin's Men.* Oxford (Basil Blackwell) 1983.

———, *Let History Judge. The Origins and Consequences of Stalinism.* Oxford etc. (Oxford University Press) 1989.

MEDVEDEV, R. A., and Zh. A. MEDVEDEV, *Khrushchev. The Years in Power.* London (Oxford University Press) 1977.

MEDVEDEV, ZHORES, *Andropov. His Life and Death.* Oxford (Basil Blackwell) 1984 (1983).

———, *Gorbachev.* Oxford (Basil Blackwell) 1986.

———, *Michail Gorbatsjov.* Houten (De Haan) 1987 (translation of the English ed.).

MLYNAR, ZDENEK, "That August of 1968", *Moscow News* 1989, No. 50, 9.

MOSKALENKO, KIRILL S., "Beria's Arrest. From the unpublished memoirs of Marshall Moskalenko", *Moscow News* 1990, No. 23 (June), 8-9.

MURARKA, DEV, *Gorbachov. The Limits of Power*. London etc. (Hutchinson) 1988.

NICOLAEVSKY, B., *Power and the Soviet Elite*. New York etc. (Praeger) 1965.

OZINGA, JAMES R., *Communism. The Story of the Idea and its Implementation*. Englewood Cliffs, N. J. (Prentice-Hall) 1991 (1987).

OZINGA, JAMES R., THOMAS W. CASSTEVENS, and HAROLD T. CASSTEVENS II, "The Circulation of Elites. Soviet Politburo Members 1919-1987", *Canadian Journal of Political Science* Vol. 22, No. 3 (September 1989), 609-617.

POND, ELIZABETH, *From the Yaroslavsky Station. Russia Perceived*. New York (Universe Books) 3rd ed. 1988.

PRAVDIN, A., "Inside the CPSU Central Committee", *Survey*, Vol 20, No. 4 (Autumn 1974), 94-104.

RAHR, ALEXANDER, "Gorbachev Discloses Details on Defence Council", *Report on the USSR* Vol. 1, No. 37 (15 September 1989), 11-12.

———, "The CPSU after the Twenty-eighth Party Congress", *Report on the USSR* Vol. 2, No. 45 (9 November 1990), 1-4.

RAPOPORT, LOUIS, *Stalin's War against the Jews. The Doctor's Plot and the Soviet Solution*. New York etc. (Macmillan) 1990.

REES, E. A., *State Control in Soviet Russia. The Rise and Fall of the Workers' and Peasants' Inspectorate, 1920-1934*. Houndmills-London (Macmillan) 1987.

RIGBY, T. H., "The Soviet Politburo, A Comparative Profile 1951-1971", *Soviet Studies* Vol. 24, No. 1 (July 1972), 3-23.

———, *Lenin's Government: Sovnarkom 1917-1922*. Cambridge (Cambridge University Press) 1979.

ROSENFELDT, NIELS ERIK, *Knowledge and Power. The Role of Stalin's Secret Chancellery in the Soviet System of Government*. Copenhagen (Rosenkilde & Bagger) 1978.

SCHAPIRO, LEONARD, *The Origin of the Communist Autocracy. Political Opposition in the Soviet State. The First Phase: 1917-1922*, Cambridge Mass. (Harvard University Press) 1955.

———, *The Communist Party of the Soviet Union*. New York (Random House) 1971 (1959).

———, "The CPSU International Department", *International Journal* Vol. 32 (Winter 1966-1967), 41-55.

———, "The General Department of the CC of the CPSU", *Survey* Vol. 21, No. 3 (96) (Summer 1975) 53-65.

SCHECTER, JERROLD L., VYACHESLAV V. LUCHKOV, eds., *Khrushchev remembers. The Glasnost Tapes*. Boston-Toronto-London (Little, Brown and Co.) 1990.

SCHUELLER, GEORGE K., *The Politburo*. Stanford, Calif. (Stanford University Press) 1951.

SHABAD, THEODORE, "Brezhnev, Who Ought to Know, Explains Politburo", *New York Times*, 15 June 1973.

SHEEHY, ANN, "Non-Russian Representation in the Politburo and Secretariat", *Radio Liberty Research Bulletin* RL 439/87, 28 October 1987.

SHREIDER, MIKHAIL, "Ivanovo, 1937. From the notes of a chekist-operative", *Moscow News* 1988, No. 48 (November), 7.

SLUSSER, ROBERT M., *Stalin in October. The Man who Missed the Revolution*. Baltimore and London (Johns Hopkins University Press) 1987.

SMITH, HEDRICK, *The Russians*. London 1976.

"So I said to Brezhnev: You'll end up in a bad way...", *Moscow News* 1989, No. 37, 16.

SULLIVANT, ROBERT S., *Soviet Politics and the Ukraine, 1917-1957*. New York (Columbia University Press) 1962.

TAAGEPERA, REIN, and ROBERT DALE CHAPMAN, "A Note on the Ageing of the Politburo", *Soviet Studies*, Vol. 29, No. 2 (April 1977), 296-305.

TALBOTT, STROBE, ed., *Khrushchev Remembers*. Boston (Little, Brown & Co.) 1970; Harmondsworth (Penguin) 1977.

———, *Khrushchev Remembers. The Last Testament*. London (Deutsch) 1974; Harmondsworth (Penguin) 1977.

TATU, MICHEL, and DANIEL VERNET, "Un entretien avec le numéro deux soviétique [E. Ligachev]", *le Monde*, 4 December 1987.

TEAGUE, ELIZABETH, "Airbrushing in These Days of Glasnost'", *Report on the USSR* Vol. 2, No. 45 (9 November 1990), 11-14

TOLZ, VERA, "Alexander Yakovlev Provides New Information about the Mystery of Kirov's Murder", *Report on the USSR*, Vol. 3, No. 8 (22 February 1991), 9-12.

TRETYAKOV, VITALY, "The Boris Yeltsin Phenomenon", *Moscow News* 1989, No. 16, 10.

———, "Politburo's Nice guy. Aleksandr Yakovlev and the left-wing alternative within the CPSU", *Moscow News* 1990, No. 26 (July), 8-9.

TROTSKY, LEON, *The Stalin School of Falsification*. London (New Park Publications) 1974 (1932).

TROTZKI, LEO, *Mein Leben. Versuch einer Autobiographie*. Berlin (S. Fischer) 1930.

TUMARKIN, NINA, *Lenin lives! The Lenin cult in Soviet Russia*. Cambridge Mass.-London (Harvard University Press) 1983.

VAKSBERG, ARKADY, *The Prosecutor and the Prey. Vyshinsky and the 1930s Moscow Show Trials*. London (Weidenfeld & Nicolson) 1990.

VAN DEN BERG, GER P., *Organisation und Arbeitsweise der sowjetischen Regierung*. Baden-Baden (Nomos) 1984.

———, "Joint Party and Government Decrees in the USSR and other Socialist Countries", *Review of Socialist Law* Vol. 11 (1985), No. 1, 47-73.

WISHNEVSKY, JULIA, "Unlikely Sources Depict Life at the Top", *Report on the USSR* Vol. 3, No. 5 (1 February 1991), 30-33.

YASMANN, VIKTOR, "The Internal Security Situation in the USSR and the Defense Council", *Report on the USSR* Vol. 1, No. 35 (1 September 1989), 8-14.

INDEX OF NAMES

For Product Safety Concerns and Information please contact our EU
representative GPSR@taylorandfrancis.com
Taylor & Francis Verlag GmbH, Kaufingerstraße 24, 80331 München, Germany

www.ingramcontent.com/pod-product-compliance
Lightning Source LLC
Chambersburg PA
CBHW050414280326
41932CB00013BA/1858